REINVENTING

THE

ORGANIZATION

ARTHUR YEUNG
DAVE ULRICH

REINVENTING

THE

ORGANIZATION

HOW COMPANIES CAN DELIVER

RADICALLY GREATER VALUE

IN FAST-CHANGING MARKETS

Harvard Business Review Press

Boston, Massachusetts

Copyright 2019 Arthur Yeung and Dave Ulrich
All rights reserved
Printed in the United States of America

10 9 8 7 6 5 4 3 2 1

No part of this publication may be reproduced, stored in or introduced into a retrieval system, or transmitted, in any form, or by any means (electronic, mechanical, photocopying, recording, or otherwise), without the prior permission of the publisher. Requests for permission should be directed to permissions@harvardbusiness.org, or mailed to Permissions, Harvard Business School Publishing, 60 Harvard Way, Boston, Massachusetts 02163.

The web addresses referenced in this book were live and correct at the time of the book's publication but may be subject to change.

Library of Congress Cataloging-in-Publication Data
Names: Yeung, Arthur K., author. | Ulrich, David, author.
Title: Reinventing the organization / Arthur Yeung and Dave Ulrich.
Description: Boston : Harvard Business Review Press, [2019] | Includes
    bibliographical references and index.
Identifiers: LCCN 2019011984 | ISBN 9781633697706 (hardcover)
Subjects: LCSH: Business enterprises. | Strategic planning. | Organizational
    effectiveness. | Organizational behavior. | Success in business. | Corporate
    culture. | Leadership.
Classification: LCC HD30.28 .Y48 2019 | DDC 658.4/06—dc23
    LC record available at https://lccn.loc.gov/2019011984

ISBN: 978-1-63369-770-6
eISBN: 978-1-63369-771-3

The paper used in this publication meets the requirements of the American National Standard for Permanence of Paper for Publications and Documents in Libraries and Archives Z39.48-1992.

CONTENTS

PREFACE

In a time of fast-changing business conditions, this book is intended to reinvent organization thinking by introducing leaders to new principles of organization design that will enable them to implement management practices and help their organizations

- Deliver innovative products and services to customers

- Create market value for investors

- Increase employee sentiment and productivity

- Provide value to a broader society or community interest

We followed three tracks to reinvent organization thinking. First, we synthesized and integrated a plethora of innovative organization ideas (holacracy, exponential, amoeba, team of teams, boundary-less, network, platform, agile, ambidextrous, lattice, and so forth). Each of these organizational innovations offers unique insights on components of what makes an organization effective in today's changing world. We combined these insights into an integrated framework that guides leaders as they reinvent their organizations.

Second, we identified some of the most innovative and successful organizations of our time from China (Alibaba, Huawei, Tencent), the United States (Amazon, Facebook, Google), and Europe (Super-cell) and did deep dives into each one to explore how they are rein-venting themselves to win. Our goal was not merely to examine what they were doing as exemplary companies, but more importantly to study the logic and principles behind their practices. Operating in a hyperdynamic environment, these iconic companies demonstrate how organizations are being reinvented. In fact, it would not be surprising if some of the companies we studied changed again, even by the time this book is published. But the principles of the new organization will remain much the same, and the practices (tools and actions) may be somewhat stable over time.

Third, we drew on our personal experiences. For the last four decades we have observed, studied, and advised organizations. After completing his PhD in organization theory, Arthur served on the senior executive teams at Acer and Tencent. He has taught for more than a decade at CEIBS (the leading Chinese business school), sits on many boards as an independent director, and has advised many CEOs to build or transform the capabilities of their companies. He also founded the Organizational Capability Learning Association and has facilitated the learning of about three hundred Chinese entrepreneurs and CEOs through quarterly meetings since 2010. Dave has taught at the University of Michigan for over thirty years, advised over half of the *Fortune* 200, and won numerous lifetime achievement awards. Together, we have published over forty books on organization, talent, human resources, and leadership. We have been instrumental in defining and shaping concepts such as organization capability, boundaryless organization, right culture, transformation, learning organization, HR value-added and HR outside-in, networks, platforms, leadership brand, leadership capital, business partner, paradox navigator, and strategic agility.

From these streams of work we have written this book to advance both the principles and practices that reinvent how to think about and build organizations. We hope these ideas will help leaders tasked with building stronger organizations and organization architects (in HR, organization development, or consulting) asked to shape and deliver this new organization form.

Writing this book has been very complex, with background research and approximately eighty interviews in China and the United States. We are grateful for the incredible help of the research team that conducted in-depth interviews and literature reviews of the eight iconic companies featured in these pages: Sharon Li, Emily Chen, Janet Huang, Devon Shu, and Wingwing Wang—all of you are great colleagues to work with. Special thanks to Kate Sweetman and Janet Huang, who turned company interviews into stories. We are especially grateful to Melinda Merino, our editor at Harvard Business Review Press, who helped shape our thinking, and to Patricia Boyd, who has been a remarkable copy editor as she masterfully turned our ideas into words with impact.

We are grateful to the interviewees who participated in our research, both for their time and their insights, and also to our close colleagues in the organizations where we work, teach, and consult. These colleagues have influenced our thinking far beyond our personal capacity. We have assimilated their ideas and made them ours (hopefully giving proper credit). Last, but certainly not least, we wish to recognize the long-term, persistent, and patient support of our families, in particular Jenny and Wendy, who are our intellectual, social, emotional, and spiritual partners.

REINVENTING

THE

ORGANIZATION

CHAPTER 1

A New Organization

How Can Your Company Deliver
Radically Greater Value?

On a sunny beach in Panama City, Florida, a mother hears her two young sons shouting for her in the surf. Urgently, she swims to their rescue, only to be caught in the same powerful riptide that is sweeping her children out to sea. The boys' grandmother jumps in, and a cousin, and another cousin, and soon nine family members struggle helplessly against the deadly current. What saves them? One quick-thinking stranger hears the commotion, grabs the hands of two other strangers, and launches what quickly becomes a chain of eighty rescuers. The human net they form stretches three hundred feet out into the ocean, captures every member of the family in peril, and returns them to safety. This story is true; a video of the event can be found on YouTube.[1]

If Olympian Michael Phelps had been the lifeguard on duty that day, for all his talent, could he have saved all nine people? Of course not. What made the difference here was not an individual hero, but an organization—the rapid, intelligent, practical, and, above all, coordinated response of many people motivated by the opportunity to save this family. Strangers with a shared purpose literally linked arms to join together. They acted quickly, innovated using boogie boards and beach balls in deep water, and succeeded against a seemingly overwhelming riptide. And imagine how the eighty people who helped save lives that day felt! Then they each went their own way.

This moving story captures the essential purpose of this book. We want to help leaders of all organizations (big or small, public or private, domestic or global) accomplish what these eighty people did for this family: anticipate and observe challenges, join together with purpose, innovate thoughtfully, act quickly, inspire people, and deliver results. But even more, we want to guide leaders on how to go beyond an isolated event like this rescue and scale their organizations to consistently accomplish desired results.

But as everyone knows, most organizations don't work this way. Today's organizations were designed for a more stable environment, which doesn't exist anymore. If you are like most leaders we talk to, you sense new requirements and rules of winning in rapidly changing markets—like the eighty beachgoers who spontaneously formed a human chain to save the endangered swimmers in a riptide. You constantly make choices and experiment with new management ideas. But you are not making the progress you both desire and need to move faster.

To better understand how organizations can become more like those eighty individuals, we set about studying the two most innovative and vital business climates in the world: China and Silicon Valley. We knew that, for different reasons, these two places incubate fresh organizational forms and practices that meet the needs of super dynamic markets very well. In China, a vibrant entrepreneurial space is filling the void between the state-owned enterprises and the multinational corporations. This space is being occupied by highly successful, privately owned organizations such as Alibaba, DiDi, Huawei, and Tencent, all four of which we have studied extensively. In Silicon Valley, the world's most famous test bed of innovators in the world, entrepreneurs are driven by the potential to create

TABLE 1-1

Companies studied

Company	Year founded	No. of employees[a]	Market value in USD billion[b]
Alibaba	1999	101,550	474.6
Amazon	1994	647,500[c]	907.8
DiDi	2012	13,000	55.0[d]
Facebook	2004	35,587	513.0
Google	1998	98,771	848.9
Huawei	1987	180,000	146.0[e]
Supercell	2010	283	10.0[f]
Tencent	1998	47,794[g]	472.0
Average	(Average age of company in 2019: 19 years)	140,561	428.4

a. Listed companies are quoted from the 2018 annual reports; others from official website
b. Market value for listed companies ended at April 15, 2019
c. Full-time and part-time employees; excludes contractors and temporary personnel
d. Information provided by DiDi external communication team
e. Reference from Hurun Report
f. Private company, information based on last round of valuation
g. Excludes contract workers as of April 15, 2019

Source: Market value of DiDi and Supercell comes from the companies' financial disclosure statements; market value of Huawei comes from Hurun Report. Other data comes from companies' official websites and financial statements.

highly successful, scalable businesses. By last count, about fifty new companies are launched in the San Francisco area every month. We were fortunate to have deep access to the top three of the leading companies in this crowd: Amazon, Facebook, and Google. In both locales, the companies were organizing themselves for success in a rapidly changing global world, unfettered by traditional organizational systems. Table 1-1 shows the organizations we studied. We had inside access to these companies and interviewed executives, employees, and alumni to find out how these organizations work.

In our studies of these remarkable companies, we found several principles and practices for delivering radically greater value in fast-moving markets. We crystallized these elements into a framework for reinvention, so that any leader in any kind of organization, especially a so-called legacy organization, could adapt them.

Of course, it is much easier to start a new organization than it is to reinvent a legacy organization. In our years of work with many CEOs and their teams, we have seen how hard it is to drive fundamental transformation in an existing organization. These challenges spurred us to write this book. We hope to offer a bridge and guide to help executives transform their organizations to ones that are faster and more responsive and that, as a consequence, deliver more value.

We also recognize that even digital companies must constantly adapt because their business world is changing so fast (AOL, Yahoo, Myspace, Netscape, to name a few, are well-known casualties of slow adaptation). These principles of reinvention apply to digital companies as well. All companies, especially those in the fastest competitive environments, need to keep their organizations nimble and responsive.

As a leader seeking to inspire employees, serve customers, delight investors, and exhibit social citizenship in this rapidly changing world of work, you need to reinvent your organization. Reinvention means more than just changing people's reporting relationships, building teams, or announcing a new strategy. You must build a fundamentally new organization, redefining how your organization works. Besides understanding and shaping your work setting, you need to change how you coordinate the work, the principles that govern it, and your own and others' leadership actions. This book offers you a complete roadmap for reinventing your organization with the principles and tools that we have found work for some of the most dynamic companies in the world today.

Before we introduce our six-step framework for reinvention, let's start with an overview of Supercell, one of the companies we studied. The company's story illustrates how a new organizational form that we saw emerging at Supercell and the other companies we studied anticipates the market and creates radically greater value.[2] As you read this, you will no doubt be thinking, "No way could my organization ever become like Supercell." Our goal with this book is to convince you otherwise and to provide you with the tools to move your company in this direction.

The Supercell Organization

Supercell, a mobile game company founded in 2010, has since developed five hit games (Clash of Clans and Hay Day in 2012, Boom Beach in 2014, Clash Royale in 2016, Brawl Stars in 2018) winning literally a hundred million loyal customers. By 2019, the company had a market value of approximately $10 billion and annual revenue of more than $2 billion. Not bad for a company with only 280 employees and with its average revenue per employee reaching $10 million.

Environment and Strategy

To achieve such rapid success, Supercell leaders anticipated the technological trend of mobile internet in 2010 and focused its game development on mobile platforms. The availability of global distribution channels through the Apple iOS store and Android stores greatly facilitated the global reach of its games.

Supercell leaders committed to make games that last for decades, have global appeal (well received in both the West and the East), and operate on mobile devices. To stay focused on its game development, Supercell recruited outside partners like Kunlun and Tencent to help with publishing in China and to outsource its IT infrastructure through Amazon Web Services (AWS).

Organization Capabilities and Structure

CEO Ilkka Paananen and the other five cofounders have rich and deep experiences in the game industry. They would call themselves "gamers," and Supercell's focus on customer satisfaction starts with them. The founders are also committed to creating a work environment that encourages creativity and innovation by independence and work in small teams supported by a platform. Supercell deeply believes that the best team makes the best games.

These small teams, or cells, are independent and self-contained: one team per game under development. The *super* suggested by part

FIGURE 1-1

The Supercell organization: platforms, cells, and strategic partners

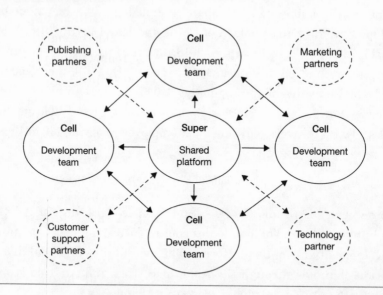

of the company name is the platform, the solid central base that provides the game-development teams or cells what they need to succeed: culture, marketing, HR, finance, and technology. The relationship between the teams (or cells) and the central platform (super) is flat (nonhierarchical), and the platform's mission is transparent: to enable the teams to concentrate on game development—period. In addition, the independent cells share insights with each other so that the whole company is stronger than any individual game. If we were to draw this organization, it would not be a traditional hierarchy but would be a platform and independent cells connected to each other (figure 1-1).

"Why the super and cell organizational design?" asks Supercell chief operating officer Janne Snellman rhetorically. "Because we saw the failure of games designed by committee elsewhere. The best [gaming] talent wants to work independently: set them on a path, give them direction, and the team will figure out the rest on its own. They cannot have a person come in to tell them what to do. The smaller the team, the faster it is." The megahit Clash of Clans, for example, began with a core team of only five people and grew over the years to seven or eight people focused on continuously adding to this highly interactive game. The larger team that supports millions of Clash of Clan players is still less than fifteen people. Like the eighty people who saved the swimmers, these individual teams bring people together to create and respond to market opportunities.

Talent

With a strong goal of keeping the company small and easy to manage, Supercell is rigorous in its hiring processes. For example, from the more than two thousand résumés received for the position of artists, the company hired only ten artists. With this level of rigor, Supercell brings extraordinary people together because it believes that one exceptional person equals a hundred ordinary people. The company then gives people freedom, removing all the obstacles it can anticipate.

Supercell empowers its creative talent by giving people the freedom to experiment with different ideas and by removing the stigma of failure. When a game idea doesn't perform as expected, the team will simply celebrate its failure with a bottle of champagne and share lessons learned with team members from other cells.

"Successful teams start with team leads, those who have proven themselves in game developing expertise," says Snellman. "When they think they have the game idea, they internally pitch their idea, and get other people to join from the other internal teams, or from the outside. There is no official approval for a team lead to form a team. People with ideas can call their own teams." Supercell, in effect, has an ongoing internal marketplace of jobs and ideas.

Connection among Teams

But beyond being an isolated independent team, Supercell teams are connected to each other both by their use of platform resources and by sharing insights across teams. Game designers can move from team to team as their interests change. Snellman says, "The best example of this is Clash Royale. When the game moved from concept to internal company playable (the step before an external beta launch), so many people got excited about it that another game team put its project on hold and moved onto the Clash Royale team. Their joining made the development of the game go faster. The thinking is, whole company first, team second. People know that when they support another team, they can expect others' support when they need it." As Snellman explains, the success of Supercell is not due to just one outstanding game or team; it comes from connected teams that move resources to new opportunities.

Culture

For this organization to work at Supercell, the overriding cultural value is respect. Snellman says, "We want a peer environment. Everyone's job is important. We have mutual respect for each other, not a king and subordinate relationship. Platform people and game-development-team people share the same bonus scale."

In this book, we will share the principles and practices—distilled into a comprehensive six-part framework—that Supercell and the other companies we studied use to operate in fast-moving environments. Supercell is the smallest and newest of the companies in table 1-1, and as we mentioned, it is much easier to create a new organization than it is to transform an existing one. But whatever your company's age or its size, these principles and practices can work for your organization. This book will show you how.

Start with the Organization You Have: Models That Best Describe Your Organization

If you want to reinvent your organization, you first need to identify the assumptions about how your company operates. To do so, you might consider which organizational model best describes how your company works (see figure 1-2). There are three traditional models: hierarchies, systems, and capabilities.

FIGURE 1-2

Evolution of organizational forms

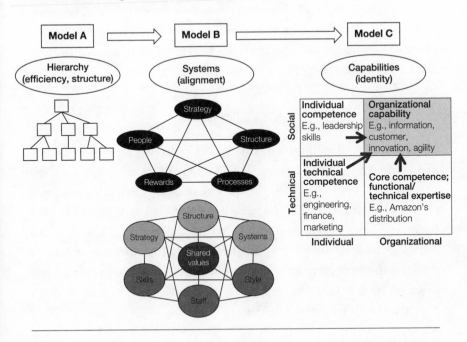

Hierarchy Model

The dominant organizational logic of your company might be best described as a hierarchy of knowledge, power, and control (the traditional organization chart; model A in figure 1-2). Model A fits your organization if leaders emphasize roles and rules and focus on improving efficiency by delayering levels, clarifying roles, and working to remove boundaries across silos. For all the talk about abolishing hierarchy, most organizations today still fall into this category.

Systems Model

If your organization has moved away from the hierarchical model and the assumptions that underpin it, your company might instead be following a systems logic approach (model B in figure 1-2). As a leader, you focus on both aligning your systems (e.g., strategy, structure, people, rewards, and processes) that will improve your organizational health.[3] If your organization operates under these assumptions, it often operates better but still responds slowly to external disruptions and may not have fully engaged people. Imagine if the eighty lifesavers had sat down to do a RACI (responsible, accountable, consulting, and informed) systems analysis before linking hands and saving the swimmers!

Capabilities Model

Alternatively, you might assume that your organization is not about hierarchies or systems, but is about its capabilities or identity (model C in the figure). In the capabilities model, you assume that the organization is effective because of what it is known for (reputation) and good at doing. That is, the model is based on an organization's identity.[4] Organizations following such a model focus on what they are good at doing and how they structure their activities to deliver value. You emphasize the creation of a unique identity that affects all your stakeholders.

Assessing Your Organization

If you want to reinvent your organization, you need to recognize your bias among these three common organizational models. Can you recognize your company's bias here? Does your organization emphasize hierarchy and clarity of people's roles? Or systems and alignment? Or does it focus on its capabilities and identity? Once you recognize your organization's predominant assumptions about who you are as an organization—whether you follow model A, B, or C—you need to let them go.

None of these organizational assumptions explains what happens with the eighty rescuers or Supercell's success. The traditional three models (hierarchy, systems, or capabilities) all focus more on the inside and who does what than they focus on the outside— where it truly counts. The traditional models also encourage predictable solutions more than they look for agile actions. So much of the epic fails of recent years—Blockbuster, Kodak, Nokia, Sears, and so on—traces back to the inability of leaders to figure out how to respond quickly to marketplace requirements or opportunities.

Are you ready to let go of your organizational assumptions and rethink how your company can deliver radically greater value? Let's now take a step toward this transformation.

Moving toward a New Organizational Model: The Market-Oriented Ecosystem

Several insights and principles from Supercell and the other companies we studied point to how you can develop a more innovative and agile organization that creates radically more value. We are clearly not the first to recognize the power of working together and to offer solutions that will anticipate customer demands, innovate thoughtfully, inspire employees, and respond quickly. Many companies have tried to redefine themselves in a post-hierarchy world. Each organizational experiment offers components of a new model. You have probably heard about and possibly even experimented with some of these ideas.

To move people around more easily, some companies experiment with a lattice structure that enables and rewards moving sideways. Other companies reframe themselves as networks to create better interconnections. If we want to unlock greater speed, can the so-called ambidextrous organization do that for us? If we want to engage others both inside and beyond our corporate borders, might the boundaryless organization be the way to go? Will the holacracy—another popular type of decentralized structure—provide the miracle cure for the hierarchy's excessive need for control, handing the organization over to self-management and self-organization by team? How about the amoeba organization or microfirms that flip organizational hierarchy upside down? Will the exponential organization respond quickly enough to market changes? And the list of organizational experiments goes on (see figure 1-3).

While we owe a great debt to these innovators and early adopters who have conducted these brave organizational experiments, the

FIGURE 1-3

Emerging models of organizations

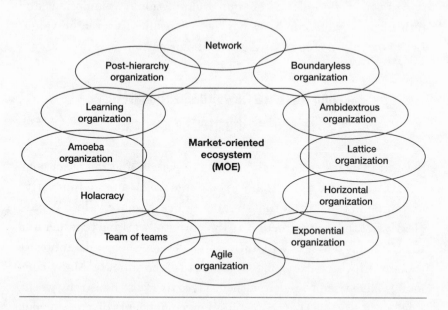

attempts are piecemeal, not integrated, solutions. They innovate organization practices, but they do not reinvent the organization.

In this book, we offer you a holistic and integrated approach on how to reinvent your organization, one based on new principles and enacted through new practices. You don't just want to run organizational experiments; you want to have real and sustainable impact.

We struggled with what to call the emerging organizational form that we saw in the companies we studied. After much debate, we decided to name the reinvented organization a *market-oriented ecosystem*. Even though it is a bit of a "clunky" phrase, the reasons for our use of this term will become clear as we go further into the book.

This emerging organization form starts with market-oriented opportunities: opportunities beyond mere market share. Market opportunities create a compelling purpose that brings people together. For the lifesavers, the purpose was to rescue swimmers; for Supercell employees, it is to create games that capture the users' imagination. Your organization's assumptions should start with an understanding of market opportunities.

Ecosystem refers to how resources and people are organized to win in the marketplace. The term is sometimes overused and has many meanings in different settings. But we will use the term as we've just defined it. For example, the lifesavers ecosystem brought together people with different skills to a common cause. At Supercell, the ecosystem is not one game or one team but how the teams connect to and learn from one another to create powerful games that endure over decades around the world. Lessons from one game's development transfer to other teams as people and ideas move from team to team. Capabilities as organizational strengths are not embedded in just the platform, cells, or strategic partners, but flourish in the connections between and within all these organizational units. With this ecosystem logic, organizations prize fluidity and the ability to pivot.

If you want an organization that acts more like a market-oriented ecosystem, many of your assumptions need to change. The ecosystem logic requires you to think of independent units (cells or teams) connected to each other through sharing information on customers, innovation, and agility. The organization doesn't achieve results through efficiencies, alignment, or capabilities. It succeeds because its participation in a broader network of teams and partners, internal and external, allows faster response to changing conditions. This evolution of organizational logic is summarized in table 1-2.

A Six-Part Framework for Reinventing the Organization

As we synthesized previous organizational research, explored front-runner companies, and drew on our decades of experience in teaching and consulting with executives in numerous organizations, we began to identify the specific choices leaders make to create a market-oriented ecosystem. In particular, for the eight companies we studied, we scrutinized the public information and conducted

TABLE 1-2

Evolution of organizational logic

Organizational trends	Defining quote	Image or metaphor	Focus	Current applications
Hierarchy: efficiency and structure	"Any customer can have a car painted any colour that he wants so long as it is black." (Henry Ford, 1909) "Take my assets—but leave me my organization and in five years I'll have it all back." (Alfred P. Sloan, 1926)[a]	• Machine with parts • Well-defined roles and areas of specialization	• Standard operating procedures and processes • Well-defined accountability, with roles and responsibilities spelled out	• Reengineering, six sigma, lean manufacturing, etc., to drive efficiency • Multidivisional firms; strategic business units; matrices; delayering
Systems: alignment	"It's not about the smartest guys in the room. It is about thinking collectively" (Peter Senge, 1990)[b]	Integrated systems aligned within the organization, which is aligned with the environment	• Ensuring that systems connect with each other • Diagnosing systems' problems	• Healthy organizations • Organizational alignment audits
Capability: organizational identity	"What the organization is known for and able to do that creates intangible value that others can't replicate" (Dave Ulrich and Norm Smallwood, 2004)	Capabilities within the organization shape its identity and intangibles	Identifying and investing in key capabilities	• Cultural audits • Process improvements
Ecosystem: interdependency among a network of partners	"Tencent manages half of our lives in our hands; the other half is in the hands of our partners in the ecosystem" (Pony Ma, chairman and CEO of Tencent, March 23, 2015)	• Organizational capabilities exist in the ecosystem • Market-oriented ecosystem	Building and collaborating with agile business teams and powerful platforms connected to each other inside and outside organization	Creating innovative and agile organizations that inspire people to win in the marketplace

a. Thomas S. Bateman and Scott A. Snell, *Management: Building Competitive Advantage* (Homewood Park, IL: Richard D Irwin, 1999), 276.
b. Peter Senge, *The Fifth Discipline* (New York: Doubleday, 1990).

FIGURE 1-4

A six-part framework for reinventing the organization as a market-oriented ecosystem (MOE)

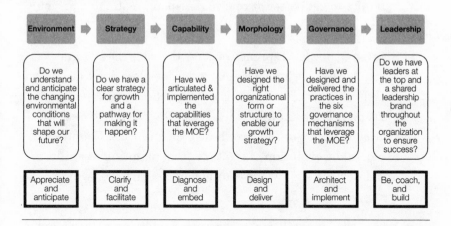

Environment ⇒	Strategy ⇒	Capability ⇒	Morphology ⇒	Governance ⇒	Leadership
Do we understand and anticipate the changing environmental conditions that will shape our future?	Do we have a clear strategy for growth and a pathway for making it happen?	Have we articulated & implemented the capabilities that leverage the MOE?	Have we designed the right organizational form or structure to enable our growth strategy?	Have we designed and delivered the practices in the six governance mechanisms that leverage the MOE?	Do we have leaders at the top and a shared leadership brand throughout the organization to ensure success?
Appreciate and anticipate	Clarify and facilitate	Diagnose and embed	Design and deliver	Architect and implement	Be, coach, and build

a series of in-depth private interviews with executives inside the companies, as well as company alumni. We walked the corridors, visited the offices, and spoke to the people. We looked at the environments in which the firms competed, the strategies they devised, the capabilities they deliberately fostered, and the leadership they showed throughout the organization. In gathering and distilling all this information, we were able to define the principles and actions that make the market-oriented ecosystem work.

Our goal is not just to describe this new organizational form but to present specific principles and practices that any leader can use to reinvent their organization. Figure 1-4 summarizes our findings on how market-oriented ecosystems work.

Our framework for reinventing an organization has six dimensions:

- **Environment:** how very successful companies appreciate and anticipate the trends and changes in their business context: social, technical, economic, political, environmental, and demographic. The pace of change in each of these areas demands ever-increasing responsiveness and innovation. These organizations look beyond current market conditions to anticipate and create what can be. In chapter 2, we take you through environmental elements that you need to understand, and we offer five actions that you and your employees can take to get better at reading, responding to, and anticipating changes in your environment.

- **Strategy:** how entrepreneurs grow their businesses and through what paths. These successful leaders don't just seek market share; they also anticipate and create market opportunity. They know how to allocate resources to create strategic agility to capture these opportunities. Chapter 3 explores the evolution of strategy from planning to agility and describes eight ways your company can become more strategically agile.

- **Ecosystem capabilities:** how cutting-edge companies win by taking advantage of and sharing information about each person's or team's knowledge and other strengths and becoming truly customer-centric, innovative, and agile. These market-oriented organizations create capabilities in the overarching ecosystem more than they do within their own boundaries. Chapter 4 traces the evolution from organizational capabilities to ecosystem capabilities and shows how four key capabilities are central to reinventing your organization.

- **Morphology:** how the most successful companies have created new organizational forms that enable their talent to nimbly capture market changes and opportunities, quickly generate ideas, experiment, close unprofitable trials, and make big businesses out of the successful ones. The form most useful in this regard consists of platforms, business teams (cells), and strategic partners (allies). This new organizational form is neither pure matrix nor multidivisional nor holding company. We offer a primer on the new form in chapter 5.

- **Governance mechanisms:** how the best companies make the ecosystem truly connected and collaborative by sharing culture, performance accountability, ideas, talent, and information. These governance mechanisms guide and reinforce the mission, vision, and operations of the firm. Chapters 6 through 11 take you through each of the six key governance attributes and show you how market-oriented ecosystems address them.

- **Leadership at all levels:** how the top leaders redesign the organization's morphology and set the context and rules for self-driven units to operate through market-oriented relationships. Leaders face the challenge of encouraging a culture that empowers, energizes, and orients the employees. Last but not least, successful organizations build leadership at all levels so that people actively take initiatives, much as the strangers did at the Panama City beach. Chapters 12 and 13 show you how to lead a market-oriented ecosystem.

By understanding and systematically addressing these six dimensions, leaders in any organization can create and scale an organization that serves customers, continually innovates, and agilely responds to opportunities and challenges. That's precisely what you'll learn in this book. For each dimension, we will explore the principles, practices, and other tools for improving your company's ability to respond to fast-changing environments.

The Roadmap for Reinventing Your Organization

This book is about what we can learn from places like Alibaba, Amazon, DiDi, Facebook, Google, Huawei, Supercell, and Tencent, which have imagined and then built organizations that truly meet the needs of the future: that are large and small at the same time and that create the conditions for success. While they understand that it is challenging to get scarce resources such as money, cutting-edge technology, and talented people, the more challenging part is how to organize and integrate these resources to create their differentiating competitiveness. There is no shortcut, but this book provides a comprehensive roadmap (table 1-3).

TABLE 1-3

Roadmap for reinventing your organization

Use of diagnosis: assess how you or your organization addresses each dimension of the market-oriented ecosystem. Give yourself a letter grade: L for low, M for medium, or H for high performing (or however you want to define these letters). You will want to put extra focus on the dimensions that scored L.

MOE dimension	Self/organization assessment question	Score (L, M, H)	Chapter and key messages and tools
Part I. The context: responding to fast-changing markets			
Environment	Do we understand and anticipate the changing forces facing our industry and organization?		Chapter 2: • Learning a disciplined process for defining environmental context • Responding to VUCA and the pace of change
Strategy	Do we have a clear strategy for growth and a pathway for making the strategy happen?		Chapter 3: • Defining a pathway for growth • Making strategic agility happen
Part II. The new organizational form: what a market-oriented ecosystem looks like			
Capability	Do we have capabilities that create our ecosystem identity? Do these capabilities emphasize information, customer, innovation, and agility?		Chapter 4: Creating the four essential capabilities in the ecosystem: • External sensing • Customer obsession • Innovation throughout • Agility everywhere
Morphology	Do we have the right organizational form or structure to make growth happen?		Chapter 5: Clarifying the operational requirements for all parts of the ecosystem: • Platform • Cell (team) • Allies (strategic partners)
Part III. Governance: how a market-oriented ecosystem works			
Culture	Do we have the right culture embedded in our organization?		Chapter 6: • Defining the right culture as an identity (what do we want to be known for by our key customers?) • Embedding culture throughout the organization
Performance accountability	Do we have clear and positive performance accountability for activities and outcomes?		Chapter 7: • Tying standards and incentives to key outcomes • Holding people accountable in a positive way, with Eastern and Western philosophies

MOE dimension	Self/organization assessment question	Score (L, M, H)	Chapter and key messages and tools
Idea generation	Do we constantly seek new ideas through experimentation and continuous improvement?		Chapter 8: • Generating an idea pipeline through experimentation and curiosity • Generalizing ideas through disciplined sharing
Talent	Do we have the right people with the right skills in the right roles with the right commitment?		Chapter 9: • Getting the right people into and around the organization • Creating meaning and purpose among employees
Information	Do we have radical transparency and share information?		Chapter 10: • Encouraging radical transparency • Embedding tools for sharing information throughout the organization
Collaboration	Do we know how to work together to make the whole more than the parts?		Chapter 11: • Managing tools for getting groups and people to work well together (common goals, the right people, shared processes, the right incentives) • Sharing ideas across boundaries inside the organization (learning matrix)

Part IV. Turning ideas into impact: how to lead a market-oriented ecosystem

Leadership	Do we both at the top and throughout the organization have leaders who help others achieve their best ?		Chapter 12: • Identifying key leadership competencies for MOE • Ensuring leadership depth throughout the organization
Transforming the existing organization	Do we know how to adapt ideas from successful MOEs to create a more innovative organization?		Chapter 13: • Adapting key MOE principles to transforming traditional organizations • Making any company more innovative

Note: MOE, market-oriented ecosystem; L, M, H, low, medium, or high score on your assessment; VUCA, volatility, uncertainty, complexity, and ambiguity.

The market-oriented ecosystem model and the assumptions that underpin it are not only for internet and high-tech firms. This new organizational model applies to firms in any industry, including retail, manufacturing, health care, finance, consulting, and other professional services, especially in the new era of digital and technological empowerment. By using the ideas and tools in this book, you can reinvent your organization to deliver enormous value to all your stakeholders.

As you undertake this important work in your organization, we offer a number of caveats. First, see the whole, but get started on only a part of the transformation. This book is intended as a comprehensive guide to help you see all the parts and how they all work together as a whole. The six dimensions in figure 1-4 offer a complete systems approach to creating the market-oriented ecosystem and represent the overall logic of the new organization. For each dimension, we will include principles that will inform your own assumptions about your organization. We will share stories to illustrate these principles in practice. And we will provide both some assessments to help you determine where your organization stands today on these dimensions and some effective tools for improving.

We recognize that the information provided here may seem like an overwhelming set of principles and practices. You should not expect to make progress on everything all at once. Bite off little chunks at a time. Pick one of the six dimensions, and try one assessment in your organization. Or start asking your teams some of the questions included in each chapter. If something works, try to build on it by using another tool in the book. If something you try doesn't work, look at a different part of the system. Can you find a component that is ready for change? Above all, keep coming back to the basic challenges of reinventing your organization with new assumptions and specific actions.

Second, the eight firms we explore in detail may not look like your company in terms of industry, age, size, heritage, or culture As we've said, it is easier to create a new organization than to reinvent an existing one. But we will show you how you can adapt specific principles and practices that will let you begin to reinvent your company. Start where you can start. Pick a pilot site that is best suited for experimentation. Learn, practice, and adapt these principles. Have confidence that early successes will cumulate. We hope our book serves as a guide for this journey.

Third, in a world of rapid change, the eight companies we study face ongoing challenges, too. In fact, as we write this, all of these companies are undergoing dramatic changes. Because of their sheer size and scope, some of them often find themselves in the headlines. Uncertainty looms as government scrutiny and regulation seem likely. As the saying goes, with greater power comes greater responsibility. As these companies become much more influential because of their instant access to millions of people's data, their moves into many new market spaces, and their expanded capabilities through the ecosystem, their responsibilities to users, industries, and society become greater. Market-oriented ecosystems need to use their prowess and data judiciously. Otherwise, they lose the trust of customers and the confidence of society at large. How will they manage public scrutiny as they become more visible? How do they respond to the public concerns about pervasive technology and privacy? These are the challenges that these pioneering companies need to continue to address to ensure their sustainable success.

Finally, none of these companies are perfect. Nor do all of them excel in all the principles we distilled from studying them as a group. Leaders who want to adapt the ideas from this book should focus on the principles and practices of the companies we studied more than on these companies' stories. In the face of unpredictable changes, some of these companies may be disrupted sooner or later, and their practices will evolve continuously. But the principles remain relatively stable. Looking ahead, how can successful companies avoid the liability of their own success and remember that they have to continually reinvent themselves? How do they transfer their organizational logic to the next generation of leaders? One thing we can anticipate: while some of the companies we studied will probably remain leaders, a few of them may lag behind. For this reason, the underlying principles and practices mean more than does an individual company's story.

PART I

THE CONTEXT

RESPONDING TO
FAST-CHANGING MARKETS

You start reinventing your organization by understanding the context in which you work. Not having context is like designing a building without knowing what it is to be used for. Is it a residence, an office space, a retail space, or a community center? Context defines the setting for the new organization and the strategy that determines the desired outcomes.

In this part of the book, we focus on the context of the emerging market-oriented ecosystem (figure I-1). In chapter 2, we explore the dynamic environment that gives rise to the ecosystem's form and offer you a template and methodology for examining your context. Knowing this context will help you and your employees know why you are reinventing your organization and recognize the riptides your organization faces. If the swimmers from chapter 1 had known this context (the danger of riptides), they would not have gone swimming (or would have been better prepared for the danger).

No doubt, the circumstances in our personal and organizational lives are more dynamic and complex than ever. This complexity demands the organizational logic needed for reinventing a market-oriented ecosystem. Your organization will succeed not just because of its hierarchy (structure and role clarity), alignment (systems), or capability (internal identity), but because of your ability to recognize and respond to environmental changes.

As you probably recognize in your organization, competitors may come from anywhere in the world through the internet. Customers today have enormous choice over where they acquire products or

FIGURE I-1

A six-part framework for reinventing the organization as a market-oriented ecosystem (MOE)

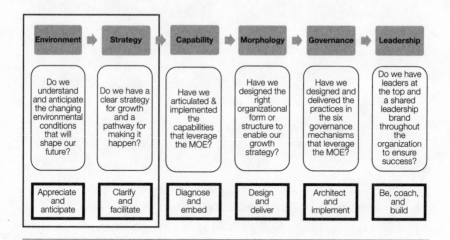

services, and employees have high work expectations around their personal and diverse lifestyles. What's more, the cycle time for new ideas is ever shorter when forums like TED talks can instantly share insights globally. The frameworks and tools in chapter 2 describe how you can understand and respond to these environmental changes.

Context also includes the internal choices that define what your organization should look like. Strategic choices offer a blueprint for where to play and how to win in the future. Many terms have been used to articulate a firm's future agenda: mission, vision, aspiration, goals, objectives, intent, themes, priorities, plans, values, purpose, kernels, and so on. While these words have different nuances of meaning (some focus on why, others on what or how), they all point to differentiating your firm from competitors in the future.

If you want to reinvent your organization, you need to change your focus to strategic agility. Market-oriented organizations challenge the rules of competition to focus less on market share and more on market opportunity. Rather than simply respond to industry conditions, these organizations pay more attention to creating new conditions. In chapter 3, we review these emerging strategic choices and suggest ways to create strategic agility for your company.

Chapters 2 and 3 will guide you toward the reinvented organization by helping you both understand your company's situation (context) and shape your appropriate responses.

CHAPTER 2

The Environment

How Can You Recognize, Respond to, and Shape It?

In the Amazon Go store, apps guide the customers to the products they want—no more hunting.[1] The internet of things tracks products and manages orders and inventory. Robots greet customers, refill store shelves, and clean floors. Amazon Go went public while it was still in the experimental stage—but that is just the start. Amazon and the other enormously successful companies we studied are willing to conduct bold experiments to learn fast and create new businesses should they succeed. The companies often lay the technology tracks in front of these experiments just in time. Even if the experiments go off the rails—as they sometimes do (witness Fire Phone, Amazon Wallet, Amazon WebPay, Amazon Local, among others)—they are staking out the space, advancing the conversation, centering themselves in the public eye, and building their company's brand. The experiments are strategically signaling the companies' intentions with a heavy focus on learning.

In other words, the successful companies we have studied have already created what others in conferences, symposia, and TED talks are calling "the future of work." The fact is, the future is here right now.

A market-oriented ecosystem like Amazon succeeds when its leaders anticipate the changing conditions of their business and turn these changes into opportunities. The ecosystem then organizes with an eye to future prospects more so than it tries to build on its historical successes.[2] This chapter offers five insights, with templates and tools, you can deploy to respond to these opportunities. When you anticipate and embrace the future, you can create a need for change and a pathway to progress.

The Impact of the Environment on the Future of Work

What do you and your employees need to know about environmental changes, and how will you handle them? Will you see these changes, embrace them, create highly adaptive organizations, and continuously support people who must deal with the always-shifting ground beneath their feet? If you fail to appreciate the context that shapes your future work, you will struggle to create the right content to respond.

The most dangerous place to be today and going forward is to believe yourself to be utterly competent and confident in a business you do not recognize as outdated. Consider the framework in figure 2-1.

Of course, we all want to be in quadrant 1: doing the right thing well. Which is the most dangerous quadrant? Most say quadrant 4 (doing the wrong thing poorly), but in fact, the place of greatest peril in a changing world is quadrant 2: doing the wrong thing well. Why? Because it is a trap of misguided excellence that once-successful companies like Kodak, Nokia, Sears, Blockbuster, Myspace, Atari, and many others fell into and never found their way out fast enough. The pace of external change guarantees that the right thing will inevitably become the wrong thing, often soon. To stay in quadrant 1, you can never be comfortable, never be too

FIGURE 2-1

Understanding environmental change

		What we do	
		The right thing	The wrong thing
How we do it	Well	1 We do the right thing well.	2 We do the wrong thing well.
	Poorly	3 We do the right thing poorly.	4 We do the wrong thing poorly.

sure of yourself. This lack of complacency is what reinvention is all about.

A fundamental paradox of our age is that you need to provide your business and your people with continuity and some sense of security at the same time that you need to stay perpetually alert to changing what you are doing and how you are doing it. To ensure that you and your employees understand why it is time to reinvent your organization, share information on the environmental demands disrupting every industry, including yours.

There are five actions you and your employees can take to understand the environmental changes building the case for reinventing your organization. These actions help you stay in quadrant 1.

Recognize Industry Disruptions

The future of work is already here. We see major changes in industry after industry, with new models emerging that run with the advances in technology, create new business models, and upend the status quo. No industry is immune: hospitality, automotive, retail, financial services, health care, education, media, and even food delivery have all experienced major upheavals. The summary of industry transformations in table 2-1 should convince you and your employees of the need to quickly reinvent your organization.

TABLE 2-1

Industry transformations

Industry	Transformations
Hospitality	• Airbnb (started in 2008) offers more lodging than does any hotel chain in the world (Hilton, Marriott, Hyatt, Intercontinental). Remarkably, the largest lodging firm in the world owns no hotel rooms. • Airbnb customers (guests) have more choice, can contact hosts directly, and often have a more intimate customer experience.
Automotive rental and taxi services	• Uber (founded 2009), Lyft (2012), and DiDi (2012) offer ride sharing that disrupts traditional taxi and car-rental industries. Today, the largest taxi companies in the world own no cars. • DiDi (part of Tencent and profiled in this book) provides services that include taxi hailing and private-car hailing. • Customers participate in the sharing economy and have more flexibility on price, service, and availability. • Drivers (independent contractors) also have flexibility of work hours and autonomy.
Self-driving cars	• Many companies are competing to create the driverless car: Waymo (part of Google ecosystem), Uber, Tesla, and most traditional automotive companies (e.g., BMW, Ford, GM, Mercedes Benz, Nissan, and Toyota). In a huge change from the old system, the car that now transports you does not have to have a driver! • Self-driving cars rely on AI, artificial neural learning, sensors, and other technologies to automate driving. • Throughout the entire transportation industry, customers—including drivers, delivery, insurance, manufacturing, and so forth—will be affected.
E-commerce; online shopping	• Every retail organization (brick and mortar, grocery, pharmacy, travel) has integrated e-commerce, which continues to rapidly expand, reinvent the retail model, and provide extraordinary shopping experiences. The store where you shop today often has no physical footprint. • Smart retail relies on technological advances in big data, the internet of things, mass customization, machine learning, AI, robotics, and the digitization of assets, operations, and the workforce. • Customers have greater flexibility, choice, and customization of products and services.
Education	• Massive open online courses and other forms of digital learning are making quality education universal; nearly all universities offer a form of online education. The setting where you learn might no longer be a classroom. • Khan Academy (a free online academy), TED talks, Wikipedia, and other information sources are readily available to customers. • Customers who want to learn can use blended learning to access real-time knowledge.
Financial services	• All forms of banking are being disrupted: depositing and investing money, paying for services (a cashless society), and insurance. Carrying cash and going to a bank are fast becoming things of the past. • Technologies like blockchain, cloud data, big data, predictive analytics, robots, and AI are shaping financial experiences. • Customers have much more control over how to manage their money.
Health care	• Vertical integration is occurring with ventures like CVS and Aetna. • Technology is rapidly changing diagnosis and treatment (e.g., telemedicine). Your doctor need not be present to serve you. • Because customers know more about their health than they used to, they can make better-informed decisions about their health.

So, why do all these industry transformations matter to reinventing your organization? First, they build a case for rapid change because disruptions are happening so quickly, everywhere. To what extent do you as a leader understand and anticipate the environmental conditions that will shape your future? The more you, and your employees, have your head on a swivel, perpetually looking outside to sense new trends, the better off you will be. Second, if you are an early adopter of the market-oriented ecosystem principles and practices, you will better serve customers, outperform competitors, inspire employees, and delight investors. Had the swimmers in chapter 1 been aware of the riptides, they would have avoided the risk. Had the eighty rescuers not been aware of the swimmers' challenges, they would have missed an opportunity to save them.

Accept the Inevitability of Change

The bottom line is that in today's world, your organizations must respond to change and adopt new ways of doing things, even if you fail in the short term so that you can learn and grow. One wise senior executive told us, "It took fifty years to build an organization that can be lost today in less than two years, if we don't change." For individuals, the half-life of knowledge (when 50 percent of what we know and do is out-of-date) is shrinking. Even in the more stable world of management knowledge, one of us (Dave) has seen that half of his teaching notes on a topic need to be changed every eighteen to twenty-four months, whereas the half-life used to be three to four years.

How fast do you need to change? Organizations and people must change at least as quickly as their circumstances do. Without the ability to change, even large organizations can falter or die (think of Circuit City, Compaq, Digital Equipment Corporation, Eastern Airlines, Enron, Gillette, Gulf Oil, Kodak, Motorola, Nokia, Philip Morris, Sears, Toys "R" Us, TWA, and Woolworths). In the last fifteen years, we found that more than 50 percent of the Standard & Poor's companies have disappeared; in the next ten years, estimates are that more than 40 percent will disappear. Similarly, employees

TABLE 2-2

Ten companies with the largest market capitalization in the world

Firm and ranking	Market cap as of April 12, 2019 (in billions of dollars)	Year founded
1. Apple	$938	1976
2. Microsoft	$928	1975
3. Amazon	$905	1994
4. Alphabet (Google)	$847	1998
5. Berkshire Hathaway	$515	1839
6. Facebook	$511	2004
7. Alibaba	$490	1999
8. Tencent	$478	1998
9. Johnson & Johnson	$362	1886
10. Exxon Mobil	$343	1999 (1870)

Source: Data from each company's official website and financial statements.

who do not learn new skills may lose their edge and find themselves unemployed and depending on others for opportunities. Even then, who will hire buggy-whip technicians? And at what wage?

What does all this add up to? New organizations have emerged and operate differently in today's world. As table 2-2 shows, six of the world's most valuable firms by market cap were founded in the mid-1990s or later when both technology and the commercial exploitation of the internet exploded at the same time with new ideas and offerings.[3]

In a world of inevitable and rapid change, it is not information that matters but how the information is accessed and applied. Size and stability are trumped by quickness and agility. What holds true for companies also holds true for individuals: many existing jobs will be eliminated and new jobs created.

The best advice we can offer in this new world of work is this: get out of your comfort zone and ask yourself, What opportunities will the new technologies offer the world and, therefore, me? Then, recognize the transformations noted above in retail, manufacturing, financial, health care, education, and see how similar disruptions are facing your business. Predict the evolution of your industry *not* from the past, but by imagining backward from the future. Become a futurist who imagines things others don't see. Surround yourself with people who are different from you. Spend more time with the younger generation to learn how this group thinks and feels. Network with geeks who are technologically savvy. Talk to founders of startups. Visit places where you are not necessarily comfortable. Go to Silicon Valley, Israel, or China periodically to see how things are moving. Constantly be looking for what is missing and what people might need.

For organizations and individuals, accept the inevitability of change. Be encouraged, not afraid of change. See change as an opportunity not a threat. Run into change, don't hide from it. And, infuse this enthusiasm in those around you.

Learn the Emerging Language of Business

Each industrial age comes with its own language. The first industrial revolution was about mechanical production, with insights on steam engine, machine tools, and factories. The second industrial revolution was the age of science and mass production, with gasoline engines, airplanes, assembly lines, and electricity and lighting. The third and current revolution is about connectivity, digitalization, and big data. Technology enables access to digital information and this information improves analytics and decision making. This information age has a unique vocabulary that becomes the basis for those involved in the new organization. To adapt to the new and changing work, leaders and employees need to learn and master the key ideas shaping this digital age. How many of the terms in table 2-3 can you and your employees define? How many of these concepts are you using in your company? (Note: The table is not meant to be a comprehensive list, but is representative of the kinds of things we hear executives talking about today.)

TABLE 2-3

Terms of the digital and information revolution

3-D printing	convergence	millennials
advanced materials	deep learning	nanotech
alternative energy	design thinking	quantum computing
analytics	digitization	renewable energy
artificial intelligence (AI)	drones	robotics/chatbots
big data	experience economy	sensors
biotech	gamification	social media
blockchain	internet of things	social networks
cloud computing	machine learning	sustainability
cognitive automation	machine vision	transportability
connectivity	mass customization	virtual reality

Use Frameworks to Organize the Chaos of Environmental Change

We can categorize six major types of change in this complex external environment: social, technical, economic, political, environmental, and demographic (STEPED). For the sake of focus, ask yourself, which two trends are most affecting our world?

- **Social:** changing lifestyles, social trends (urbanization, flexibility of where work is done, work-life balance, social mobility, globalization)

- **Technical:** increasing digitalization, the use of technology for efficiency, innovation, information, and connection (see the digital terms in table 2-3)

- **Economic:** global markets with new competitors, economic cycles, new business models

- **Political:** political unrest, regulatory policies and shifts, increased nationalism or populism, global trade

- **Environmental:** social responsibility, community reputation, effects of climate change, sustainability

- **Demographic:** changing workforces, influence of millennials, women in leadership positions, unconscious biases and cognitive styles, aging employees

These six categories can help you organize the information you have gathered on the external circumstances your organization faces. For example, we have asked leaders to complete the STEPED exercise in table 2-4 to describe changing environmental conditions. How do you gain the external knowledge and insight to complete such an exercise competently? We make it simple, having people identify what they need to learn, what they must do to learn it, and what outcomes they should be looking for because of this learning and doing.

In workshops and our consulting work, we often ask which of the six categories has the most impact on an organization's future success. Inevitably, people answer that technology or digitalization has the greatest effect. Digitization particularly is changing everything. As discussed earlier, digitization can touch every aspect of a business, speeding it up and making it more capable of handling both volume and complexity with low error rates. In industry transformation, we see the digitization of assets (infrastructure,

TABLE 2-4

Changing environmental conditions: a STEPED assessment tool

Identify a geographic location or an industry, and answer the questions to describe the environmental conditions.

Category	What are the industry trends in each category?	What opportunities and threats will these trends imply?	What actions could we take to anticipate and respond to these trends?
Social conditions			
Technology			
Economics			
Politics			
Environment			
Demographic			

connected machines, data, data platforms); operations (processes, payments, business models, customer and supply-chain interactions); and the workforce (digital tools, digitally skilled workers, and new digital jobs and roles).

To prepare for the future, spend some time looking at these six trends and how they might affect your organization. Organizing and understanding the world of change enables you and your employees to not be threatened by the changes ahead but to be prepared for and excited about them.

Help Employees Experience the Positive Impact of Rapid Change

Perhaps the most important consideration of these six trends that necessitate the organization's reinvention is their impact on the people directly responsible for this reinvention. In our work, we found that when employees have a positive experience at work, customer engagement and better investors' results follow. In study after study, employee engagement, though stabilizing in the 60 to 65 percent range and rising slightly in recent years, falls short of what it could be.[4]

There are many barriers to better employee work experiences, but clearly some obstacles come from traditional organizations that box in their employees, limiting their opportunities, energy, and passion. A reinvented organization liberates employees to engage in work that excites them. They shift from boxes that constrain them to open areas that give them opportunities to grow.

If anything, the digital world only exacerbates this employee limitation. The very technologies that are creating so many opportunities have, in many ways, made the world more difficult to live in as well. Social media is particularly blamed for increasing amounts of personal malaise and social isolation. In various studies of millennials, researchers found that increased use of social media platforms (more than two hours a day) bred more perceived social isolation and lower well-being.[5]

In addition, loneliness is a higher cause of mortality than is high blood pressure, high cholesterol, inactivity (lack of exercise), drinking, anxiety, or depression.[6] And technology that should connect people actually isolates them. The US surgeon general recently stated that loneliness is more serious a health problem than are opiates.[7] The United Kingdom has just named a minister of loneliness to create policies to deal with the challenge of social isolation.[8]

So, what does this employee and personal malaise have to do with reinventing your organization? Organizations are a primary setting for people to find a sense of belief (meaning and purpose), an ability to become (learning and growth), and a community of belonging (connection and teams).[9] When your reinvented organization delivers belief, enables learning and growth, and advances belonging, your employees will have a greater sense of well-being and increased productivity. Again, imagine how the rescuers must have felt after saving the family caught in a riptide. Do you think they felt that way at work the next day?

At Tencent WeChat, employees always look deep beyond activity and experience to understand the meaning of why people are using WeChat. When brainstorming new features or applications, they do not position WeChat as just an instant messaging tool (activity), or strive to improve its efficiency, user-friendliness, or stability to enhance user experience, but look at it as a means to address people's

TABLE 2-5

Self-assessment of your organization's understanding of the environment

Diagnostic question: to what extent do we . . .	Assessment*	How could we improve?
Recognize industry disruptions		
Accept the inevitability of change		
Learn the emerging language of business		
Use frameworks (such as the six environmental trends) to identify and assess the sources of environmental change		
Engage employees to have a positive response to change		

*On a scale of 1 to 5, where 1 = very poorly and 5 = very well, how are we doing?

need for social acceptance, to reduce loneliness, and to raise self-esteem in a connected world.[10] The access to enormous user data and the enabling technologies can help employees address user needs, starting at the activity level, moving to experience level, and ultimately reaching the meaning level. When we are helping consumers to find meaning, we get meaning ourselves.

All the market-oriented ecosystems we studied give employees a strong sense of purpose. Aligning employee purpose with company purpose and offering employees opportunities to make a difference at their jobs can make work more engaging and fulfilling.

Managerial Implications

Organizations operate within a context. When you and your employees appreciate the shifting context of your work, you build a case for change and can better align your organization to those changes and transform it. We suggest rating and discussing the five actions in table 2-5 to increase your understanding of environmental trends.

CHAPTER 3

Strategic Agility

How Can You Define a Pathway for Growth?

Think back to 1999. China is on the move. Applying the six-trend STEPED tool we introduced in the previous chapter, we see changes in the six categories. *Socially*, urbanization is well under way as more and more people move into the cities, and dual-income families are on the rise. *Technologically*, the internet is becoming increasingly widespread and utilized. *Economically*, China's gross domestic product and personal disposable income are on the rise. *Politically*, the country is opening up more and more, joining the international community and removing various barriers. *Environmentally*, China is also changing due to economic takeoff: traffic jams in large cities make shopping (and selling) time consuming and inconvenient. *Demographically*, the one-child policy in place for a generation has brought a sharp decline in the level of poverty, and those well-cared-for children are enjoying greater wealth and educational opportunities. Middle class is burgeoning because of better employment opportunities in the cities. And, as is the case everywhere else, everyone likes to shop.

Now imagine that you are Jack Ma, the famed founder of Alibaba. You are fluent in English, you believe in the power of the internet, and you have tried your hand at several small ventures before. True, you have been unsuccessful, but you have learned. You are intensely curious, always seeking more information and ideas. You have a passion for helping small Chinese businesses grow, and you have a deep desire to succeed yourself. In light of your experience, you see an opportunity to connect the vast ocean of Chinese manufacturers to a globe awash in potential buyers: an infinitely large online marketplace, just waiting to be tapped. You launch your new company Alibaba.com in your apartment, energized by the vision of helping Chinese small businesses export overseas, just to begin with.

Now imagine that it is 2019. Alibaba has long been the dominant force in Chinese e-commerce. Your company has earned a market value of approximately US$490 billion, serves some 450 million customers in over two hundred countries, and offers a host of successful businesses related to e-commerce. As of today, Alibaba is one of the ten most highly capitalized business in the world.

How did you climb this high in just nineteen years?

Environment creates the space. Strategy defines the choices to fill the space. Organization makes the strategy happen. In a very dynamic environment—like China in the case of Alibaba—the key strategic challenge is to transform your company as fast as, or faster than, the environment changes. We call the ability to make these necessary choices quickly, creatively, and intelligently *strategic agility*. As the saying goes, organizations are perfectly designed to get the results they get. In the market-oriented ecosystem, strategy shapes the organization in ways that enable it to win. Sometimes, when the strategy is as powerful as Alibaba's, it even shapes the environment in which the competition is taking place. So, how do you as a leader learn from market-oriented ecosystems to become strategically agile?

Strategy Is about Choice

The fundamental goal of strategy is to make informed choices that help a firm win. No company has unlimited resources. Skill and judgment allocate scarce resources to capture evolving opportunities for profitable growth. Firms fail all too often because they stick around too long in a business space that is no longer profitable. In fact, as discussed in chapter 2, when you consider the list of the top ten most successful businesses in the world, most were founded to capture the rise of the great computing and communication technologies in the last few decades (see table 2-2). Microsoft was founded in 1975, Apple in 1976, and Amazon in 1994, followed by Alphabet (née Google) and Tencent in 1998 and Alibaba a year later. Facebook was founded in 2004. Where are the colossi of the twenty-first century? Not at the top. Many are not even alive.

Pivoting from Strategic Choice to Strategic Agility

If you want to reinvent your organization, you need to improve your ability to make choices that lead to strategic agility. Reflect on how your organization has approached strategy, and compare your work to the strategic agility choices made by market-oriented ecosystems to see which part of the evolutionary wave you are in (figure 3-1). Note also how this evolution of strategy matches the evolution of organizational logic and structure (see figure 1-2 and table 1-2). This connection makes sense, because structure generally follows strategy. Let's now consider the four evolutionary stages of strategy.

FIGURE 3-1

Evolution of strategic choice

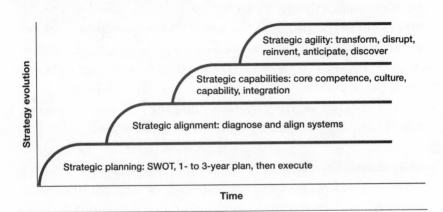

Strategic agility: transform, disrupt, reinvent, anticipate, discover

Strategic capabilities: core competence, culture, capability, integration

Strategic alignment: diagnose and align systems

Strategic planning: SWOT, 1- to 3-year plan, then execute

Strategy evolution

Time

Stage 1: Strategic Planning. This stage represents the traditional top-down, hierarchical (or even bureaucratic) model in which strategic work is centralized within a dedicated group in the senior ranks of the organization. This group largely focuses on serving the internal logic of the organization with little regard for external factors like competitors or even customers. The leaders often plan strategy in off-site meetings using SWOT analysis (a focus on strengths, weaknesses, opportunities, and threats). Once the strategic plan is set, the agreed-on time horizon is considered sacrosanct: one year, three years, or even five years. And the strategy is often treated like a trade secret, known only to the few. (In one case, we worked with a company that would number the printed copies of its strategic plan. Leaders had to "check out" a copy of the strategy but then had to return it.) The strategy is then enacted through objectives and performance targets cascaded through the hierarchy, with little connection to market opportunities. The organizational system is built through investing in practices, and the company seldom takes marketplace opportunities into account.

Stage 2: Strategic Alignment. In the next advancement, business leaders try to think through the impact that the strategy has—or could have—on the inner workings of the organization: its structures, systems, and culture. Strategic work is not considered complete until the organization is aligned around delivering it. The alignment decisions are based on the judgments of a few key people at the top who manage the integration. Classic frameworks like the star model (from the 1970s), the 7S model (developed in the early 1980s), or organizational health (an updated alignment model) provide checklists of organizational levers to be synched in ways that are, one hopes, mutually reinforcing of the strategy. Employees may or may not understand why they are being "aligned," and factors outside the firm are not considered in most alignment models.

Stage 3: Strategic Capabilities. In more recent work, a number of scholars, such as C. K. Prahalad and Gary Hamel, have redefined strategy as *core competences* or *capability* in recognition of the need for organizations to provide their customers with key intangible know-how or other intangibles: important competitive qualities that mattered to customers, like innovation or customer responsiveness. Capabilities result from the collective skills, abilities, and expertise of an organization—and represent the ways that people and resources are brought together to accomplish work. They form the identity and personality of the organization by defining what it is good at doing and, in the end, what the organization *is*. In a capability model, strategy work is not done until the systems are aligned around a few key organizational (internal) capabilities. The key strategic question in this organization is, What capabilities do we require to win?

Stage 4: Strategic Agility. What these high-performance, high-growth firms we studied share is their focus on strategic agility, or the ability to move quickly to define, anticipate, and penetrate new market opportunities. They focus on the outside more than the inside, on stakeholders more than processes, and on moving with agility even more than perfect accuracy. These agile organizations are guided by their mission and broad strategy. They are informed by their own external orientation and are held together by their common capabilities (more on this in chapter 4). Agile organizations take advantage of the tools of instant and ubiquitous information and data sharing. Your key leadership question for strategic agility is, How can we as an ecosystem make exceptionally good and dynamic choices through swift and self-initiated experimentation (like the riptide rescuers)? Strategy and execution occur simultaneously in close iterations, not preset in clearly laid-out annual plans.

This strategic agility comes from a mindset positioned to win in the future. Table 3-1 lists the mindset shifts you can use to achieve strategic agility. From this list, pick the two or three mindsets your organization must shift to make progress.

The evolution of strategic choices is clearly driven by the business context in which the company is operating. When one of us (Arthur) worked as head of human resources in Acer Group in the 1990s, the

TABLE 3-1

Strategic agility mindset in the market-oriented ecosystem

Shift from	Shift to	How to do it	Priority (pick 2 or 3)
Industry expert	Industry leader	Create a reputation as the innovator, not a follower, in the industry.	
Market share	Market opportunity	Appreciate and act on trends in the environment (see chapter 2).	
Who we are	How we are known by future customers	Define internal identity (reputation, values, culture) through the eyes of future customers.	
Our goals or ideas	How customers respond to our goals or ideas	Cocreate goals and outcomes with targeted customers' goals and outcomes.	
Penetrating existing markets	Creating new, uncontested markets	Experiment often with new ideas.	
Beating competition	Moving ahead of competition by focusing on customers	Strive to leapfrog competitors and to worry less about competitors' current opportunities.	
Blueprints for action (SWOT analyses, followed by strategy and key performance indicators)	Dynamic processes for agile choices guided by mission and broad strategic direction	Assume strategic agility by not locking into a definitive agenda	

Note: SWOT, strengths, weaknesses, opportunities, and threats.

PC industry had been going through major radical strategic changes every ten years. During that time, strategic alignment or strategic capability was adequate to handle the competitive environment Acer was facing. However, demand for strategic agility grows as the environment becomes more volatile, uncertain, complex, and ambiguous (VUCA). When he was working as senior adviser at Tencent in the last ten years, he witnessed radical changes for the internet industry every three years. Embrace the change, or meet your doom. Many leading internet players in China fell behind or died, simply because of their failures to make the right strategic choices in today's VUCA world. Some ventured into the wrong space (e.g.,

Baidu's entry into food delivery), remained in the shrinking market too long (e.g., Sina's focus on a PC portal), or moved too aggressively into new markets beyond their capabilities (e.g., Ofo in bike sharing service, Groupon in group-coupon purchasing). Knowing which stage best reflects your strategy and which mindsets have to shift will help you reinvent the organization in ways that help you win.

Alibaba's Strategic Agility

To illustrate strategic agility, look at how rapidly Alibaba grew in nineteen years, from 1999 to 2018, by basing its choices on a belief in the power of the internet and a shared mission. From the start, Alibaba's overall mission was "to make it easy to do business anywhere."[1] Here are some key business milestones for Alibaba that demonstrate the strategic agility of a market-oriented ecosystem:

1999   Jack Ma founds Alibaba.com to create China's first online B2B marketplace.

   The vision: Use an online business platform to give small Chinese export companies global reach.

2003   Company adds C2C Taobao Marketplace.

   New vision: Enable Chinese small and medium-sized enterprises to catch business opportunities in the Chinese consumer market.

2004   Company releases Alipay (secure payment system) and AliWangwang (instant messaging between buyer and seller to negotiate terms).

   New vision: Build the online business infrastructure in a way that improves consumer trust and security in online transactions.

2010   AliExpress, an online retail service enabling Chinese companies to offer products to international buyers, is established.

   New vision: Globalization!

2011   Taobao splits into three parts: Taobao Marketplace (C2C), Tmall.com (B2C), and eTao (for group
purchases).

New vision: Explore different business models of future
online e-commerce

2013   Company founds Cainiao Smart Logistics Network (logistics inside and outside China).

New vision: Build the logistic infrastructure for
e-commerce

2014   Alipay expands into Ant Financial Services Group.

New vision: Upgrade the payment and financial infrastructure for e-commerce. Go beyond payment and move
into new areas, such as loans to consumers and small
and medium-sized enterprises, investment products, and
investment services.

2015   Alibaba Cloud

New vision: Further expand and deepen the e-
commerce infrastructure by empowering technological
capabilities of companies to do business online and
offline.

2017   Five new strategies are unveiled in these areas: retail,
technology, finance, manufacturing, and energy, all taking full advantage of the digital world.

New vision: Build new business ecosystem, augment the
infrastructure to transform traditional industries in the
future.

Alibaba made major strategic moves and milestones to get to
where it is today. Alibaba's mission had been consistent and clear:
"To make it easy to do business anywhere," with small and medium-
sized businesses as its targeted customers. The conglomerate demonstrated strategic agility by pivoting from online B2B (Alibaba
.com) to C2C (Taobao, like eBay) to Alipay (and Ant Financial Ser-

vices Group) to logistics (with Cainiao) to Tmall and to the future of retailing.

Market-Oriented Ecosystem Principles and Practices That Can Be Adapted to Your Organization

What can you learn from Alibaba about creating strategic agility in your organization? Consider the following eight key principles demonstrated by Alibaba and the other market-oriented companies we studied.

Establish a Consistent Set of Priorities

Strategically agile firms establish and maintain a consistent set of priorities, resisting the temptation to chase whatever is in front of them. Most companies have a vision statement, but these firms live theirs. Alibaba stays focused on its mission "to make it easy to do business anywhere," initially paying attention to small businesses and then expanding to consumers and more-established businesses. Amazon espouses the same three priorities it started with in 1994—customer obsession, innovation, and be patient—and constantly evolves its business activities to be consistent with its mission statement: "To be earth's most customer-centric company, where customers can find and discover anything they might want to buy online." Google's mission is "To organize the world's information and make it universally accessible and useful." Facebook says, "People use Facebook to stay connected with friends and family, to discover what's going on in the world, and to share and express what matters to them." Huawei says, "To focus on our customers' market challenges and needs by providing excellent communications network solutions and services in order to consistently create maximum value for customers."[2]

As the mission statements of these market-oriented ecosystems show, their priorities remained relatively constant as the organizations evolved. So, to reinvent your organization, you need to have a mission or purpose statement that articulates your direction, is commonly understood, guides your company's actions, and is stable over time.

Create the Future by Anticipating What the Market Will Be

Strategically agile firms are a step ahead of the market. They anticipate and respond to marketplace trends (see STEPED analysis from table 2-4) that are critical to the company's future success. The great firms that we investigated have leaders who are ahead of the curve in envisioning the future. Amazon's Jeff Bezos believes that when you think about business three years down the road, you have a lot of competitors. If you can think seven or eight years further away, you encounter little competition.[3] To envision this future, market-oriented ecosystems not only rely on the strategic agility of people at the top but also count on the distributed leadership of smart people throughout—people who are empowered to think, not just execute. When anyone in these ecosystems sees an opportunity, he or she speaks up, suggests ideas, and takes risks, knowing that the ideas are greeted with respect.

How do firms like Amazon, Alibaba, Google, Facebook, Tencent, and others create their future before others even see it? Rule number one: remember your principles. They are your guide; keep them front and center.

There are other rules for creating a future. For example, rule number two: forget your past. You don't need to build on it, unless the future rewards it. Do not base your budget on past performance or tweak products that *used to* work brilliantly. That kind of strategic thinking led Nokia to fall off the cliff.

Third, anticipate your future by quickly letting go of anything that is outdated, outclassed, outmaneuvered, or outlasted. Accept that things go out of fashion. Everything, including your products, services, business model, and technology, has an expiration date. Only your principles survive. This means actively shedding the burdens of legacy structures, systems, and cultures. Position yourself in the future, and figure out how to get there regardless of what got you here.

Under the leadership of CEO Satya Nadella, Microsoft is doing exactly this. Building on Microsoft's leadership in PC Windows and Office, Nadella has redefined Microsoft's mission "to empower every person and every organization on the planet to achieve more." Instead of staying stuck in the PC mindset, Nadella embraces change by shifting the company's strategic priorities to mobile and the cloud. Instead of assuming, "We know it all," Nadella challenges the team to "learn it all." Instead of looking down on others' operating systems (e.g., Linux and Apple iOS), he adopts an open strategy to collaborate with other platforms and players. The future is clearly different from the past. Nadella honors the past and looks forward to the future, rescuing Microsoft of its last two lost decades. As a result, Microsoft has tripled its share price in four years and has outperformed Google as one of the most valuable firms in the world.[4]

Fourth and finally, accept the uncertainty of being a pioneer. Pioneers have a direction without the need for a clear destination. When you are a pioneer leader, the horizon will always recede in front of you because the nature of strategic agility is ongoing change. And this uncertainty is fine, as long as the direction is toward the right markets, which will also be ever evolving. It is the nature of pioneers to pioneer. It is the nature of settlers to settle. We live in the age of pioneers.

Win through a Focus on Growth

Strategically agile market-oriented ecosystems have a clear strategic focus on growth. So, how well are you growing your business? To grow, you must challenge what you know, do, and have done, and engage in creative destruction to focus on future growth.

In our studies of strategically agile companies, we saw the three traditional pathways for growth—through deep knowledge of customers, products, or geographical locations. Most of the companies we

TABLE 3-2

Pathways for growth with strategic agility

Customers	Products	Geographic locations
Facebook Gained new users and users' attention through personalization and new devices	• Expanded from social networks on campuses to other social networks • Offered new product apps to make that possible (WhatsApp, Instagram, Facebook Messenger)	• Expanded from the United States to worldwide, from developed countries to developing countries; now the world's largest social network platform
Huawei Entered the market with small-scale switching equipment in the early 1990s	• Developed large-scale switching equipment, wireless and optical networks, and more • Expanded into mobile consumer devices and enterprise services like the internet of things and cloud computing	• Started with third- or fourth-tier cities and moved upward to first- and second-tier cities in China • Entered overseas markets after 2000, starting with developing countries and then moving to developed countries
Amazon Grew customer base and loyalty through low prices, large selection, convenience, personalized recommendations, and Prime membership	• Started with self-operating e-commerce in books, expanded into other product categories, opened Amazon to other merchants through marketplace, offered logistics and cloud services to other merchants • Recently offered smart devices, digital content, and solution for smart retail stores (Amazon Go, Whole Foods Market)	• Has expanded out from North America to over a dozen countries

Source: Compiled by Arthur Yeung and Tencent Research Team, case studies of Facebook, Huawei, and Tencent; Facebook, Huawei, and Amazon founders' and senior executives' various public statements.

studied grew rapidly in all three pathways. Table 3-2 shows how Facebook, Huawei, and Amazon used these three pathways for growth.

Let's take a deeper look at the Amazon growth pathway. The company's story of growing *customers* is that of a virtuous "flywheel" whose starting point is to offer customers the best value. In every case, the three sources of momentum on the flywheel are lower prices, broader choices, and greater convenience. These customer advantages attract a bigger user base, which in turn attracts more merchants to offer products with lower prices at Amazon.[5] In addition to customer value, Amazon is also obsessed with improving the customer experience and realizing this through data, automation, and other technology. Amazon treats every problem as a puzzle to be solved through software that will automate things as much as possible. Self-service is common, especially when coupled with the recommendation engine and other tools on the Amazon Web Services platform.[6] This flywheel logic not only drives the scale and customer base of its retail business, but is also evident in *all* its businesses, including AWS and Amazon Prime membership.

In addition, Amazon pursues a growth pathway of new products and services. In the words of a former Amazon general manager: "The reality of innovation at Amazon is more of execution and persistence—you try a lot of things and you respond quickly. Agility is very important in innovation. You try fifty things, and even then, you don't know what will be a success. After that, you think, 'Wow! That was a good idea.' [And you run with it.] Originally, Prime was two-day shipping. Five years later, it became fifty thousand movies, thirty thousand television episodes, four million music tracks, unlimited photos. An explosion of digital benefits."[7]

While the market-oriented companies experimented with all three growth pathways (customer, product, and geographic location), they each had a dominant agenda. What is your primary growth pathway? Are you investing the resources to make this pathway work?

Stay a Step Ahead of the Market by Anticipating Targeted and Future Customers

Strategically agile firms run to where the ball will be, skate to where the puck will be, aim their bow where the deer will bolt, and venture to where the customer is not . . . yet. Agile strategy is not stuck in the past or the present but anticipates the future. Because markets change, agile strategy positions you to be there, primed and ready, before the opportunity arrives. The fundamental shift that the agile strategist needs to make is to move away from serving today's customers or simply gaining market share. Instead, leaders must dream of new prospects within fresh markets—continuously driving the organization to get to a new place before anyone else, realizing market opportunity.

For example, enabled by internet technology and an artificial intelligence (AI) personalization capability, VIPKid at China taps a huge unserved market of Chinese millennials (more than half a million students at this moment, and the number is still growing fast) who aspire to learn native English-speaking skills and a global mindset. By connecting them with fifty thousand high-caliber teachers in North America, the innovative learning approach is, so far, rewarding for both teachers and students, as many teachers passionately testify on YouTube.[8] To be an agile strategist, imagine who the customers of the future will be. What would amaze them?

Effectively Use Different Options to Execute a Growth Pathway: Buy, Build, or Borrow

Strategically agile firms deliver on the product, customer, or geographic pathway through the three fundamental means of equipping the organization: buy, build, or borrow. Since agile strategies, by definition, require rapid changes in the organization, most organizations select some combination of all three means. Which approach you choose depends on your strategy, capabilities, timing, and financials.

- **Build:** The companies that we studied worked hard to build the core of their business. By *core*, we mean the fundamental sources of their identity and competitive ability. This core quickly becomes the platform on which other strengths are built and that allows adjacent competencies to develop. This central structure must perfectly fit the needs of today and be designed to shift and scale into the future. No one can create the core but the company itself: the core is too tightly tied and critical to the vision and mission. Only Google could have built its search engine and its advertising infrastructure. Only Amazon could have built its e-commerce business and

AWS. And only Tencent could have built its QQ platform and WeChat platform, from which it was able to build its online businesses including games, music, shopping, movies, payment, and cloud.

- **Buy:** With the core in place, bringing in other proven or promising businesses and technologies can make good sense. Buying can accelerate the development of the core business, and speed matters. All the highly successful market-oriented ecosystems that we studied grew in part by acquiring new firms and quickly integrating these acquisitions by investing in them and helping them grow. Google acquired YouTube, Android, and Nest to instantly enter existing spaces that also hold great promise. Tencent did the same thing when it invested in Riot and Supercell to strengthen its game portfolio. Amazon has accelerated the flywheel it created in e-retail, AWS, and digital content by acquiring businesses in new product categories, new regions, and new technologies like Bookpages (UK), Joyo (China), Zappos, and most recently Whole Foods Market.[9] Facebook added WhatsApp, Instagram, and Oculus to its social media as well as its gaming line-up very quickly through purchase.

- **Borrow:** Sometimes it is not worth buying a business, a technology, or another resource, as the resource lies outside the core competencies of a company. Maybe there is no way to quickly get the talent and know-how from scratch. Or perhaps the management of making a purchase and integrating it is simply too time-consuming. If you need to enrich the suite of offerings to the customers, sometimes the best choice is a joint venture or a strategic alliance that can quickly lead to growth. Borrow means working closely with other companies to complement your resources or products and extending your reach to customers through an ecosystem beyond your own organization. Tencent makes excellent use of this option as it enriches its service offerings with strategic partners like JD.com, Meituan, DiDi, 58.com, and Netmarble. Google works with developers to enrich its technological platforms and business partners to build its advertisement business. Similarly, Amazon is forming close relationships with external partners that are able to expand its ecosystems in smart homes, digital content, and the marketplace.

Table 3-3 shows how Amazon conceives its growth agenda. In the rows, it defined its growth pathways through new customers and products; in the columns, Amazon used buy, build, and borrow approaches to move along each path.

Whatever pathway (customer, product, or location) and means (build, buy, or borrow) you choose, don't let your strategic story get too complicated. Reinventing strategic agility requires looking at your past growth agenda and then anticipating your future. Which pathway and means will help you maintain the simple storyline of

TABLE 3-3

Amazon's growth pathways and approaches

Customer channel or offering	Develop core businesses by building strategy		Accelerate the flywheels by buying and borrowing strategy	
	Build		Buy	Borrow
	Top-down	Bottom-up		
Retail	• Amazon.com • Fulfillment by Amazon	• Prime • Prime Now • Prime Air • Amazon Go	• Bookpages (UK) • Joyo (China) • Zappos • Whole Foods Market	• Regional partners • Ecosystem partners: marketplace merchants and third-party developers
Digital and entertainment	• Amazon Publishing • Amazon Video	• Amazon Music	• IMDB • CDNow • Audible • Twitch	
Device	• Kindle • Fire Phone	• Echo • Fire TV • Dash		
Technology		• AWS	• TouchCo • Yap • Kiva	

Source: Compiled from Amazon annual reports, proxy statements, and shareholder letters; employees and former Amazon employees, interview by Tencent Research Team; Brad Stone, *The Everything Store: Jeff Bezos and the Age of Amazon* (New York: Little, Brown and Company, 2013); Amazon Web Services, AWS introduction video at AWS re:invent 2014, Las Vegas, November 11, 2014, www.youtube.com/watch?v=QZwo35viW3g; Daniel Buchmueller, cofounder Prime Air, www.linkedin.com/in/danielbuchmueller; Dina Vaccari, owner Prime Now, www.linkedin.com/in/dinavaccari.

what you are trying to accomplish in the future marketplace with future customers?

Seek and Inspire Agile Employees

A strategically agile firm inspires its employees through the exciting opportunities it offers. Our observation, substantiated by research, is that the best firms have the most engaged employees, even though they need to work very hard. Why? These employees are trusted to have an impact on the company at their highest level of contribution, not just expected to live in a box.

A thoughtful and successful executive told us that "strategy follows people." He said that if he (and his organization) could put the right leader with the right skills in the right business role, the right strategy would naturally follow. These agile individuals replace negative self-talk ("I can't do this") with opportunity talk ("I can't do this . . . yet"). They have a growth mindset, with which they are continually experimenting, learning, failing (and succeeding), and improving. They are comfortable with paradoxes that require divergent and convergent thinking. That's exactly the kind of mindset that Nadella tries to instill in all Microsoft employees, shifting from know-it-all to learn-it-all.

At Amazon, in addition to the visionary leadership of Bezos, many successful ideas for new strategic choices come, surprisingly, from the bottom up. These ideas include highly successful products or businesses like Amazon Prime, AWS, Amazon Echo, and Amazon Go stores (see table 3-3). For instance, the idea of the Prime subscription service was initiated by an Amazon software engineer named Charlie Ward, who suggested the idea of a free shipping service via a suggestion box on the internal website (called Idea Tool) in late 2004.[10] Looking at the frequent-flier loyalty programs from the airline industry, Ward suggested treating customers according to their time sensitivity in product delivery.

To create strategic agility, you need to continually learn and grow. You need to become the industry pioneers who forge new paths for your organization. Your personal learning agility shows up when you are curious, ask questions, seek options, and experiment continually. You and other leaders should spend time understanding the six types of environmental opportunities laid out in chapter 2, visiting leading customers, and probing for market opportunities. You need to be brutally honest with yourself on what works and what does not. As an agile leader, you need to never settle, never perch, never land, never relax. It is the early adopters—the seekers—who grab the best space and make it into something that matters.

Use Scorecards and Data to Drive a Growth Mindset

Strategically agile firms have scorecards that reflect a commitment to growth. How do you know that you are meeting your objectives—that you are on the right path and skating to where the puck will be? An old saying, often incorrectly attributed to Peter Drucker, is "What gets measured gets done." In fact, Drucker was quite skeptical of measurement and the dangers of bean counting. What he also reportedly said was, "If you can't measure it, you can't improve it"—a dynamically oriented statement that was less about hitting a target and more about ongoing learning and improvement. American statistician Edward Deming, who shaped Japanese management practices, was credited with the following humorous statement (though its true source remains unknown): "In God we trust; all others must bring data." Whatever its source, notice that this statement does not include the term *measurement*. The true goal of data is to reveal trends, to enable businesspeople to learn and to make quick, educated, data-driven decisions that have real impact on the business. All the market-oriented organizations we studied use metrics (e.g., daily revenue, daily and monthly active users, and new users) to gauge daily development of different products or services to enable rapid product iteration and marketing adjustments.

As a leader, you should make sure to evolve your scorecards so that they promote deep thinking about the future: How do the results we are getting today inform us about tomorrow? Financially, yes, of course, you want to make money today. But how are your financials positioning you for tomorrow, next year, or the next decade? What is your customer feedback telling you about your market opportunities tomorrow, next year, or in the next decade? Are you getting the necessary insights on the needs and desires of future customers? Will they see you as uniquely positioned to meet their needs? Who else might compete in that future space?

Always Reinvent Strategy Because Strategy Is Never Finished

As part of reinventing the organization, strategically agile firms believe that strategy is an ongoing, iterative process of discovery, disruption, experimentation, and learning. As such, strategy is not a fixed object; it is invention in motion. Agile strategy means that you know when to diverge, zoom out, and explore options and when to converge, zoom in, and focus on priorities. Strategically agile leaders bring clarity on some key questions about the strategy process:

- **Who is involved in shaping strategy?** As a leader, you shape strategy, but you need to seek the broad involvement of customers, investors, and employees. Even more, you uncover and partner with industry provocateurs and pioneers who anticipate what's next. You spend time as an anthropologist investigating offerings that future customers may value but that are not yet defined. You experiment with and use the products or services you might offer (e.g., Tencent leaders are heavy users of their own products to gain firsthand experience with them).

- **How much dialogue and dissent is encouraged?** Market-oriented ecosystems clearly employ a balance of divergence to get new ideas and convergence to get a focus. As a strategically agile leader, you welcome tension without contention, or disagreement without being disagreeable. You encourage employees at all levels to challenge the status quo and to provoke new ideas. Navigating this divergence-convergence paradox enables you to create an agile strategy that wins in changing market conditions.

TABLE 3-4

Principles and practices of strategic agility of Alibaba and Amazon

Principles of strategic agility	Alibaba in action	Amazon in action
Having clear and consistent priorities to guide strategic choices	• Mission: "To make it easy to do business anywhere"	• Build the most customer-centric company on earth • Focus on cardinal rules: customer obsession, innovation, patience
Anticipating and creating new market spaces in light of STEPED contextual trends	• Believe in the disruptive power of the internet and technology • Envision how retail will look in the next thirty years; formulate "Five New" strategies • Anticipate changes in demographics and lifestyle of consumers (e.g., rising middle class, increased consumption power)	• Believe in the disruptive power of the internet and technology • Develop deep insights on unserved customer needs for price, selection, convenience in all kinds of shopping
Clarity on which pathways (customers, regions, or products) to take to grow the business in the next three years	• Focus on acquiring new customers in the early stages • Improve customer conversion and purchasing power through personalized recommendations • Move into adjacent businesses to build e-commerce infrastructures • Venture into overseas markets in Southeast Asia, Japan, and elsewhere	• Grow customer base, and improve customer value through flywheel • Use technology, data, and automation to improve customer experience • Use core platform to move into adjacent businesses • Go global to a dozen overseas markets
Anticipating the changing or unserved customer needs, and turning these gaps into new businesses	• Heavily target online female shoppers in fashion category • Extend online shopping capability to offline shopping experience	• Use better customer value and experience to increase Amazon penetration from single to multiple categories, from self-operating businesses to marketplace businesses, from physical products to digital products, and from online shopping to offline shopping
Effectively using build, buy, and borrow options to execute growth pathways	• Use "build" for core businesses in e-commerce in B2B business, Taobao, and Tmall • Use "buy" to move into new areas like digital content (e.g., movies and games) • Use "borrow" for logistic and overseas expansion of network through partnership	• Use "build" for core businesses in e-retail and AWS • Use "buy" to accelerate flywheel by supplementing new categories like shoes or by moving into new regions like China; buy different technological firms to strengthen AWS services • Use "borrow" to enrich developer community in AWS and merchants in e-commerce

Principles of strategic agility	Alibaba in action	Amazon in action
Seeking agile employees, and inspiring employees at all levels to have strategic agility	• Empower employees to be more agile in smaller business teams • Use monthly business meetings to tap good ideas from the front line	• Use PR&FAQ exercise to encourage employees to come up with new ideas anytime* • Encourage bottom-up ideas, many of which, like Prime, and Amazon Go, succeeded
Encouraging and rewarding people for growth rather than for merely meeting goals	• Use data to spot trends, to review progress, and to revise products or strategies	• Use data to spot trends, to review progress, and to revise products or strategies (Bezos only believes in facts and data for decision making)
Having the right atmosphere for strategic reinvention	• Empower leadership teams at different small business units • Cocreate with customers new businesses or ideas (e.g., Single's Day shopping festival)	• Form S-team (abbreviation for the core senior leadership team) as strategic decision-making body • Consistently push leaders at all levels to generate new ideas for the future • Encourage contention and debate using data and customer insights

*PR&FAQ is Amazon's exercise of having employees write simulated press releases and FAQ documents to help the team be clear on the customer value in any innovation.

Source: Compiled by Arthur Yeung and Tencent Research Team, case studies of Alibaba and Amazon; Alibaba Group, home page (English), accessed January 15, 2019, www.alibabagroup.com/en/global /home; Amazon, "Our Company," accessed January 15, 2019, www.aboutamazon.com/our-company; Martin Reeves, Ming Zeng, and Amin Venjara, "The Self-Tuning Enterprise," *Harvard Business Review*, June 2015; Jeff Bezos, quoted in Paul Farhi, "Jeffrey Bezos, Washington Post's Next Owner, Aims for a New 'Golden Era' at the Newspaper," *Washington Post*, September 2, 2013; Amazon annual reports, proxy statements, and shareholder letters.

- **How will the strategy evolve?** Strategy is less what is shared in presentations or reports and is more an integrated set of continuous choices being made, assessed, and remade. An agile strategy is an ongoing process more than a finite plan, an ongoing dialogue more than a document, and a series of learning experiments more than a set of explicit rules. A leading firm we studied has a mantra for strategic agility: think big, test small, fail fast, and learn always.

Reinventing Organization with Strategic Agility

The market-oriented ecosystems we studied embedded strategic agility through the preceding eight principles. Table 3-4 summarizes how Alibaba and Amazon use these eight principles and practices.

Managerial Implications

In an environment of constant uncertainty and change, reinvented organizations have to embark on strategic agility to respond. Strategically agile organizations seek to define market opportunity more than they seek market share. They anticipate what can happen more than they build on what has been. And they take risks and

TABLE 3-5

Self-assessment of your organization's strategic agility

Principles and practices of strategic agility: to what extent do we . . .	Assessment*	How could we improve?
have clear and consistent priorities to guide strategic choices?		
anticipate and create new market opportunities?		
know which pathways (customers, regions, or products) to take to grow our business in the next three years?		
anticipate changing or unserved customer needs, and turn these gaps into new businesses?		
effectively use build, buy, or borrow options to execute our growth pathways?		
seek out agile employees, and inspire employees at all levels to have strategic agility?		
encourage and reward people for growth rather than for merely meeting goals?		
have the right atmosphere for strategic reinvention?		

*On a scale of 1 to 5, where 1 = very poor and 5 = very well, how are we doing?

learn more than they have plans and actions. The eight principles of strategic agility lay out lessons learned from the market-oriented organizations that have redefined the nature of strategy. By examining and improving on these eight principles, you can move up on the strategic-agility ladder.

Table 3-5 provides a self-assessment tool on your firm's strategic agility. You or your leadership team can candidly assess where you stand on the eight principles and practices of strategic agility. Understand where you are, then find ways to improve it.

PART II

THE NEW ORGANIZATIONAL FORM

WHAT A MARKET-ORIENTED ECOSYSTEM LOOKS LIKE

hapter 1 reviews how organizations can evolve from a focus on hierarchies (i.e., efficiency) to systems (i.e., alignment) to capabilities (i.e., companies' identities) to market-oriented ecosystems. In part I, chapters 2 and 3 examine why a new organizational form is required and how the companies we studied have mastered a dynamic understanding of their environment.

Organizational form follows strategy. Today's complex, uncertain, and super dynamic business environment calls for new strategic thinking, evolving from strategic planning, strategic alignment, core competency to strategic agility.

In this section, we deep dive into the function and form of the reinvented organization (figure II-1). Chapter 4 identifies the critical capabilities that companies must magnify through their ecosystems in this era of uncertainty, disruption, and transformation. In this chapter, we build on the work that defined organizations as capabilities. Here we focus on the capabilities embedded in the network or ecosystem. We identify four of these critical capabilities that our market-oriented organizations demonstrate: external sensing, customer obsession, innovation throughout, and agility everywhere. This chapter offers insights and audit tools for creating ecosystem capabilities.

Chapter 5 introduces the organization design choices that market-oriented ecosystems use to reinvent their organizations. It offers deep insights into how these ecosystems operate. We show how they differ from, and can enhance, both the traditional holding company

FIGURE II-1

A six-part framework for reinventing the organization as a market-oriented ecosystem (MOE)

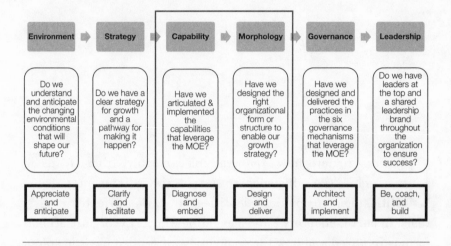

and the multidivisional firm. We then offer details on how to design the three building blocks of these ecosystems (platforms, cells or teams, and allies or partners) and how to combine them in different archetypes to deliver different ecosystem capabilities, enhance strategic agility, and create market opportunities.

The insights and tools in these chapters help you think through and reinvent the kind of organization you need if you are going to succeed in the years to come. You can assess the extent to which these capabilities exist within your ecosystem and how you use organizational design to enable these capabilities.

CHAPTER 4

Ecosystem Capabilities

How Can You Develop the Critical Capabilities of a Successful Ecosystem?

North Africa, 1941. Rommel's Deutsches Afrika Korps is winning the war in the Western Desert. Convinced by the evidence that the British cannot win in North Africa by conventional military means, an aristocratic junior officer from Scotland, notorious for his irreverence, irresponsibility, and charm, uses his social advantage to inveigle a meeting with the top military brass in Cairo. David Stirling proposes a new approach, the antithesis of military hierarchy and chain of command. His idea is based on small, self-led units using stealth, agility, and cunning to engage the enemy where they least expect it. His insight: while the Germans and Italians guard themselves from possible attack by Mediterranean Sea—the only danger they perceive—their broad desert flank is exposed and unprotected. They see no reason to prepare for an attack from a hostile, trackless, unmapped ocean of burning sands when it is impossible for an army to mass there. Stirling asks instead, why not unleash a nimbler force from the desert, one that can survive on very little and can split into tiny units that carry out raids on foot completely unexpectedly? This force, he argues, can also infiltrate an enemy position, quickly grasp the situation, and radio back key facts about men and material to the conventional forces to inform their strategies and tactics. The force would also be free of the often-cumbersome command-and-control decision-making apparatus. He proposes, in other words, the Special Air Service (SAS).

First in North Africa and later in Europe, the SAS conducts experiments quickly with both its purpose and its approaches throughout the remainder of World War II. It invents new weapons, like the compact, lightweight, high-impact Lewes bomb for disabling parked airplanes. It creates new tactics, for example, quickly abandoning its original approach of having paratroopers jump into the desert and instead pioneering capabilities around long-distance treks on foot and highly mobile desert jeep warfare. Sometimes, the SAS mission is to hike three hundred miles across the brutal Sahara Desert, creep into German and Italian air bases, and blow apart as many parked planes as the forces could carry munitions for. At other times, its role is to gather intelligence on enemy strength and position and call in strategic air strikes. Eventually, its job is to disrupt transportation and supply lines and demoralize the retreating German army during the Allied offensives in Italy, France, and Germany. At its best, wherever it is, the SAS remains an intelligence-gathering, innovative, agile, and highly disruptive force.

The SAS pioneered a form of combat that has become central to modern warfare. Although it began life as a raiding force in North Africa, it grew into the most formidable commando unit of World War II and the prototype for special forces around the world, notably the US Delta Force and US Navy SEALS.[1] Today, the SAS remains a legend of toughness, fitness, intelligence gathering, mission obsession, innovation, and adaptability. These attributes give SAS units tactical influence disproportional to their own size.[2]

Why are we describing this rascal version of a military unit in our discussion of market-oriented ecosystems? The SAS vividly illustrates how reinventing the organization can make a radical difference on combative strategy and outcomes. Instead of relying on the traditional military organization, which depends on a hierarchical chain of command, the SAS takes a different approach. Buttressed by strong back-end support bases, this agile and elitist force both responds to and shapes its environment for maximum impact with few resources, much as the basic units of market-oriented ecosystems like Supercell do. In many ways, the SAS and other special forces units have "scaled" the innovative organization that saved the swimmers in the riptide in chapter 1.

If you want to respond to rapid environmental changes and create strategic agility, you will need to create an organization that moves quickly. Increasingly, this organization is not just deploying independent and isolated teams, but also integrating individual teams into an ecosystem. The special forces teams seem independent, but they are highly interdependent with an ecosystem that enables their predictable success.

In this chapter, you will learn that the conceptual underpinnings of the market-oriented ecosystem are the capabilities embedded within it. Then we will describe four key capabilities that we found in our research and that you can apply to your organization.

The Organization as a Set of Ecosystem Capabilities

The capabilities of the market-oriented ecosystem are not derived from just the organization itself, but come from all the parts of the ecosystem. Consider special military forces. In the idealized version, a small team of elite military members is given a special and difficult assignment, which they carry out brilliantly. For example, the movie *Captain Phillips* chronicles the story of a US Navy SEAL team that rescued a Maersk boat captain held hostage by Somali pirates. In the movie, the SEAL team sweeps in and overcomes the pirates, saving Captain Phillips.[3] This story and others depict the autonomy, bravery, and cunning of this remarkable team. The stories are true, but incomplete. In reality, the SEAL team's capabilities were made possible by a host of shared resources. The members had been rigorously trained and had access to technology and information about the setting. The team learned from other similar SEAL teams how to accomplish their mission, and more importantly, the SEALs were backed up with additional support from the US Navy vessel standing by. They were not independent, but very interdependent, or part of what we call an ecosystem. Had the crew members gone to rescue Captain Phillips (or carried out any of their other missions) without being part of a broader network of training, information, and back-end support, they would have probably failed.

The Composition of Your Ecosystem

The ecosystem for an organization may include many forms of collaboration, alliances, and other affiliations. In chapter 5, we will discuss organizational design choices around the platforms (shared resources and back-end support), cells (autonomous teams), and allies (partners with shared resources and stakes in the ecosystem) that make the ecosystem work. But in this chapter, as mentioned above, we emphasize that an organization's capabilities are embedded throughout this ecosystem, not just in any one part of it. As organizations create autonomous teams, these teams need to be connected with each other by sharing a commitment to develop critical capabilities.

High-performing ecosystems must have integrating capabilities that enable them to win in the marketplace. For Amazon, the critical capabilities are customer obsession and innovation, first created within the organization and later magnified throughout its ecosystem. For Tencent, user experience and innovation stand out as critical capabilities. For Google, technology-driven innovation guides its sustainable success. For Huawei, it is also customer obsession.

Furthermore, our research of successful companies reveals that their ecosystem capabilities are very market oriented not only because the companies focus their resources and capabilities to win in the external marketplace, but also because these firms demonstrate strong market orientation inside their ecosystem. Different parts of the ecosystem interact (or transact) with each other using market mechanisms: transparent, win-win collaboration rather than command and coordination from the top.

To reinvent your organization, your job is not only to lead those inside your company, but also to create and take advantage of your alliances with suppliers, partners, distributors, customers, and others who form your ecosystem. You lead this reinvented ecosystem by establishing unique capabilities within this network of relationships. To understand how to do so, let's examine three market-oriented ecosystems.

Ecosystems in Action: Tencent, Amazon, and Alibaba

Founded in 1998, Tencent was first known for its instant-messaging service QQ, and its peers included ICQ, AOL, and MSN in the west. It is now one of the biggest technology companies in the world.[4] From its beginnings of introducing licensed games for the Chinese market, Tencent has grown into the largest online game operator and publisher in the world, and in 2018 was the second-largest social networking company after Facebook. With the strategic partnership with Sogou (the second-largest search-engine company in China) in 2013 and JD.com (the second-largest e-commerce company in China) a year later, Tencent started to build its ecosystem strategy by clearly defining what products and services to develop inside Tencent (social platforms and digital content like games, music, news, and movies) and what to do through its strategic partners to enrich the product and service offerings of its social platforms. The company's WeChat app, with over a billion active users per month in 2018, owes its popularity to a wide range of frequently used services. With WeChat, for example, you can message a friend to join you for dinner, book a taxi to get to the restaurant, order dishes by scanning a QR code while seated at a table and then pay via the mobile wallet in your smartphone for the food at the end of it all. In short, WeChat is a super app that not only connects people to people (social media) but also services to people (e.g., dining, entertainment, and payment) and, more recently, enterprises and organizations to people (e.g., paying taxes, fines, and paying for public transport). By 2019, as of the writing of this book, WeChat is available in more than 200 markets. And, of course, the plan is to grow.

But these facts are only headlines. Tencent is a large and thriving ecosystem of many entities sharing capabilities that create mutual success. For example, Tencent has a large number of product or business teams inside the company, plus hundreds of strategic partners in its larger ecosystem. Each of these business teams and strategic partners is expected to be a category leader on its own while sharing key resources and capabilities with other groups at the same time.

What does Tencent's high level of mutual support mean? At the resource level, Tencent can direct its user traffic to strategic partners such as JD.com, DiDi, Meituan, or PinDuoDuo while these strategic partners enrich the service offerings on Tencent platforms and increase the user base of WeChat Pay or QQ Wallet (Tencent's mobile payment). In terms of competency sharing, Tencent also shares its expertise and resources in technology, legal affairs, government affairs, and talent and organizational management with its strategic partners. For instance, Tencent offers technological and service infrastructure through Tencent Cloud, AI applications, advertisement and marketing services, location-based services, and WeChat Pay to its strategic partners. An in-house consulting team overseen by one of us (Arthur) also offers consulting, training, and coaching support to help key strategic partners upgrade their leadership, key talent, and organizational capabilities. By helping each other in resources, products, and competencies, Tencent and its strategic partners become stronger and more competitive as an ecosystem, not just as separate organizational entities.

Tencent is not alone. All the winning companies that we studied shared and embedded their capabilities across units to make the ecosystem stronger. They recognize that no company can be strong in everything. Amazon, one of the most innovative and powerful companies in the world, collaborates with key strategic partners in its retail business (through Whole Foods Market to share insights on customers and innovations that may help others in the ecosystem), in AWS (to share technological insights with technology startups), and in Echo (to entice more developers to build applications to make smart homes more powerful and useful).

Alibaba also needs many important business partners to sell products at Taobao and Tmall so that more users will visit the site. To attract the right partners to sell at Alibaba e-commerce platforms and to help them succeed, Alibaba exchanges data with them, for example, what kind of users visit their online shops and how they might offer more-personalized marketing resources using AI. Combining online user data at Taobao or Tmall with user data from these business partners' offline retail shops, Alibaba can help the partners develop integrated and personalized marketing programs to target their users. Alibaba calls this approach "thousand users, thousand appearance," offering different users different product or service advertisements that are relevant to the users' unique interests and needs at the right time and place.[5]

From Organizational Capabilities to Ecosystem Capabilities

So, what underlies these successful market-oriented ecosystems that you can adapt to reinvent your organization? Over the last twenty years, one of us (Dave) and his colleagues have worked to identify the key capabilities that an independent firm must have to succeed. The right capabilities lead to investor confidence, customer commitment and improved revenue per customer, and employee commitment and higher productivity.[6]

In addition, Dave and his colleagues studied which organizational capabilities have the most impact on business results. In 2016, using a survey of twelve hundred companies that identified eleven basic organizational capabilities, Dave and his colleagues plotted these capabilities on a matrix (figure 4-1). The x-axis shows the relative impact on business results; the y-axis shows how well the business is deploying or focusing on that capability. By highlighting the capabilities that have the most business impact and that are delivered

FIGURE 4-1

Business impact of capabilities

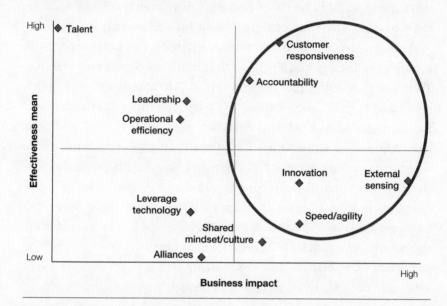

the most effectively, the chart helps prioritize which capabilities deserve attention going forward. External sensing (described below), customer responsiveness, innovation, and speed/agility are clearly identified as capabilities that have the strongest business impact in today's environment.

Meanwhile, Arthur has developed another stream of work related to organizational capability in teaching, consulting, and executive learning in China. In 2010, he founded the Organizational Capability Learning Association (OCLA), which has served more than 250 entrepreneurs and CEOs in China so far. The association is an ongoing learning platform for prominent Chinese entrepreneurs in both high-tech and traditional industries, including fashion, retail, manufacturing, financial services, logistics, and internet services. By working closely with the CEO participants in OCLA, he can identify the capabilities that matter the most to these rapid-growth companies. He also sponsors a large-scale survey through the annual National Organizational Capability Survey in China. The survey has enjoyed the participation of more than two hundred businesses and a hundred thousand respondents every year since 2016.[7] From both the case studies of OCLA members and the large-scale national survey, Arthur has discovered that the key capabilities for business competitiveness have been changing over the years. Although low cost, high quality, and quick delivery times were critical to many firms in the industrial era, customer obsession, innovation, and agility have become much more critical to firms today.[8]

From our decades of research on, and consulting experience with, organizational capabilities in the United States, China, and other parts of the world, both of us have, surprisingly, come to the same conclusion. Four capabilities are critical in today's super-dynamic and uncertain environment: information, customer, innovation, and agility.

Finally, and most importantly, as we examined the critical capabilities from the eight market-oriented ecosystems we studied, we identified similar ecosystem capabilities. From our multiple research studies, we are confident that these four capabilities are critical for firms and ecosystems to thrive and survive in today's business context. These capabilities, laid out in figure 4-2, will be

FIGURE 4-2

Ecosystem capabilities required in the environment of disruption

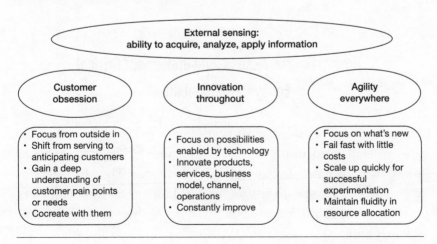

discussed in greater detail in this chapter. But first, we'll define these capabilities:

- **External sensing:** the ability to acquire, analyze, and apply information about trends and shifts in your marketplace.

- **Customer obsession:** the ability to relentlessly focus on fulfilling the unserved needs of current and future customers, and the mental shift from serving customers to anticipating or even creating their needs.

- **Innovation throughout:** the ability to foster creativity and ingenuity in products, services, business models, distribution systems, and so forth, with a special focus on the opportunities that digitalization and other new technologies present.

- **Agility everywhere:** the ability to improve and experiment fast. When something fails, you learn from it; when something succeeds, you scale it. When you are agile everywhere, you can quickly move scarce resources around the enterprise to make the most of the best opportunities.

The successful organization embeds these capabilities in its ecosystem, and so can you.

How to Define, Assess, and Implement Critical Ecosystem Capabilities

These four key capabilities show up in our research, but they can also be embedded into your own ecosystem by thoroughly examining them in light of your own circumstances. The next sections describe why these capabilities matter, how successful companies create such capabilities, and how you can use them to reinvent your organization.

External Sensing

The ability to sense, interpret, and act on critical information is at the heart of nearly every organizational transformation. The digitalization innovations of AI, the internet of things, robots, the cloud, and big data revolutionize the ability to access and process information quickly. Market-oriented ecosystems aggressively manage data through their digital strategy.

In our work on external sensing, we draw on exceptional work by Wayne Brockbank, of the Ross School of Business at the University of Michigan. Professor Brockbank found that leading firms excel in their ability to acquire, access, and apply information that creates market opportunities. Managing this information leads to information asymmetry.[9] Enjoying this information asymmetry (having better information than their competitors have), the organizations are more likely to win in changing markets. In the organizations we studied, this information is shared between the core platform and the individual cells and among the cells.

The process for information acquisition and application generally follows five steps (figure 4-3). First, you must identify the sources of key information for new market opportunities. Such information comes not only from thoroughly understanding today's customers and competitors, but also from examining the key environmental trends like those laid out in chapter 2. For example, by foreseeing the advances in technology, Amazon has anticipated that smart retail has great potential for growth and the enhancement of the user experience. Similarly, VIPKid witnessed China's rise of its affluent middle class and this group's willingness to invest in the education of a family's single child. With this understanding, and enabled by interactive technology, the online education company has created market opportunities by hiring the best teachers around the world to teach Chinese kids English. By constantly scanning external trends, VIPKid employees can anticipate future possibilities and the business implications of these possibilities.

Second, you and other leaders should import key information into your organizations. Companies are finding creative ways to

FIGURE 4-3

External sensing capability

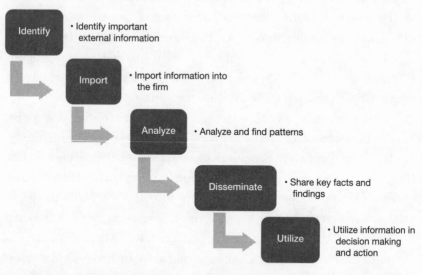

Source: Thanks to Wayne Brockbank for these insights.

ensure that the most important information is brought into the firm and that the less important information is filtered out. In addition to the typical electronic means of capturing structured information about customers from multiple sources, successful organizations find unique way to gather unstructured information. By *unstructured information*, we mean (1) electronic media such as YouTube videos, online chat rooms, email, speeches by industry leaders and other influential people, and news articles; (2) social interaction such as hallway conversations, friendship networks, phone calls, and town halls; and (3) observations made when leaders and all employees act like anthropologists and observe others' actions.

While structured data tends to be stable, predictable, fact based, and readily categorized and interpreted, the overwhelming proportion of available global information is unstructured. This type of information is harder to capture and analyze. In spite of this difficulty, unstructured data can often yield greater insight than what ready-to-read data offers. Structured data often captures what has been; unstructured data identifies what can be. To benefit from unstructured data, the organization or ecosystem will find that immersed observation, deep dialogue, and experience sharing are more useful vehicles.

Third, once you have identified and gathered important information, you then face the challenge of analyzing it to develop useful insights. In *What the Dog Saw*, journalist Malcolm Gladwell has pointed out that competitive advantage is frequently found in really smart "slightly batty geniuses" who find patterns in unpredictable, chaotic, but pervasive information.[10] In successful market-oriented ecosystems like Supercell, Amazon, Google, and Tencent, a handful of smart creatives can gain insights or make key findings through personal intuition or AI using both structured and unstructured information.

Fourth, companies need to disseminate useful information and insights throughout the organization. In market-oriented ecosystems, this dissemination may occur through many means, including automatic reporting of key data trends, town halls, and customer-focused discussions in which market and other information is widely communicated. At Google, weekly town halls between senior leaders and all employees have been conducted in the form of TGIF (thank God it's Friday) or TGIAF (thank God it's almost Friday) sessions. Facebook holds a weekly All Hands meeting between CEO and cofounder Mark Zuckerberg and employees.[11] In addition, market-oriented ecosystem leaders can facilitate interactions that produce collaborative insights both within and across silos.

Fifth, all the above practices have little impact unless the information is used to improve the organization's decisions. The information may be used in experimentation with new products or services, in the iteration of current products or services, for more precise targeting of customers, or for greater efficiency in logistics and inventory management. Another more subtle use for information is to help employees at all levels find that their personal purpose matches their organization's purpose by serving genuine customer needs or solving broader social problems.

In summary, to evaluate how well you and your team acquire external information and apply it to reinvent your organization, you need to ask two overarching questions. First, how well does your current organization identify, import, analyze, disseminate, and utilize structured and unstructured data to reveal unserved customer needs, identify opportunity for innovation, and generate quick insights for decisions? And second, what can you do to improve the five-step process?

Customer Obsession

Competitiveness requires that an organization obsessively seek new ways to add value to customers. In the market-oriented ecosystem, creating market opportunities takes the lead over grabbing customer share, but these market opportunities work when the organization can deeply understand customer needs and anticipate what people want even when they themselves cannot articulate it. In a famous example of this phenomenon, Apple created the iPhone, a product that no customer had (yet) asked for—but that a customer would fully appreciate—and the rest is history. The goal is to mentally shift from serving customers to anticipating their needs. This change requires a comprehensive understanding of customer needs or pain points, and is best served by cocreating offerings with them. In the companies we study, Amazon and Huawei are by far the most customer-obsessed companies.

To become more passionate about its customers, your organization has to investigate the following questions: What are the hidden wastes and costs for your customers to access and use your product or service? How can you be more user-friendly and efficient with your customers through the use of technology? Which users are not currently buying your product or service, and why not? How can you attract potential users by being cheaper, faster, easier, more accessible, or otherwise better?

We discovered four levels of customer interaction (figure 4-4). The highest order of customer interface, as well as the most strategically powerful, is the fourth and highest level: anticipation. Customer anticipation may come from structured data, where statistics highlight what innovative and lead customers are doing, but

FIGURE 4-4

Levels of customer interaction

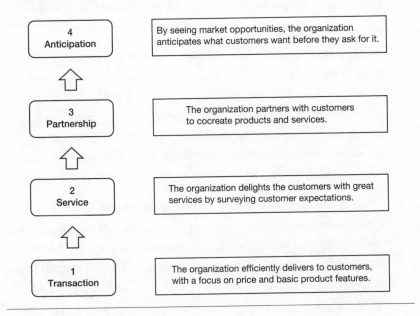

may also come from market sensing, where leaders and employees become anthropologists who detect what customers may need even beyond what they want.

Mobike, recently acquired by Meituan, is one example of a customer-obsessed company. While public transportation (like buses and subways) are very convenient in China, they seldom connect from door to door. Commuters must walk ten to twenty minutes between the bus or subway stop and their home or destinations. Although taxis offer door-to-door service, congestion during peak traffic hours makes them an inconvenient alternative. Seeing hundreds of millions of people facing such challenges when commuting to work or school, Mobike has been offering a solution to the so-called last-mile problem (the long walk between mass transit and home, school, or office). With Mobike, people can pick up a bike anywhere and drop it off anywhere. By simply scanning a QR code, you can unlock the bike and can ride it to your office, school, or home. When you relock the bike, the typically small fee (usually less than US$0.50) is automatically deducted from We-Chat Pay.[12]

The most successful market-oriented ecosystems anticipate customers' needs in any of the following ways:

- **Seeing their customer's customers:** When a firm has external information about its own customers' clientele, the company can find new ways to serve them both. For example, Amazon AWS starts by serving internal customers (retail business groups) and moves on to supports its customers' customers (business partners that the retail business groups are serving).[13]

- **Sharing customers across cells and partners:** Sharing customers means that customers from one cell may work with customers from other cells. For example, Amazon's Whole Foods Market can serve as a distributor of online retail business by being a place customers can pick up their products rather than having them shipped. By doing this, it also generates traffic and creates new sales opportunities for Whole Foods Market. Similarly, Tencent and its strategic partners generate user traffic with each other.

- **Having deep data on customers to anticipate their buying patterns:** When this form of big data can be shared across business partners, a huge amount of value can be created. Alibaba in particular does an exceptional job of data exchange across different business teams and strategic partners to form an integrated profile of users and their buying preferences and behaviors.[14]

- **Being a customer:** It is rather obvious, but by being customers themselves, leaders and employees of market-oriented ecosystems recognize what product or service is and is not currently available. For example, Tencent leaders and many employees are also heavy users of their own products who know firsthand what is expected of them.

As this section has shown, to gain a deep understanding of your customers, you must continuously think like a customer and think about your customers. Ask these questions about your organization's customer obsession: How closely is your organization interacting with customers and other users? Does it stick to the basic levels of a transaction or service, or does it engage in higher levels, like partnership or anticipation? What can you do to improve the level of customer intimacy and centricity?

Understanding the customers' real (often unspoken) needs is one of the first steps in reinventing your organization to be market oriented. New market opportunities cannot be created unless you see their pain points.

Innovation Throughout

Business today is all about examining every aspect of what you do and asking yourself, "Can we do better? Can we go about this in a whole new way?" In the digital age, the willingness and ability to continuously improve (at a minimum) or shatter current reality and bring forth something truly disruptive and new (in the best case) means that market-oriented ecosystems innovate in all aspects of their overall work throughout the value chain: business models, supply chains, product performance, the systems surrounding the offering, channel distribution, manufacturing, service, talent development, brand—everything.

Innovation is embedded as a capability in the ecosystem when each cell experiments with new ideas and shares those ideas with other cells. Together, the cells should be questioning, observing, and experimenting with new ideas and putting various ideas together in new ways. At Amazon, for example, an innovative idea is articulated in its so-called PR&FAQ exercise (a simulated press release and FAQ document that force employees to clearly articulate customer value in any innovation). This practice forces everyone to base their innovation on customer needs. Then, Amazon experiments with the new idea using what it calls its *two-pizza teams*, meaning that no team should have more people than can be happily fed with two pizzas. Keeping the teams small becomes easy for the company with the support of AWS. Also at Amazon, both successful and unsuccessful innovation is captured in a postmortem document called *a collection of errors*; this document can be openly shared with other units.[15]

At Supercell, game developers can always propose new game concepts that are based on their interests and passions. Once a game idea is approved with agreed-upon metrics, a small development team of five to seven people will be formed. New games will then be judged against pre-agreed metrics and either successfully launched or, more often than not, disbanded. To encourage innovation, however, Supercell still acknowledges team efforts, even if a team, after working hard for several months, fails to achieve its agreed-upon targets. The team will nevertheless celebrate failure because the members have learned something new. They will freely share with other teams what did and didn't go well.[16]

Innovation requires organizations that think big, test small, fail fast, and learn always by failing forward and learning from failures. Of these four mantras for innovation, the most difficult are the admonitions to fail fast and learn always. Recognizing when it is time to move on from a failure and to transfer this learning to future initiatives is difficult. In the market-oriented ecosystem, the marketplace's response to a product or a service answers the fail-fast dictum. And the easy formation of new cells in the ecosystem enables people to fail forward as their ideas may then move to another team.

Innovation also requires people who are curious. Curious people innovate by asking questions, probing options, seeing potential, experimenting, and viewing failure as the opportunity to learn. If you want innovation in your company and ecosystem, above all else, do everything you can to hire for curiosity, and then support and reward it.

To ensure that creativity, curiosity, and openness to change permeate your organization, ask yourselves these questions about your approach to innovation: How capable is your organization at innovating? How broadly do you innovate (i.e., just in product development or throughout the entire value chain)? How disruptive is your innovation (i.e., is it incremental or radical?)? And how fast? What can you do to provide the right atmosphere and support for people at all levels to think big, test small, fail fast, and learn always to fail forward? How well do you share successes and failures with others to promote quick learning?

Agility Everywhere

How can you iterate fast to upgrade a current product or service? How can you fail fast and cheaply to test a new idea? When something new works, how do you scale up quickly to take advantage of the opportunity (and keep competitors out)? How do you move scarce resources around the enterprise to make the most of the best opportunities?

Agility seems to be the capability du jour. It is the ability to quickly respond to and anticipate emerging market opportunities. Agile companies embrace change, learn continually, and act quickly and flexibly. In a world of unrelenting change, where strategic agility differentiates winning business strategies from losing ones, organizational and personal agility make change happen even faster. More-agile organizations win in the customer and investor marketplaces; more-agile individuals find personal well-being and deliver better business results.

Organizations that cannot change as fast as their external demands change can quickly fall behind, never to catch up. When WeChat was launched in 2011, another product called MiLiao was launched by Xiaomi around the same time. With the lightning speed of product iteration on a weekly or even daily basis, the WeChat team rapidly improved on its functionality and user-friendliness, and eventually took lead of the market. Agility magnifies a company's customer and innovation capabilities. Rapid response to future customer opportunities and fast innovation differentiate organizations that win. The market-oriented ecosystem is uniquely positioned to foster agility, as customer-oriented teams like WeChat team are fully empowered with authority, responsibility, and information to rapidly penetrate new opportunities with the support of a strong platform. For example, the technological infrastructure of Tencent helped WeChat rapidly scale up in storage, computing, and bandwidth power. In market-oriented ecosystems, independent cells are also connected with each other to share resources to ensure agility.[17]

Organization agility requires team members who can learn and grow as leaders or employees. Individual agility is both a mindset that embraces growth, curiosity, and other creative qualities and a set of skills that support this mindset (e.g., the ability to ask good questions and the ability to connect business skills with imagination). A leader's learning agility, i.e., ability to learn fast, is a key indicator of effective leadership.

Because individual agility comes in part from a person's predisposition, or nature, an organization can hire individuals who are naturally agile (they learn, change, and act quickly). But an organization can also enhance individual agility through training on asking questions and taking risks, experimenting with new ideas and actions, continuously improving by auditing what worked and what did not, observing others, embarking on stretch assignments, and so forth. For example, Facebook intentionally hires people who are bold, fast, and builders. Microsoft, under the leadership of Nadella, emphasizes a growth mindset for learning and experimentation.

Agility everywhere ensures that the different units of market-oriented ecosystems and the individuals who occupy themselves to learn, change, and move quickly. Like military special forces, these elite teams adapt quickly to opportunities and requirements as agility everywhere becomes a way of life.

As you work to spread agility everywhere in your ecosystem, ask these questions to assess where you are now and how you can improve: How agile is your organization in capturing new market space or improving existing products or services? How agile is your organization in redeploying and sharing internal resources around new opportunities? How can you and your employees improve your organizational agility and individual agility?

Critical Capabilities of Market-Oriented Ecosystems We Studied

In the ecosystems we studied, the preceding four capabilities—external sensing, customer obsession, innovation, and agility—were often embedded in some of the individual organization units. But even more, these attributes were regularly and systematically shared across individual units so that the capabilities permeated the overall ecosystem, not just the individual units. Table 4-1 summarizes our assessment of the capability strengths of the market-oriented companies we studied. Two caveats should be noted in our assessment. First, these companies rate far better on the four ecosystem capabilities than do average companies. The ratings here only compare the eight companies we studied. And second, there is substantial variation on the capability strengths of different units within these ecosystems. The table shows our assessments of the overall ecosystems' capabilities.

TABLE 4-1

Dominant core capabilities of eight market-oriented ecosystems

Dark gray, strongest; medium gray, medium strength; white, lower strength.

Ecosystem	External sensing	Customer obsession	Innovation throughout	Agility everywhere
Supercell	dark gray	medium gray	dark gray	dark gray
Facebook	dark gray	white	dark gray	dark gray
Google	dark gray	medium gray	dark gray	medium gray
Huawei	dark gray	medium gray	medium gray	dark gray
Tencent	dark gray	dark gray	medium gray	dark gray
Alibaba	dark gray	dark gray	medium gray	dark gray
Amazon*	dark gray	dark gray	dark gray	dark gray
DiDi	dark gray	white	dark gray	dark gray

*Core retail business.

As the table shows, all these successful companies are adept at external sensing. This capability makes perfect sense. External sensing enables ecosystems to see their market opportunities and to acquire, analyze and apply information. Strengths vary around the other three capabilities, depending on priorities:

- **Customer obsession:** Amazon strives to become "Earth's most customer-centric company." At Tencent, improving the user experience infiltrates everything the company does. In contrast, Google places relatively less emphasis on this core capability because the company is more technology driven than customer driven. Supercell, whose core strength is creativity, is leading the customers rather than following them and so does not focus as much there. Facebook rates relatively lower on customer obsession because of its excessive use of customer data for monetization. The overriding priority on growth at ride-sharing conglomerate DiDi relegates passenger safety to a lower priority. The eroding capability of Facebook and DiDi in customer obsession has cost both companies dearly in investor confidence, customer commitment, employee engagement, and social responsibility.

- **Innovation throughout:** Amazon is constantly rated as one of the most innovative firms by Fast Company because of its ability to constantly roll out new winning products and businesses one after another. Relatively speaking, Huawei has not been renowned for technological innovation until recently. Its core strengths used to be serving and responding to customer needs by offering lower costs and responsive service.

- **Agility everywhere:** Supercell forms and dissolves development teams with great speed, quickly scaling up or dropping new games according to the games' success. Alibaba is also remarkably flexible in initiating organizational changes and rotating people across units. DiDi captures and dominates new market space with admirable agility. And Huawei, having a telecom equipment manufacturer as its core business, focuses less in this domain because its priority is to offer complex, proven, reliable products and solutions to telecom operators around the world.

Managerial Implications

Autonomous, high-performing, and responsive teams matter. But when these teams are interconnected with each other, they multiply their impact. As this chapter has described, the high-performing market-oriented ecosystems we studied have four critical capabilities that weave autonomous teams into connected networks. External sensing allows teams to capture and act on current and future opportunities and threats. Customer obsession helps teams anticipate who future customers will be and how to serve them. Innovation throughout enables teams to experiment and improve. Agility everywhere helps teams to act quickly and iterate ideas with impact.

To summarize, several assessments and actions will help you and the rest of your organization create, or improve on, these four capabilities. First, determine which critical capabilities your company needs if it is to win in your industry in the next three to five years. Are your current capabilities, such as quality, cost, and delivery, good enough to help you achieve competitive differentiation in your industry, or do they just afford competitive parity? How critical to your sustainable success in this era of disruption are external sensing, customer obsession, innovation throughout, and agility everywhere? The relative importance of these capabilities is tied to your company's industry (e.g., Supercell in game development, Amazon and Alibaba in e-commerce, Tencent and Facebook primarily in social media, and Huawei in telecom equipment manufacturing) and its mission.

Second, spread these critical capabilities throughout your ecosystem, not just within one organizational unit. Identify critical alliances or partners that your company should work closely with to better serve customers; to innovate models, products, or services; and to act with agility.

Next, define the boundary and components of your ecosystem. Which functions should go to the platform as shared resources and capabilities? Which functions should be operated autonomously as business teams? Which businesses should not be run by your company alone but should be run as a collaboration with your strategic partners? Which strategic partners need to be acquired as one of your business teams? As a leader, you need to make all these critical organizational decisions when designing your ecosystem.

Fourth, audit the current capabilities of your platform, business teams, and strategic partners. Identify the weak links. How strong is your platform? How agile and empowered are your business teams? How closely do your strategic partners work with you? For the units that need improving, develop initiatives to build up their organizational capabilities.

Fifth, build linkages and other mechanisms to share resources, data, ideas, and competencies with your business teams, platform, and strategic partners. Identify any opportunities to collaborate, and aim for win-win successes (e.g., internal pricing mechanisms, shared mission and values, shared incentives, shared databases or tools).

Finally, have individual unit leaders meet regularly to share experiments, initiatives, insights, and lessons learned on the journey of capability building. Celebrate success, and reflect on failure. Encourage unit leaders to adapt insights from others in the ecosystem to their unit and to share their experiences with others. Confidence and success are the most precious resources you can have to reinvent your organization!

CHAPTER 5

Morphology

How Should You Be Organized to Deliver Key Ecosystem Capabilities?

Both of us own condominiums. As owners, we have the autonomy to remodel and use our units as our families wish. But our individual units are parts of condo associations. Each association sets guidelines and covenants about our personal units. For example, the rules prohibit pets and subletting (i.e., no Airbnb types of use) and require contractor approval for any work done on the condos. Each association also manages the public and shared features of the condo building (e.g., parking, lobby maintenance, the satellite connection, the exercise room, utilities, and landscaping). Although we are owners with the freedom to buy, use, and sell our units, both associations' guidelines ensure that the condo buildings operate effectively.

The organizational logic of having autonomous units with shared resources exists in other settings, such as the following:

- **Professional sports associations:** The Union of European Football Associations represents the national football (what Americans call soccer) associations of Europe. It runs national and club competitions and controls prize money, regulations, and media rights to these competitions. Likewise, the National Basketball Association, National Football League, and other professional associations set guidelines for competition. Owners of individual teams have autonomy about buying, managing, and selling their teams, but the association ensures that the leagues are effective.

- **Shopping malls:** In this physical arrangement, the individual store owners buy, manage, and sell their spaces, but the overall mall management sets guidelines that govern how the mall operates.

- **Private equity:** Since around 2004, the number of publicly traded firms in the United States has declined by about 50 percent, partly because of the rise of private-equity firms.[1] These firms create a fund, acquire companies, and set about to transform them. The acquired companies remain independent but draw on financial, strategic, and organizational support from the private-equity partners to better manage their business.

In each of these cases—condos, sports associations, malls, and private-equity firms—the "bigger" organization manages the independent units while offering oversight and resources that make the whole more valuable than the individual parts. A condo is worth more if the condo building is well maintained. The individual sports teams gain value through wise association governance. Well-managed malls attract more customers for individual store owners. Acquired companies who avail themselves of the financial, strategic, and organizational support of the private-equity partners become more successful.

This chapter focuses on how to structure the market-oriented ecosystem through organizational design choices that build the right skeleton to sustain and scale critical ecosystem capabilities. Too often, organizational reinvention starts here, with a focus on organization morphology: an organization changes its form without knowing the environmental context to explain why (chapter 2), which strategy choices to drive agility (chapter 3), and whether it has put in place the four core ecosystem capabilities (chapter 4). Without incorporating the insights from these previous chapters, organizational reinvention is a random event, not a sustained pattern.

To redesign the organization, we will introduce the three building blocks of the market-oriented ecosystem: platform, cells, and allies. We will show how this new approach reinvents traditional organization design thinking and then examine how the eight ecosystems we studied manage each of these design elements.

As a leader, you do not need to become an organizational design aficionado. But you should recognize organizational design choices to better deliver the four key capabilities of external information, customer, innovation, and agility.

A Primer on Market-Oriented Organizational Design Logic and Language

Market-oriented ecosystems organize through platforms, cells, and allies to deliver critical capabilities:

- **Platforms:** These building blocks provide an ecosystem's various cells with valuable common activities and resources (e.g., user traffic, big data, cloud computing, R&D, supply chains, logistics, and customer services) to succeed in their respective markets. They enable the cells to focus on their core activities. Platforms are like condo associations, sports leagues, mall management, or private-equity groups; they are hubs whose support, resources, and governance make the whole more than the individual parts.

- **Cells (or business teams):** These parts of an ecosystem are like the individual condo units, sports teams, mall stores, or firms acquired by private-equity partnerships. In an ecosystem, these cells anticipate and serve customers, capture new opportunities, and outperform competitors by offering better or differentiated products or services. They also generate ideas, conduct experiments, create businesses where they make sense, and close down a trial business where it does not.

- **Allies (or strategic partners):** These ecosystem building
  blocks supplement the activities of the platform or the cells.
  For example, condo owners might hire contractors to renovate
  their individual condos, sports teams might form a partnership
  with experts to help them win in their league, and store owners
  might contract with experts to better manage their stores. In
  market-oriented ecosystems, the allies or strategic partners
  provide other key contributions—expertise, products, services,
  access—that can make all the difference because they offer
  specialized insights into the success of the individual cells.

Figure 5-1 is a generic image of what this organization might
look like with platforms, cells or teams, and allies connected within
an ecosystem (see figure 1-1 for how Supercell adapts these terms).
The connecting lines represent sharing capabilities and resources
to make the whole more than the parts. If you were asked to draw
your own organization, what would it look like? Would it reflect the
ecosystem logic in figure 5-1?

As discussed in chapter 4, the unique strength of the market-
oriented ecosystem is its ability to build capabilities not just in the

FIGURE 5-1

**Overview of the market-oriented ecosystem structure with
different businesses**

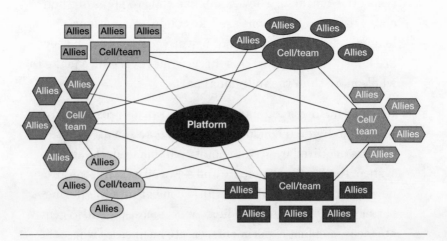

individual cells or teams but throughout the ecosystem. How do platform, cells, and allies work together to deliver critical ecosystem capabilities?

- **External sensing:** The platform captures, integrates, and analyzes big data from different cells. This information helps individual cells make better decisions that cannot be done on their own. A platform, with its broad expertise and access to wide-ranging information of relevance to the entrepreneurial cell, can feed that information to the cell in useful ways. For example, great platforms like Amazon or Alibaba share integrated customer profiles with their business teams for more-personalized recommendations. And DiDi collects real-time traffic data from different services (e.g., taxi hailing, private-car hailing, chauffeur, bus, minibus, and luxe) into its main app to guide better route recommendations.[2]

- **Customer obsession:** Information-rich platforms, combined with the inherent expertise of the creative business experts in the cell, can pinpoint the current needs of the customer and even anticipate future needs and desires, from their joint analysis. Using big data, for example, DiDi can accurately predict the pattern of passenger demands and direct adequate cars to the right place at the right time. Similarly, Amazon and Alibaba can remind customers of their latent needs by using targeted recommendations.

- **Innovation throughout:** Deep customer insight captured through superior attention to external information, combined with the entrepreneurial spirit of cells or teams, drives innovation. For example, noting the Chinese custom of exchanging red packets during Chinese New Year, WeChat Pay used this customer insight to come up with the innovative idea of virtual red packets to share blessings with friends and families not only during important festivals like the Chinese New Year but now for literally many occasions of celebrations. Such innovation would not have been possible without the platform support of WeChat, which links hundreds of millions of friends and families together.[3]

- **Agility everywhere:** Less impeded by resource constraints and armed with knowledge and access to key functions, data, and technologies, cells or teams can improve and innovate new businesses much faster than before when an ecosystem platform offers plug-and-play support to cells. For example, new ideas at Amazon can be experimented with a small two-pizza team with a strong AWS platform. This allows the team to start small and fail fast with little costs and resource commitment.

As a leader, you can make and oversee choices about platforms, cells, and allies (strategic partners). These abilities will enable you to reinvent your organization to deliver radically greater value.

Market-Oriented Ecosystems and Other Organizational Logic

To clarify how the market-oriented ecosystem reinvents the organization, let's compare it with a holding company and a multidivisional firm. Some observers see the ecosystem as merely a rehash of the traditional organizational forms. But we are articulating a new organizational form substantially different from these two traditional models both in structure and in substance (table 5-1). In reviewing the table, you might put an X where you see your company today with each dimension to assess where you stand relative to the market-oriented ecosystem.

Holding Companies

If you work in a holding company, the market-oriented ecosystem advances your approach by creating more synergy and support between and among business teams and platforms. The holding company has a hub-and-spoke strategy: a small hub, a shared resource, is surrounded by spokes, each of which represents a business opportunity. Examples of hub-and-spoke companies abound:

TABLE 5-1

Comparison of holding companies, multidivisional firms, and market-oriented ecosystems (MOEs)

Traditional conglomerate or holding company	Traditional multidivisional firm	MOE
Roles of top leaders Manage the portfolio, setting output goals and KPIs	The big brains who set the direction from the top and tell others what to do; primarily concerned with creating shareholder value	Set the mission and the boundaries of the ecosystem, specify the roles and functions of different units, and define how units and people collaborate
Roles of unit leaders Are hired and work as professional managers in different companies	Assigned as agents of their headquarters to ensure compliance and execution of approved strategy	Cell or team leaders who define and probe market opportunities as entrepreneurs; agents unto themselves, with personal accountability and responsibility for their career choices and success
Formulation of strategy Portfolio strategy at holding company to decide which companies to invest in and which to divest	Decided from the top or with some bottom-up engagement from the business units; primarily internal, up-down discussion	Based on frontline people's ability to anticipate market opportunity (customer needs) and on technological enabling; strategy rapidly evolves according to results (shown in data)
Roles of headquarters Primarily focus on financial leverage and control	A governing group that allocates resources and rewards and holds people accountable; primary roles of control and compliance	A platform of competencies and resources to empower teams to win in the marketplace rather than ensuring the control and compliance of teams
Roles of business units A collection of highly independent businesses acting on their own	Corporate units that are organized around a product or service, industry, or geographic region, often leading to a matrix	Teams or cells that act more like small businesses that respond to market opportunities; also connected within the ecosystem to grow faster and better
Control Control from holding company primarily through financial return	Control through rules, approvals, and objectives (management by objectives, KPIs): "shackled by rules and policy"	Control through market (reward based on market success and contribution) and self-driven mindset: "unshackled and autonomous"
Coordination Little coordination across companies	Decision rights negotiated, often in a RACI matrix; time spent inside the organization to figure out who does what	Clear roles of platforms and teams, loose coupling and market-based relationships among teams to ensure cross-unit collaboration and network capabilities

Note: KPIs, key performance indicators; RACI, responsibility, accountability, consultant, informee.

Berkshire Hathaway, Virgin Group, Tata Group, and Danaher. But the businesses represented by these spokes are independent and not connected to each other, so there is little information sharing of customers, innovation, or how to act with more agility. The challenge of most of these companies is the lack of synergy. The whole is worth less than the sum of the parts, or the breakup value is worth more than the current market value of the parent company. And many holding companies have been broken up to realize this full market value.

The market-oriented ecosystem is not a holding company, because of the platform support the ecosystem offers. A pure holding company has autonomous businesses that send resources (profits) to headquarters. In an ecosystem, the opposite occurs. Most cells draw resources because the platform actively supports their success. Traditional holding companies primarily focus on the financial results of their portfolio of businesses. In market-oriented ecosystems, information and resources are shared from the platform to and from the cells and among the cells. These resources are not only about financial success, but also about anticipating environmental opportunities, strategic agility, and ecosystem capabilities.

Private-equity firms are using this ecosystem logic, because they have evolved from a pure holding company model, in which a firm is acquired and financially reengineered so that it can be returned to the public market. Today, most private-equity firms provide strategic and organizational insights to transform the individual firms and to make the private-equity parent firm more valuable.

Another way that a market-oriented ecosystem differs from a holding company lies in the connections between cells. While each ecosystem cell or team operates independently, the cells also contribute to the success of the larger network by cooperating with each other. In an ecosystem, the cells share key capabilities—even codevelop them, as discussed in chapter 4.

Multidivisional Firms

If you work in a multidivisional firm, the market-oriented ecosystem advances your approach by fostering agility, market orientation, and entrepreneurship in different business teams. In a traditional multi-divisional firm, divisions are formed to allocate responsibility and work. These divisions often create silos for control and coordination. Sometimes, these divisions represent functions, each division having deep expertise (e.g., R&D, supply chain, manufacturing, marketing, and customer support). Because of the challenge of collaboration across functional units, organizations create cross-functional teams, liaisons, or other mechanisms to work across functional silos. Or the multidivisional firm creates separate businesses by product, customer, or geographic area, although the businesses are still controlled by strong corporate oversight, with internal mechanisms for resource allocation. The multidivisional firm sometimes becomes a matrix of accountabilities for function, product, customer, and geographic area. Such a matrix requires complex and often time-consuming decision-making processes to govern the work.

Regardless of its form (functional, divisional, or matrix), the multidivisional organization cannot be confused with the market-oriented ecosystem. Instead of focusing internally on control and compliance at the headquarters of multidivisional company, the platform of an ecosystem like Supercell or Alibaba focuses externally on empowering and enabling teams to win in the marketplace. Leaders and others in multidivisional firms often look upward on the hierarchy for guidance; in a market-oriented ecosystem, they look outward to market opportunities for direction. In market-oriented ecosystems like Supercell or the game-development studios at Tencent, the cells or teams are run more like self-driven startups led by a leader with an entrepreneurial spirit. Accountability, authority, and reward for performance all align in cells. In MOEs the relationship between platforms and cells is a win-win collaboration based on an internal market relationship instead of command and control. The power shifts from platforms to teams, because teams are considered internal customers to be served.[4]

Just as reinvention is occurring for industries, products, and customer experiences, so too is organizational reinvention. Organization forms today are neither holding company nor multidivisional, but the market-oriented ecosystem logic and emerging practices offer a novel way to think about and create organization success. There will be first-mover advantage as leaders recognize and adapt this new organizational form.

Both Large and Small Firms

Market-oriented ecosystems solve the classic organizational dilemma of being both big and small. Every organization strives to grow big as it enjoys economies of scale in market influence, brand image, access to resources, costs, and so forth. However, growth can create the problems of a slow and wasteful bureaucracy. It reduces the entrepreneurial drive of people at all levels because of the strong, built-in control-and-compliance mechanisms seen in many multidivisional firms.

By investing and building a strong platform to offer the best shared resources and expertise in common functions (IT, AI, supply chains, HR, and finance, to name a few), the market-oriented ecosystem exploits the strength of big firms. On the other hand, by empowering autonomous, self-driven teams that are facing customers and competitors in the battlefields, the ecosystem unleashes the entrepreneurial drive of the leaders and members of these teams. Until the evolution of the market-oriented ecosystem, these two conflicting advantages—the power of larger firms and the responsiveness of smaller ones—could not coexist. (You might use the terms *centralized* for "big" and *decentralized* for "small.") The market-oriented ecosystem brings these two essential elements together in incredibly synergistic ways, allowing small businesses to grow at unprecedented rates and big organizations to move with astounding speed.

How to Manage the Market-Oriented Ecosystem Platform

The primary organizing principle for platforms is this: everything that can or should be shared is on the platform. In carrying out its main mission, a platform offers shared resources and competencies to support a set of self-driven, highly autonomous cells and business allies to win in the marketplace. Using the Special Air Service analogy from chapter 4, we consider platforms similar to carriers or air bases that support the operation of elite special forces on the battlefield.

The platform empowers rather than controls. It must create the right structures and incentives to align with the needs and priorities of the teams. Business teams or cells are customers for platforms to serve and empower. To create synergy, a highly successful platform sets common standards so that tools, data, coding, and processes can be easily shared. These common standards facilitate the interconnections that the ecosystem needs. Since ecosystems are, by intention, highly dynamic, the platform needs to be as flexible as possible while also providing essential resources reliably enough for others to depend on.

Types of Platforms

As businesses evolve and grow with their business cycles, more activities will migrate to the platform because great degrees of professionalism are required for the firm to be truly world-class. We have identified three basic types of platforms:

- **Core business support:** This support is intertwined with the daily business operations of business teams. Typical functions include basic research, procurement, logistics, customer reach, and other services. For example, Huawei has four elements on its platform: basic research laboratories; supply chains, procurement, and manufacturing; and Huawei University and Huawei Internal Service.[5] Tencent's two social media platforms, WeChat and QQ, generate user traffic for its business teams and allies.

- **Technology support:** These platforms provide technological and data prowess for business teams. Typical functions include IT storage and computing infrastructure, security, coding, user data, AI, and development tools. At Amazon, for example, AWS offers software developers a highly scalable, reliable, and fast and accessible data storage infrastructure at a very low cost. It is the same data storage infrastructure that Amazon uses to run its own global network of websites, and the AWS platform makes the infrastructure available to any developer. By modularizing its different technical capabilities into microservices (such as storage, payments, and search), AWS provides technical support for business teams and allies to experiment with new products or services or to scale up mature operations quickly and cheaply. The infrastructure is designed as a plug-and-play service.[6]

- **Functional support:** Typical functions offered by platforms include strategy, HR, finance, branding, public relations, investor relations, government relations, and business development. Huawei, for instance, has a function platform that includes HR, finance, corporate development, strategy marketing, quality, cybersecurity and user protection, PR, government relations, legal affairs, internal auditing, ethics, and compliance as well as a joint committee on regions.

Alibaba's Platform Design

Alibaba integrates the two layers of business support and technology support and offers what it calls a midplatform (or middle platform, between the front end and the back end) to its business teams and allies.[7] The platform fulfills many support roles in the ecosystem:

- It offers integrated customer profiles to different business teams and allies for targeted marketing.

- It works as a technical service platform that offers IT infrastructure, algorithms, and database and computational support to teams.

- The midplatform identifies the commonality in data and technology requirements of all businesses and turns these common requirements into standardized service modules to be used by teams like merchant management, user management, shopping cart, payment, search, and security.

- It offers support in user account management and profiling and sets rules in coding, sharing, and using data.

Tencent's Platform Design

Positioned as a connector and digital assistant, Tencent makes the most of its traffic-generating platforms (e.g., WeChat, QQ, its browser, and its app stores) and technological infrastructure (e.g., the cloud, payment apps, and social media advertisement). These platforms transform the user experiences and operational efficiency for its business teams and partners in various industries, including retail, health care, finance, transportation, dining, entertainment, municipal services, logistics, education, and more.

In 2014, the fiercest battle of Chinese taxi services (like Uber and Lyft) happened between DiDi (Tencent backed) and Kuaidi (Alibaba backed). During that period, DiDi experienced several system downtimes when it was overwhelmed with information from the dramatic increase in the number of customer requests. In coping with such unexpected growth, Tencent rapidly answered DiDi's request to help upgrade its IT infrastructure. Tencent sent a task force from its Technology and Engineering Group (a platform) to DiDi (a strategic partner). They were able to prepare extra servers overnight to handle the exploding demand. With close cooperation between Tencent and DiDi R&D teams, DiDi was able to handle the exploding information demand and beat Kuaidi in user access and user loyalty. Tencent's technological platform allowed its partner, DiDi, to move quickly and win this business battle.[8]

Key Success Factors for Platforms

For the platform to fulfill its mission and strategic roles in the ecosystem, several critical factors need to be in place:

- The platform must, above all else, be best in class in its expertise. Unless it is providing exceptional value and expertise in the resources it offers, it will not fulfill its promise to the teams to help them become successful in their domains.

Without offering superior expertise, the cells might as well be on their own or find another source to fulfill their needs.

- Part of providing world-class expertise is a thorough understanding of the needs of business teams and the ability to offer products and solutions that turbocharge their efforts. In a fast-paced, highly competitive world, an ill-fitting solution is no solution at all. You might as well offer mismatched shoes to Usain Bolt. He will kick them off and find another provider before he ever reaches the starting blocks.

- The platform also needs to be responsive to internal customers instead of asking them to wait in line for their requests. Otherwise, the platform only impedes the cells' and allies' agility and innovation rather than empowering these groups.

- Finally, the more that a platform can facilitate cross-network learning so that the cells hugely benefit from being in the same community, the more valuable the platform. Establishing common standards and protocols for information and resource sharing is important. Effective platforms also offer menus of choices, depending on the unique needs of the businesses, rather than recipes that everyone has to follow.

In a nutshell, the platform works for the business teams, just as an excellent consultant would, and needs to prove its value every day, just as a consultant must. When the platform and teams work together, both elements benefit hugely, and the ever-changing needs of the business teams provide constant challenge for the platform to improve—sometimes slowly but steadily and at other times very rapidly.

How to Manage the Market-Oriented Ecosystem Business Teams or Cells

The business teams are the business drivers for growth and profitability in the ecosystem. While the platform plays the vital roles of strong back-end support and synergy sharing, the teams most directly create the value. Like elite special forces in the field, they are self-contained units to capture and ride on environmental opportunities that shape new markets. From the point of view of the ecosystem, individual teams should focus on specific product niches and should fit together like jigsaw pieces—each compatible with the others with little overlap, if any. Each team will have embedded within it the functions or expertise that it needs for its own special purpose, such as product design, product development, operation, sales, and product marketing. Depending on the nature of the business, teams can assume various roles. There are development teams (e.g., new games in Supercell) and product category teams (e.g., electronic products, fashion, appliances, books, and fresh food at the e-commerce firm JD.com). There are also product teams (e.g., music, online games, reading materials, animation, and video in Tencent) and service teams (e.g., taxi hailing, private-car sharing, and chauffeur services in online-to-offline businesses like DiDi).

Types of Business Teams

Business teams operate according to the market opportunity they are pursuing. We have identified three types of teams.

- **Hierarchy teams:** These are founded on mature businesses with a focus on efficiency more than innovation. For example, DiDi forms hierarchy teams to grow market share and become market leaders in those well established businesses (e.g., taxi, private-vehicle sharing, luxury, bus). These teams are relatively stable, reporting to a unit leader. Their mission is to grow the business in new cities and to improve efficiency by matching the best car with the passenger through the fastest route.[9] Similarly, Amazon has stable hierarchy teams to run retail businesses inside the United States and to run warehouse and logistic operations.

- **Project teams:** These teams focus on delivering against a specific client opportunity or cross-functional task (e.g., consulting assignment). Often, customization is required to meet the specific needs of clients. Huawei's project teams, for example, work to capture and fulfill business opportunities. To that end, the company organizes customer-facing teams in country offices. These so-called iron triangle teams comprise three critical roles: account manager, solution expert, and delivery expert.[10] Working together, they anticipate, profile, and quickly respond to customer needs. Project teams are widely used in consulting, private-equity funding, architecture, and investment banking.

- **Innovation teams:** When a business focuses on creating new products or services at the experimental stage, it is more likely to form innovation teams that are smaller and more fluid and can either grow bigger or dissolve if the concept doesn't work out. For example, the goal of many Amazon teams is to continuously innovate and experiment with new ideas to serve unfulfilled customer needs and become the world's most customer-centric company. They use a two-pizza innovation team logic, with which the team is designed to be small and comprises only members with core expertise. After a new idea is approved by a director or vice president, a newly formed team typically includes a team leader, technical experts, and engineers. Operating like a small startup, the team has the full autonomy to develop, prototype, and test the ideas with platform support in cloud computing and other tools. In light of a periodic progress review, the team will either further grow or dissolve.[11]

Most market-oriented ecosystems use a mix of these prototypical team types. For example, Tencent has several core business groups (WeChat, Interactive Entertainment, Cloud and Smart Industries, Platform and Content, Technology and Engineering) and uses an assortment of hierarchy, project, and innovation teams within these business groups, depending on the nature of the work and the stage of the business life cycle.

Key Success Factors for Teams

The primary organizing principle for teams is that everything that is idiosyncratic, or uniquely designed for the particular business, product, or customer, goes on the team. Successful cells need the same attributes that any other high-performing team needs:

- **Purpose:** High-performing teams require a clear sense of purpose with an ability to articulate outcomes and goals clearly and precisely and to have explicit accountability. At Supercell, each game-development team is chartered with a clear mission to develop a certain genre of game and is given clear performance metrics before the game can be launched on a full scale.

- **Governance:** Teams operate best with clarity about who is on the team, what their contribution needs to be, how decisions are made, and where accountability resides. Governance ensures that the team has adequate authority to make business decisions and to invest resources to win in the marketplace. At Supercell, a game-development team with five to seven core members (who typically include a game lead, a design lead, an art lead, a client lead, a server lead, and a product management lead) has full autonomy to decide the direction and fate of the game before the product goes online for its testing phase.

- **Relationships:** Teamwork makes people behave better when there are high levels of trust and mutual commitment and where team members care for and support each other. Trust allows the members to disagree without being disagreeable, prevents tension from creating strife, and sees conflict as enabling change. At Supercell, all team members are expected to contribute by voicing their thoughts and opinions. The belief is that the best teams develop the best games.

- **Rewards:** To create a strong incentive for teams to succeed as a whole and to achieve breakthrough goals, team members' rewards should be clearly and strongly linked to the performance of the team. Business teams must align accountability, authority, and incentives if they are to operate like small startups with agility and entrepreneurial drive. Such practice proved successful in helping Tencent roll out blockbuster games one after another.

- **Leadership:** Given the autonomy and resources that the cells or teams are endowed with, each team must be led by a well-rounded business leader who can make sound business judgments and who has strong aspirations to succeed and grow the business. To some extents, such a leader plays the role of owner or entrepreneur (not a professional manager) of the business team.

- **Learning:** Teams constantly improve by evaluating what works and what does not work. Agility in learning is developed both with the team as it constantly improves and with each individual who adjusts and grows. At Supercell, teams share lessons about all their efforts. As mentioned earlier, whether the new game effort was launched successfully or failed, the members still celebrate with a bottle of champagne.[12]

When cells or teams possess these attributes, they not only move quickly into new market opportunities with new products or services, but they also become sustainable as high-performing team insights move from team to team.

How to Manage Strategic Allies in the Market-Oriented Ecosystem

Outside business allies or partners expand the scope and competencies of the ecosystem. They can form networks with the platform or the cell and can enrich the products and offerings of the cell to which they are aligned. Accessing competencies through alliances expands the reach of the platform or cell when the outside partners have unique skills and experiences that can do better than the cells can, in terms of both domain knowledge and cost efficiency. These complementary allies allow market-oriented ecosystems to move quickly to shape or fill a market opportunity. They enrich product or service offerings according to user needs. They can also serve roles along the value chain, upstream (e.g., content) or downstream (e.g., channels), or in different vertical domains (e.g., finance, dining, and entertainment). These business partners often have great autonomy and flexibility to run their businesses, and they are often more productive because of their deep domain expertise and their entrepreneurial drive to run their own businesses rather than be acquired and managed as a company's business unit.

Types of Strategic Allies

In today's knowledge-based economy with great connectivity, allies or partners can have myriad roles. For example, a strategic partner might have a single focus (e.g., working with single app developers) or an organizational focus (e.g., working with more-established firms with a wide range of services). They may enter into a short-term, fee-based relationship or a long-term equity partnership. Or they might help with cost efficiency or might add service offerings. Table 5-2 captures these many options into five categories and shows each category's defining characteristics. Market-oriented ecosystems use all five types of alliances because the work in ecosystems is more defined by the tasks to be done than by people's roles in the organization. Focusing on the actual tasks allows for a host of configurations to deliver the work.

Key Success Factors for Strategic Allies

Allies and partners enable the cells in ecosystems to seize market opportunities quickly, to enrich content and service offerings, to augment the cells' own critical skills and competencies, and to scale up to meet market demands. As allies become more prevalent,

TABLE 5-2

Major types of alliances and partnerships

Type of alliance or partnership	Example	Criteria for success	Challenges
Individual free agent	Collaboration based on expertise (e.g., professional or user-generated content in short videos or articles)	Insight or content	Long-term stable freelance relationship
Project collaborators	Customized, large-scale solutions from multiple firms (e.g., in consulting, architecture, and IT services); partnerships with academic institutions on cutting-edge technologies like AI and robotics	Seamless integration	Customizing a solution rather than combining current products or services from multiple parties
Outsourcing partners	Hiring buffer or seasonal workers for noncritical activities	Cost and buffer (flexible) workforce	Sharing culture and quality standards and ensuring security and IP protection
Business partners	App developers for Apple stores; game developers for Tencent game platform; independent service vendors for customer reach, project implementation, and service support in different industries	Clear rules of profit sharing or fees according to win-win expectations	Creating value for each other for a sustainable relationship
Strategic partners	Complementary partners with equity relationships (e.g., Cainiao with Alibaba; JD.com or Metituan with Tencent)	Long-term alliances; mutual gains for each party	Maintaining boundaries, creating synergy for ecosystem success

market-oriented ecosystems need to know how to best access and use this alliance organization model. The following practices will help you make the most out of your strategic partnerships:

- Decide on your boundary. What types of activities or businesses need to be operated by your business teams, and which can be outsourced or worked through allies? This important decision affects which businesses need to be acquired or majority-controlled (like WhatsApp and Instagram

at Facebook, Android and YouTube at Google) and which
businesses should be spun off as business partners (like the
search business and e-commerce business at Tencent).

- Contract with the partners or allies to ensure that they are
  focused on the right issues. The collaboration agreement
  includes expectations and goals (which are often framed in
  market-opportunity terms); financial arrangements (e.g.,
  fees, commissions, or equity participation); resource commitment (e.g., user traffic, sharing of data, marketing, and
  promotion); and governance (who makes what decisions).
  Work out collaboration protocols so that the relationship
  is win-win for both parties rather than imposing on your
  allies to comply with cell or platform demands. For example,
  key strategic partners of Tencent include DiDi, which offers
  transportation convenience to Tencent users and increases
  the number of users in the ecosystem's payment business. In
  return, Tencent generates user traffic for DiDi. Tencent sold
  its e-commerce business to JD.com in 2014 and joined hands
  with the e-commerce giant to fulfill the e-commerce needs of
  its users. In return, Tencent provides additional traffic for
  JD.com's sales leads.[13]

- Know when to use which type of partners (e.g., free agents,
  project collaborators, outsourcing partners, business partners, or strategic partners). The time horizon for the collaboration, the type of work you want done, and the knowledge
  required to discover market opportunities may shape which
  type of alliance you'll want to form.

- Be selective in picking individuals and partners who will
  deliver the requirements of each business team domain.
  Assess a potential partner's compatibility according to the
  prospect's expertise, resources available, and cultural fit.

When these criteria are met, market-oriented ecosystems can
better deliver on the four critical ecosystem capabilities: external
sensing, customer obsession, innovation throughout, and agility

everywhere. For example, Amazon partners enhance the organization's mission to be the most customer-centric company in the world. To create more choices for its users in product and price selection, Amazon not only opens its e-commerce platform to outside retail companies (its external allies), but also supports them with logistic services and cloud computing. This collaboration enables Amazon to rapidly grow in new market opportunities (e.g., Amazon Marketplace e-commerce, Fulfillment by Amazon, and AWS). In return, these partners offer better products and services to enrich the Amazon ecosystem.[14]

As you review these descriptions of platforms, cells, and allies, ask yourself which principles and practices you could adapt to your organization. As you adapt these principles and practices, the concepts of platforms, cells, and allies become real. In the next section, you will decide which market-oriented ecosystem fits your organization's overarching mission.

The Three Archetypes of Market-Oriented Ecosystems

With our exploration of the building blocks of market-oriented ecosystems—platforms, cells, and allies—we can begin to look at how the ecosystems combine these components into an overall structure. The eight companies we studied may have at least three variants as evidenced in table 5-3.

Creativity-Driven Market-Oriented Ecosystems

These are the companies making best-selling games and blockbuster movies: truly creative endeavors. This type of market-oriented ecosystem is all about having strong, creative people in the cells, because strong people with insight driving creative actions make all the difference. Not only are the dynamics in creative cells hard to standardize, but you would not even want to try. The

TABLE 5-3

Three archetypes of market-oriented ecosystems (MOEs)

Creativity-driven MOEs	Technology- or product-driven MOEs	Efficiency-driven MOEs
Examples: Supercell; Tencent (game studios); Amazon (digital content in movies or TV)	Examples: Tencent (WeChat, Tencent Cloud); Facebook; Google; Alibaba (Ali Cloud); Amazon (AWS, smart devices)	Examples: Alibaba (e-commerce); DiDi; Amazon (e-commerce)
• Production of block-buster games or movies is most critical. • Products are online and digital, with the primary focus on content creation rather than on publishing or distribution. • Teams are typically small but very strong in expertise. • The platform is lighter.	• Product innovation and user experience are most critical. • Products are online and digital, with the primary focus on product development and management. • Teams are flexible and fluid and are based on products or projects. • The platform offers shared support in tools, data, and technological infrastructure.	• Conversion rate and accurate matching are critical. • Engages in both online and offline business activities. • Business teams are relatively stable, focusing on growing users and merchant partners. • Strong middle platform to empower internal business teams and external partners with technological support and user data.

Source: Compiled by Arthur Yeung, case studies of Supercell, Tencent, Facebook, Google, Alibaba, DiDi, and Amazon.

magic comes from creating uniqueness time and again. Only special people, set free in a cell structure and supported by a platform supplying a limited number of essential resources (talent, IT infrastructure, and marketing support, for example), can be truly creative. Would Netflix ever have created its wildly popular series *Stranger Things* if the company had straitjacketed the creators Matt Duffer and Ross Duffer? Of course not. Supercell, Tencent's Interactive Entertainment Group (IEG) game studio, and Amazon's digital content are also great examples of success based on wonderfully talented teams that are both free to do what they do best and supported in their basic needs by the platform. Customers are delighted by the unique offerings, the teams seek out or create the information they need, innovation soars, and things happen very fast—these groups are superagile. Figure 5-2 depicts the Supercell ecosystem (on the left) and a close-up of an individual game cell (on the right).[15]

FIGURE 5-2

Creativity-driven structure of a market-oriented ecosystem at Supercell

The platform has these characteristics: (1) all support functions are designed to allow front-end R&D cells (teams) to focus more on products; (2) to ensure the effectiveness of support functions, personnel in support services are recruited for certain characteristics (e.g., a sense of service instead of a desire for self-realization); (3) to control company size, all job responsibilities are cautious, focused business choices; and (4) the platform prefers to use partner's resources.

The cells have these features: (1) each cell has five to eight members who have overlapping responsibilities and who cooperate closely; (2) each cell operates independently and, to the greatest extent possible, maintains control over its products (creative ideas, when to launch, when to terminate, operation activities, etc.); and (3) the cells follow a professional sports model in which no management level is required and all the staff can do their jobs and make rapid decisions.

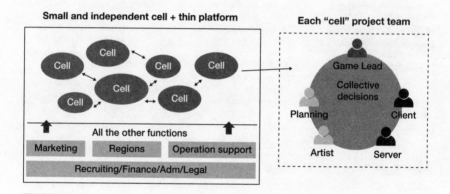

Technology- or Product-Driven Market-Oriented Ecosystems

Google, Facebook, Huawei, Tencent's WeChat, and Amazon AWS earn much of their success from their technology- or product-driven ecosystems. In this type of ecosystem, most daily activities occur within the teams, which are self-contained; there is minimal cross-unit work. The team leaders and platform leaders are both important and demanding in their areas of expertise.

Facebook, for example, has three types of teams (hierarchical teams, cross-functional project teams, and flash teams). Flash team is the most fluid team formed by a few individuals on their own to focus on a specific challenge. Facebook also has three types of platforms: technology platforms like shared coding, data, and tools; business platforms like unified advertisement and sales; and functional platform like HR and finance. For its allies or partners, Facebook cooperates with data providers Epsilon, Datalogix, Acxiom, and BlueKai to improve the accuracy of its targeted advertisement.[16]

Facebook's teams have weak organizational boundaries by design: there is no formal organizational structure in the company. All the staff are managed by functions and work on cross-team projects. These small teams constantly work on new products and features, continuously experimenting. The teams, usually consisting of six or seven people (mostly engineers and a product manager), form around a concept. For example, on the larger Facebook Messenger team, smaller teams work on different features to improve effectiveness—for example, adding a new payment transaction feature. This small group of people will see a customer need, get approval, expand on the idea, get further approval, and roll it out. Typically, team members stay together as a dedicated group for about six months before completing the task, disbanding, and moving on. Since engineers are often problem solvers who like to be exposed to different challenges, this process is satisfying for them personally and professionally. They also participate in hackathons to solve existing problems more radically.

Facebook's product-driven ecosystem offers three forms of technical support for these teams (figure 5-3).[17] First is an infrastructure platform, where tools that are repeatedly used in different teams are openly shared. These tools cover all areas, including research, site support, and daily management. Second, the database or code platform is updated weekly and is open to changes by anyone. These code changes will be evaluated by assessment engineers and the top leaders. Every engineer is encouraged to actively report and fix code bugs. Third, technologies for the future are led by top scientists in their field to create a more connected world. These technologies often focus on AI, virtual reality, and connectivity.

FIGURE 5-3

The product-driven market-oriented ecosystem at Facebook

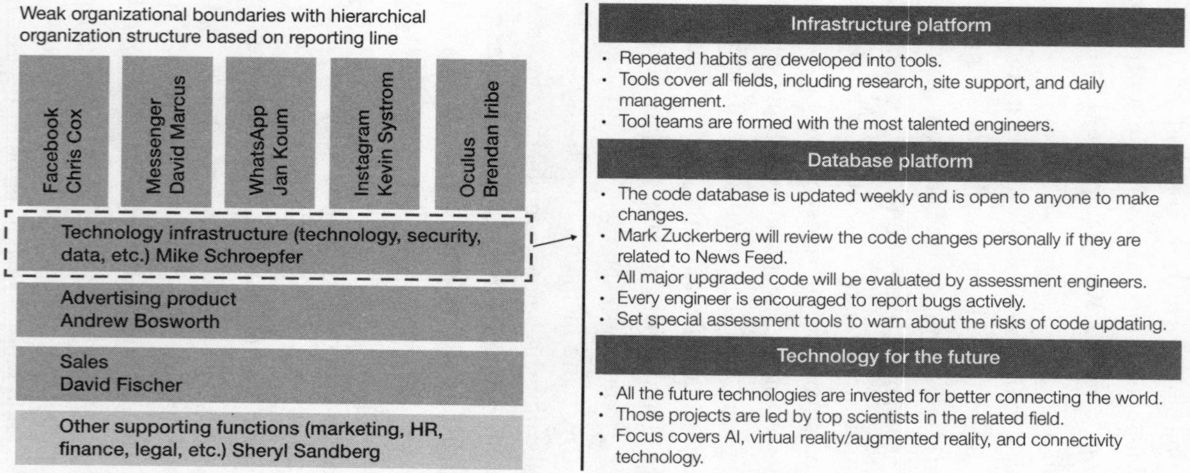

Weak organizational boundaries with hierarchical organization structure based on reporting line

Facebook
Chris Cox

Messenger
David Marcus

WhatsApp
Jan Koum

Instagram
Kevin Systrom

Oculus
Brendan Iribe

Technology infrastructure (technology, security, data, etc.) Mike Schroepfer

Advertising product
Andrew Bosworth

Sales
David Fischer

Other supporting functions (marketing, HR, finance, legal, etc.) Sheryl Sandberg

Infrastructure platform

- Repeated habits are developed into tools.
- Tools cover all fields, including research, site support, and daily management.
- Tool teams are formed with the most talented engineers.

Database platform

- The code database is updated weekly and is open to anyone to make changes.
- Mark Zuckerberg will review the code changes personally if they are related to News Feed.
- All major upgraded code will be evaluated by assessment engineers.
- Every engineer is encouraged to report bugs actively.
- Set special assessment tools to warn about the risks of code updating.

Technology for the future

- All the future technologies are invested for better connecting the world.
- Those projects are led by top scientists in the related field.
- Focus covers AI, virtual reality/augmented reality, and connectivity technology.

Efficiency-Driven Market-Oriented Ecosystems

Market-oriented ecosystems driven by efficiency focus on the conversion ratio of user traffic to effective sales leads, cost efficiency through shared services, and rapid scalability of the business. Amazon, Alibaba, JD.com, and DiDi all focus on delivering highly accurate recommendations to the right customers at the right time. Such targeted recommendations require strong IT and data support offered by the midplatform, which is typically headed by technically capable leaders with a deep understanding of business needs. Efficiency-driven systems have the strongest platform capability and structure among the three archetypes of market-oriented ecosystems. These platforms sets standards for data, tools, usage, and collaboration so that their support can be used across teams, and the team leaders subsequently focus on exploiting these resources and competencies to grow their own business. The platforms are incredibly customer focused through their information-rich data sets and the algorithms that allow them to both capture and anticipate customers' needs in nanoseconds.

Alibaba delivers on this efficiency logic (see figure 5-4).[18] At the front end, the ecosystem comprises approximately thirty highly autonomous business teams that offer different products and services to Alibaba's users. For example, Taobao mainly sells products provided by many small businesses, while Tmall offers products from more established brand companies like Procter & Gamble or renowned fashion designers. Analyzing customer needs and buying behaviors, these teams customize the products or brands they carry and recommend them to the right users. Relying on big data and sophisticated algorithms, Alibaba business teams can display on their web pages completely different products to different users.

There are four layers in Alibaba's midplatform. First, the platform provides business support resources that are critical to the business operations of most cells, including a member platform (how to manage membership and user accounts and how to interact with users), a merchant platform (how to support merchants that do business at Alibaba), a content platform (how to produce and

FIGURE 5-4

The efficiency-driven market-oriented ecosystem at Alibaba

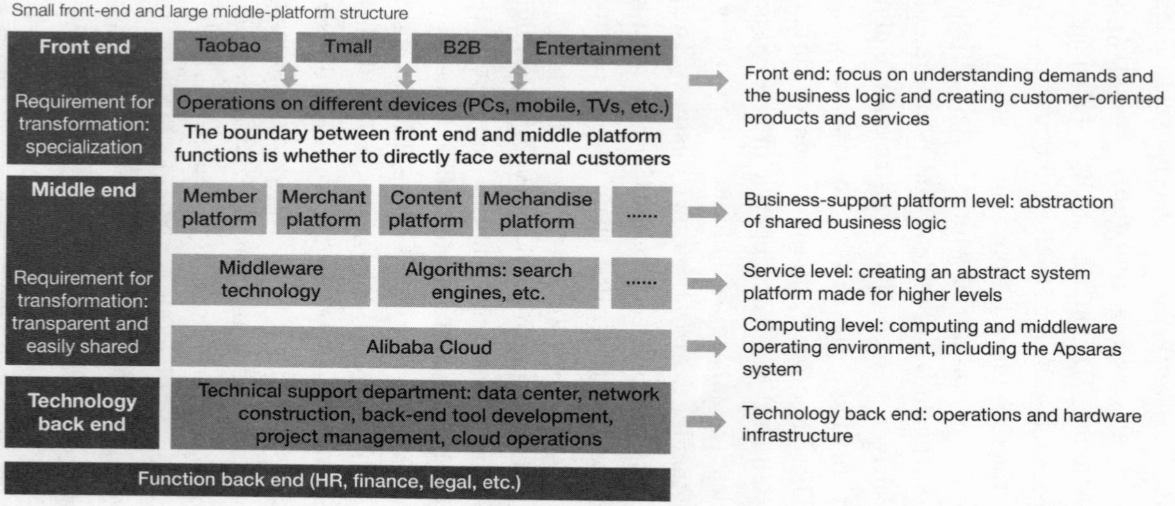

Small front-end and large middle-platform structure

Front end	Taobao	Tmall	B2B	Entertainment

Operations on different devices (PCs, mobile, TVs, etc.)

Requirement for transformation: specialization

The boundary between front end and middle platform functions is whether to directly face external customers

→ Front end: focus on understanding demands and the business logic and creating customer-oriented products and services

Middle end	Member platform	Merchant platform	Content platform	Mechandise platform	......

→ Business-support platform level: abstraction of shared business logic

Middleware technology	Algorithms: search engines, etc.	......

→ Service level: creating an abstract system platform made for higher levels

Requirement for transformation: transparent and easily shared

Alibaba Cloud

→ Computing level: computing and middleware operating environment, including the Apsaras system

Technology back end

Technical support department: data center, network construction, back-end tool development, project management, cloud operations

→ Technology back end: operations and hardware infrastructure

Function back end (HR, finance, legal, etc.)

display product marketing materials), and a merchandise platform (how to organize products and merchandise). These basic tools need to be customized in different business teams. The second and third layers provide the service and computational capabilities through application software and Alibaba Cloud with numerous microservice modules, AI, and user profiles. The fourth layer offers basic IT infrastructure, such as servers, networks, security, and data centers. The midplatform is one of the critical initiatives Alibaba has adopted to overcome the highly decentralized business silos that didn't share data and tools in the past. This lack of a centralized platform resulted in inefficient, inferior technological support during the pre-platform era. With the building of the midplatform since 2016, Alibaba's sales growth and profitability has taken off, with better conversion rates and more-personalized recommendations.

As with most companies, the back-end platform at Alibaba includes typical functions like HR, finance, strategy, government relations, and public relations. These platforms offer guidelines and professional support to Alibaba's business teams. Though they are not closely intertwined with the daily operations of the business teams, these functions empower the business teams with their functional expertise and facilitate cross-learning of best practices across teams.

Summary of Market-Oriented Ecosystem Archetypes and Structures

The eight market-oriented ecosystems that we studied used platforms, cells, and allies to deliver the results (e.g., creativity, new products, efficiency) that are critical to business success in their industries. While these basic structural components are the same in every ecosystem, how they are deployed depends on the strategic goals of each company (see, for example, table 5-4). In each of these market-oriented ecosystems, the organizational form has allowed the firm to quickly deploy resources to capture market opportunities, to reduce the cycle time from idea to action, and to fully engage the passion of employees who have the freedom to act and who

TABLE 5-4

Summary of market-oriented ecosystems: strategic priorities, platforms, cells, and results

Strategic priorities	What the platform does	What the cells offer	Results
Supercell (creativity driven) Apply the company motto "The best teams make the best games."	Allows the team to concentrate on game creation itself Provides essential support in marketing; traffic generation in key markets; and HR, financial, and legal support	Focus on the development of high-quality games	Five games are all once listed in the global top-ten list of most popular games One of the best and most valuable mobile gaming companies in the world
Google (technology driven) Mission: to organize the world's information and make it universally accessible and useful Start from search at websites to search at contents (books, news, maps, videos etc.) to generate user traffic that provides opportunities for advertisement Create new tools and platforms (like Gmail, Chrome, Android app stores) to create new user traffic Google X to incubate technology-driven innovations in AI, autonomous driving, medicine, energy, etc.	Very strong IT infrastructure through shared codes, tools, and key technologies like TensorFlow Shared platform to provide support through advertisement PA, sales, marketing, and Gtech (to manage strategic partnerships) Back-end platforms in HR, finance, legal, etc.	Organize by product areas like search, ads, maps, Android, YouTube, Cloud Frequent use of flexible, self-contained project teams (around 7 people with different expertise) under product areas to work on OKR projects or feature improvement	One of the most valuable companies in the world, exceeding USD 800 billion Constantly selected as the "best employer" by *Fortune* magazine
Facebook (product driven) Apply the company motto "Connect the world." Growth is driven by boosting the number of users in different apps around the world, lengthening user time, and improving ways of monetization.	Provides strong technical platform, tools, and shared data to make everyone's work easier; provides a shared advertisement and sales platform to support the monetization of user traffic in different apps	Facebook, Messenger, Instagram, WhatsApp, and Oculus to target different users	With more than one billion users, the largest social media company in the world

Tencent (product driven)

Make connection and digital content the core businesses. Work with ecosystem partners to use two social media platforms (WeChat and QQ) to offer more products and services in different vertical domains.

- Use two social media platforms (WeChat and QQ) to generate user traffic
- Create a technological and engineering platform to provide computing, algorithms, and other technical support to assist user data protection and sharing of data analytics, which benefit decision making

- Dozens of product teams to enhance user experiences in different offerings (games, music, mobile payment, digital books, news, videos)
- Growth of more than 50 percent in the last two years
- Widespread users: WeChat and QQ serve over 1 billion and 800 million monthly active users respectively
- One of the top ten most valuable firms in the world

Huawei (product driven)

Start as a telecom equipment provider in China (from digital switches to end-to-end solutions). Develop five new strategies in retail, finance, manufacturing, and energy. Grow into both adjacent and disruptive businesses.

- Developed regional platforms that offer the key product and technical competencies to business teams in different countries
- Developed an HQ platform as a service provider that enables continuous transformation in basic research, supply chain, service delivery, and financial services; enhances the project teams' ability to create value for customers

- Iron-triangle customer facing team consists of account manager, solution expert, and delivery expert
- Project director and manager nomination is based on the importance of the project
- Project team members come from the country and regional resource pool
- Ranked 72 in *Fortune* Global 500 Companies in 2017
- Top telecom equipment provider worldwide based on market share and sales revenue in 2018
- Second-highest mobile phone provider worldwide based on shipment and market share in 2018

Alibaba (efficiency driven)

Predict and embrace changes to fulfill the mission. Develop five new strategies in retail, finance, manufacturing, and energy. Grow into both adjacent and disruptive businesses.

- Build a strong mid-platform for shared technological and data support
- Offer IT infrastructure, algorithms, database and computational support, unified user account management, and profiling and coding rules
- Enable teams and strategic partners to make more-targeted business decisions and to innovate

- About thirty empowered and self-contained business teams that serve customers for different products or services
- Substantially more accurate personalized recommendation from integrated user profiles across all teams
- Better conversion ratio of internet traffic, leading to more effective sales leads and faster sales growth
- Strong support for new businesses inside China like fresh food delivery service (He Ma Sheng Xian) or overseas like Lazada in Indonesia
- Growth of more than 50 percent in both 2017 and 2018

(continued)

TABLE 5-4 *(continued)*

Summary of market-oriented ecosystems: strategic priorities, platforms, cells, and results

Strategic priorities	What the platform does	What the cells offer	Results
Amazon (efficiency driven) Become the world's most customer-centric company by continuous innovation to serve unfulfilled customer needs. Start from core retail business and relentlessly expand into adjacent enterprise and consumer businesses.	Through AWS, provides microservices (both internally and externally) to scale up existing core businesses and to enable two-pizza teams to quickly prototype new ventures	Different teams to build businesses in e-commerce, AWS, digital content and devices, and offline retailing; wider selection, lower prices, and greater convenience for customers	Ranked number one in innovation by *Fast Company* Among the top three most valuable firms in the world
DiDi (efficiency driven) Offer smart transportation through ride sharing and autonomous driving Expand from taxi hailing to multiple types of ride sharing services, from serving passengers to car owners (e.g., leasing, insurance) and drivers (e.g., gas station, maintenance) and from serving individual users to corporate customers and municipal governments (e.g., smart city)	Integrate product management and core technologies in the midplatform Capture real-time user data from millions of networked vehicles on the road, analyze big data through AI, and predict passenger demands and traffic flow for improved services	Organize into different self-contained service teams like taxi hailing, private car hailing, hitch, chauffeur, bus, minibus, luxury service	Became the biggest on-demand transportation platform on the planet based on number of rides served Market valuation exceeds USD 50 billion

can find meaning in their work. These ecosystem configurations of platforms, cells, and allies have created different strengths in four ecosystem capabilities (see table 4-1) that are essential to sustainable success in their respective industries.

Managerial Implications

Traditionally, organizational design choices have been about things like roles, responsibilities, processes, reporting relationships, and alignment. These choices would lead to the organizational models of hierarchies, holding companies, multidivisional firms, and so forth.

In today's rapidly changing world, where strategic agility replaces strategic planning, the emerging choices pivot around platforms, cells, and alliances and how to design them to create and sustain ecosystem capabilities. This emerging organizational form advances both the traditional multidivisional firm and the holding company. Market-oriented ecosystems that can truly master the challenges of what the platform offers and how the cells and strategic partners support and reinforce each other, will have a decided competitive advantage that others might only hope for.

The ecosystems we studied started fresh by making these new organizational choices. If you are a leader of a newer or startup firm, you can begin with a clean sheet to create the right platform, cells, and allies and integrated capabilities that anticipate and grasp market opportunities.

But if you lead a more traditional organization, the transition to a market-oriented ecosystem is often difficult because of embedded patterns and culture. In chapter 13, we present three detailed case studies of firms that have made, or are making, this transition. In the interim, however, you can ask about choices that lead to more agility in your organization.

- Overall market-oriented ecosystem agenda:

  - What competitive differentiators (creativity, new products, or efficiency) are critical to your businesses?

- Which of these three differentiators would lead you to the best growth and success within your industry?

- Platform:

  - What work should be shared on a platform and what else can then be allocated to cells or allies?

  - How can platform work be organized into menu options that a cell leader can access to move quickly into a new market?

  - How do you ensure your platform deeply understand the needs of business teams and strategic partners, maintain superior expertise, and be responsive to needs of internal customers?

- Cells or teams:

  - What work should be kept within cells to ensure agility and innovation?

  - How do you quickly form teams that can explore and exploit new opportunities?

  - How do you encourage individual teams to innovate new ideas as well as adapt ideas from others to create new markets?

- Allies and strategic partners:

  - Which businesses should be best kept within your company, and which should be best run by allies or strategic partners?

  - How can you structure win-win alliances with your strategic partners (e.g., through fees, commissions, minor equity participation, or managing the right partner participation)?

  - How do you cocreate with your partners and customers so that you can use and access their resources, capabilities, and information to win in the marketplace?

- Ecosystem capabilities:

  - How can you design and combine platform, cells, and partners in ways that strengthen or magnify critical ecosystem capabilities (external sensing, customer obsession, innovation, and agility) that are critical to the sustainable success of your business?

  - What type of ecosystem (creativity-driven, product- or technology-driven, or efficiency-driven) fits your company or business group best?

By asking and answering these questions, you may be able to adapt some of the organizational design choices to reinvent your organization.

PART III

GOVERNANCE

HOW A MARKET-ORIENTED
ECOSYSTEM WORKS

I f you want to adapt market-oriented ecosystem principles to reinvent your organization, you have to understand business context (part I), create the right organization anatomy (part II), and manage the day-to-day operations of your organization. This part of the book explores how the market-oriented ecosystem operates through six governance mechanisms that you can adapt to reinvent your organization (figure III-1).

Organizational governance used to mean exclusively, in a word, control. Oversight committees established rules and internal regulations at the top, and these rules frequently created time-consuming and often-convoluted approval processes as checks not only on potential malfeasance but also on what *not* to do.

In the market-oriented ecosystem, governance is more about what *to do* so that the ecosystem moves rapidly to respond to market opportunities. This governance helps with the coordination of shared beliefs and priorities; the alignment of actions and outcomes through performance accountability and incentives; the generation of new ideas; the fluid movement of talent; the rapid sharing of knowledge, data, and insights; and the collaboration of units throughout the entire ecosystem. This sort of governance supports success under today's extreme conditions; it does not simply keep the organization from failing. As the saying goes, a market-oriented ecosystem worries less about doing the right thing and more about doing things right by bringing external sensing, customer obsession, innovation, and agility to life.

FIGURE III-1

A six-part framework for reinventing the organization as a market-oriented ecosystem (MOE)

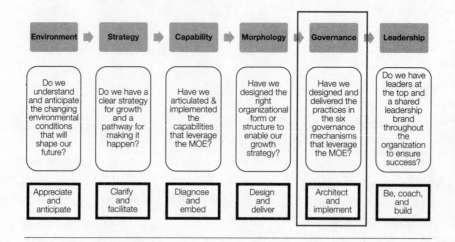

Part III discusses in six targeted chapters how the eight market-oriented ecosystems we studied guide everyone's actions and behaviors not through edicts but through governance choices. When these mechanisms are well devised, people and organization will naturally do the right things because the system supports and encourages them to do so. Unobstructed by an underbrush of bureaucracy, the organization and the people in it have a clear line of sight into the larger environment. They also enjoy the elbow room to maneuver and find alternative approaches to customers and each other as collaborators and colleagues on an ongoing basis. Governance in this sense is more about guidance than it is about rules.

Our research uncovered six key governance attributes that have an impact on how successful companies deliver on the four key capabilities (figure III-2). Here are brief explanations of these six influences:

Culture: As described in chapter 6, culture takes place on three levels: (1) as symbols, rituals, stories, and other organizational events; (2) as thoughts, feelings, and behaviors expressed in the organization's values and norms and in people's emotional responses to how things are done in a company; and (3) as the identity of a company as perceived by its best custom-

FIGURE III-2

Six governance mechanisms in market-oriented ecosystems

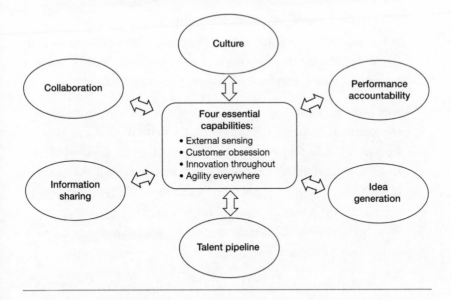

ers from the outside in. Culture defines the key priorities and behaviors people should pursue collectively in an ecosystem.

Performance accountability: This attribute, discussed in chapter 7, links business plans to individual actions to business outcomes. In a world of extreme speed, change, uncertainty, and experimentation, accountability matters more than ever. But accountability is less in the traditional complex performance management processes and more in daily conversations between leader and employees and among employees.

Idea generation: Market-oriented ecosystems maintain their winning capabilities in customer obsession, innovation, and agility by encouraging the generation of new ideas from everywhere and quickly turning them into experimentation (chapter 8). This pipeline of ideas starts to flow when personal curiosity turns into organizational creativity.

Talent pipeline: Obviously, organizations with better overall talent have a clear advantage over those with lesser talent. As chapter 9 shows, the talent pipeline is all about bringing in the right people and helping them to succeed: setting the right standards and sourcing, screening, securing, and orienting the talent. Through the talent pipeline, organizations also develop, move, engage, and retain the right talent so these people can support experimentation on new ideas and flexibly execute on proven ideas. Inspired people produce exceptional results.

Information sharing: All market-oriented ecosystems excel at external sensing. In chapter 10, we explain that information sharing as a governance mechanism deals with what information and data to capture and then share, who to share it with, when to share it, and how to share. Radical transparency exists in these ecosystems. The norm is that more, not less, information is shared among all people, and valuable data flows easily across units.

Collaboration: Chapter 11 explains that collaboration deals with the challenge of making the whole more than the parts. Collaboration occurs when teams combine the skills of individuals into team performance and when individual teams in a network work with each other to make the network better than any single team. Instead of relying on a command-and-control approach prevalent in traditional hierarchies, market-oriented ecosystems use market mechanisms to facilitate win-win collaboration.

Each of the eight companies we studied designs and uses governance mechanisms in slightly different ways. In the six chapters in part III, we briefly review the latest thinking on governance mechanisms, share examples of how the companies are using these mechanisms, and offer tools that can be adapted to any organization. Each of these six governance mechanisms has been the topic of extensive research and practice. As we distill these ideas through the lens of a market-oriented ecosystem, we provide a host of practices and tools to help you adapt market-oriented principles to your organization. Table III-1 provides an overview of the six governance mechanisms of the eight firms we studied.

Governance mechanisms of market-oriented ecosystems (MOEs) studied

Company and key MOE capabilities	Culture (chapter 6)	Performance accountability (chapter 7)	Idea generation (chapter 8)	Talent pipeline (chapter 9)	Information sharing (chapter 10)	Collaboration (chapter 11)
Creativity-driven MOE						
Supercell: external sensing, innovation, agility	• Setting high standards • Bold experimentation • Admitting mistakes • Celebrating failures	• No formal grading; assessment based on calibration discussion to compare employee performance across teams. Emphasis on company first and team second in talent rewards	• Bottom-up innovation, celebrating failures	• Extremely high hiring standards • Easy mobility	• Internally transparent data (e.g., number of users in each game is released every day)	Each cell's establishment and operation are highly autonomous, but all decisions are based on the company's best interests
Technology- or product-driven MOE						
Facebook: external sensing, innovation, agility	Hacker culture + five core values: • Be bold • Focus on impact • Move fast • Be open • Build social value	• Focused on value and impact, not just result • Peer review and calibration • Reward: high pay and good working conditions and employee benefits (free lunches, free snacks, etc.)	• Hackathons: idea generation and experimentation • Monthly review by Zuckerberg or Boz: everyone has the chance to propose ideas and get feedback and resources	• High recruitment standards • Retain "brilliant jerk" • Free movement of talent according to project teams and internal job market	• Transparent information sharing (unified code base, data, tools, technical information and support)	• Very strong technology platform to make everyone's work easier • Facebook@ Work to facilitate collaboration
Google: external sensing, innovation, agility	Ten principles in a strong engineering culture: • Respect for engineers: innovation based on tech insight • Respect for individuals: transparency, internal mobility • Do no evil	OKR + calibration meeting • Pay "unfair" to reward people very differently based on performance • High fixed salary, good working conditions and employee benefits	• 10X thinking big to encourage destructive innovation • Strategy summits • Concept of 20 percent of time spent on what excites team members	• High hiring standards • Recruitment committee that calibrates or compares new hires across teams • Easy talent movement according to project teams and internal job market	• Weekly meetings • Transparency in most information and data within the company	Cross-functional teams in product area work together

(continued)

TABLE III-1 (continued)

Governance mechanisms of market-oriented ecosystems (MOEs) studied

Company and key MOE capabilities	Culture (chapter 6)	Performance accountability (chapter 7)	Idea generation (chapter 8)	Talent pipeline (chapter 9)	Information sharing (chapter 10)	Collaboration (chapter 11)
Huawei: external sensing, customer focus, innovation	Core values: • Customer first • Dedication • Long-term hard work	• Rigorous performance management and consequence management • Promotion, demotion, and separation clearly tied to results	Learning from world-class benchmarks, consulting firms, external partners to drive transformation in new product development, supply chain, service delivery, and finance	• Recruiting fresh graduates from best universities • Rotating talent across functions and regions	• Regional platforms to share knowledge and competence • HQ platforms as service provider and enabler	Collaboration between project teams and platform based on internal market settlement (project has P&L accountability, pays for internal services)
Tencent: external sensing, customer focus, innovation, agility	Company priorities: • User value • Employee growth • Integrity • Proactive • Collaboration • Innovation	• Employee bonus tied directly to team performance at game development studio • Hall of Fame for products ranked first in industry (each team gets generous bonus)	Incubation process at mobile internet group to drive bottom-up innovation during the period of 2014–2018	• High recruitment standards based on job and cultural fits • Internal mechanism that allows employees to apply for new internal jobs	Technological engineering group enables business team with technical support (e.g. big data, security, and AI)	• Collaboration in game business based on market relationship • "Internal race mechanism" allows multiple teams to work in similar area to ensure winning in the marketplace
Efficiency-driven MOE						
Alibaba: external sensing, customer focus, innovation, agility	Company core values: • Customer first • Teamwork • Embrace change • Integrity • Passion • Commitment	Dual system of employee assessment, integrating both performance and six core values	Innovative ideas from customers, frontline people, and mission-driven business innovation from the top	Proactive job rotation by company to nurture well-rounded talent and leaders	Middle platform provides business teams and allies with integrated data and technology	Front-end business teams and middle platform relationship: customer relationship with service mindset

Amazon (core retail business): external sensing, customer focus, innovation, agility	Customer-centric leadership principles: • Customer obsession • Ownership • Invention and simplicity • Are right. A lot (in decisions). • Hiring and developing the best people • Highest standards • Thinking big • Bias for action • Frugality • Learning and curiosity • Earning trust • Diving deep • Willingness to disagree and commit • Delivering results	• Leadership principles constitute 50 percent of evaluation • Peer review plus calibration to compare employee performance across teams • Toleration of failure and company-first decisions	• Innovation funnel • PR&FAQs as tool to suggest new ideas from all levels any time • Formal three-year planning process to seek big new ideas	• High recruitment standards: leadership principles + job-specific skills • High standards and cultural fit • Easy flow of internal talent	AWS offers various microservices and shared tools	• Self-contained teams with "single-threaded" leaders • Easy access to existing AWS services via a platform
DiDi: external sensing, innovation, agility	Core values: • Listening to customers • Safety, experience, and efficiency • Frequent communication • Leading technology • Diversity • Attention to growth	• Peer review constitutes 10 percent of assessment • Compensation for top technical talent is much higher than for other talent	Mainly based on top-down innovation at this phase	High-end talent strategy	Build a shared technology platform to integrate data and tools	• Support-oriented relationship between platform and business teams • Internal market mechanism to govern relationship based on transfer price

Note: OKR, objectives and key results; P&L, profit and loss.

Source: Compiled by Arthur Yeung and Tencent Research Team, case studies of Supercell, Facebook, Google, Huawei, Tencent, Alibaba, and DiDi; and employees and former employees of these same companies, interviews with Tencent Research Team.

CHAPTER 6

Culture

How Can You Shape the Right Priorities and Behaviors in the Ecosystem?

The business literature is filled with pithy ways of saying that culture trumps strategy. For example, there's a well-known saying, often (erroneously) attributed to Peter Drucker: "Culture eats strategy for breakfast."[1] Few leaders would today deny the importance of organizational culture. It shapes and sustains employee well-being and productivity, business results, customer reputation, and investor confidence. Culture is more difficult to copy than is accessing financial capital, implementing a new technology system, making customer promises, or even creating a strategic plan. For these reasons, culture is central to competitiveness. It ensures sustainability, which by definition outlives any single individual. It makes the whole organization more than the individual parts (or the ecosystem more valuable than the separate cells).

As a governance mechanism, culture shapes personal behavior by moving beyond incentives (markets) and rules (hierarchy) to norms and values.[2] Employees do the right things because of the cultural norms dictating what they are expected to do. Employees *belong* to a culture when they embrace its ways. When people love their culture, they meet the written and unwritten expectations because they long to be valued members of the tribe.

As Eric Schmidt, former Google CEO and chairman, said, "Google is run by its culture and not by me . . . Google is probably the best example of a network-based organization. Very flat, very non-hierarchical, very much informal in culture and ideas—ideas come from everywhere . . . Part of the job of being a CEO in a company like Google is to have an environment where people are constantly throwing you their best ideas as opposed to being afraid to talk to you."[3]

But while culture matters to an ecosystem's success, managers trying to transform their organizations, and even auditors trying to document culture, it is often ambiguous and hard to define.[4] For you as a leader to effectively use culture as a governance tool, you'll want to (1) define the right culture and how it fits into the governance process; (2) learn how to think about and use culture, using the examples presented in this book; and (3) apply specific tools for creating the right culture.

How to Define the Right Culture

You know culture when you experience and feel it. It is the difference between walking into a McDonald's and entering la Tour d'Argent; between a performance of Lady Gaga and one of *La Traviata*; between a visit to Boston and a trip to Berlin, Bangkok, Beirut, or Beijing. Do you like where you are? Do you fit in? Does it fit you? Families have cultures, regions have cultures, countries have cultures, and so do organizations. Culture is more than food, music, language, architecture, and clothing. It is *everything* that happens in a place. Culture is what gives the people inside a group or a place a distinctive feeling and a set of expectations—sometimes conscious and sometimes not—about what to do, how to do it, and what is going to happen.

Any organization has a culture. The challenge lies in defining the right culture that governs the organizational processes and employee actions. Many visualize culture as the roots of a tree. We disagree. The roots reinforce the past and offer a fixed view of culture. We see culture as the leaves of the tree, drawing energy from the sun and growing into the future.

Defining the right culture requires clarifying four concepts: purpose, values, brand, and culture. Satya Nadella, Microsoft CEO, recently said, "Last week in my email to you I synthesized our strategic direction as a productivity and platform company. Having a clear focus is the start of the journey, not the end. The more difficult steps are creating the organization and culture to bring our ambitions to life."[5] With Nadella's words in mind, we'll outline the four concepts of culture:

- **Purpose:** We've already discussed purpose in chapter 3 as the basis for strategically agile companies; it represents an aspiration for what can be. It includes an idealized vision of what you want to become and is often expressed in a tagline ("the world's best X"). The purpose also includes a mission statement of why you exist, your strategies and goals, and statements about where and when you should invest to reach these goals. Your organization's purpose envisions a future that inspires people and offers direction. All the market-oriented ecosystems we studied have purpose statements. As mentioned earlier, Google's mission is "to organize the world's information and make it universally accessible and useful," while Alibaba's mission is "to make it easy to do business anywhere." Amazon's mission, though a little long, is clear and compelling: "To be Earth's most customer-centric company, where customers can find and discover anything they might want to buy online, and endeavors to offer its customers the lowest possible prices."

- **Values:** These represent core beliefs, what you stand for, and how you go about doing your work. In the tree metaphor,

values are the roots. They are generally articulated by the
founder, are stated in a value statement, and remain stable
over time. Values determine acceptable employee behaviors.
They are also often generic and consistent across companies
and include such noble values as integrity, empowerment,
excellence, accountability, service, and passion. At Tencent,
the four core values are integrity, proactive, collaboration,
and innovation, while Amazon describes leadership principles that highlight the desired behaviors and mindsets that
leaders should demonstrate.

- **Brand:** A brand represents what you are known for in the
  marketplace and the promises made to customers about a specific product. It also represents how your firm will interact
  with its customers.

- **Culture:** This idea refers to the identity of the firm in the
  mind of your key customers made real to employees. This
  definition moves an internal-value focus to an external,
  customer-value focus because it connects culture to the
  marketplace. Such a view of culture also ensures that the
  firm's brand and promises to its customers become major
  considerations in the firm's internal actions. For example,
  this outside-in view of culture represents how your employees understand the key customers' impression of your firm's
  identity.

Taken together, these four concepts capture the key process
for defining the right culture as more than a generic set of embedded values and more than a tailored and isolated set of customer
promises.

As shown in figure 6-1, once the right culture is defined, it establishes governance expectations that lead to the right organization
processes and the personal actions that increase both employee well-
being, ecosystem cohesiveness, and organizational performance.
You can ask yourself how well your company does on these four dimensions of defining the right culture.

FIGURE 6-1

Defining the right culture in an organization

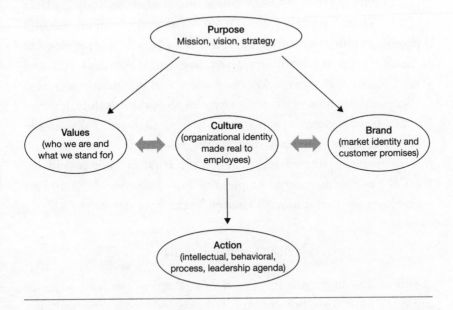

The Multifaceted Nature of Culture

With culture as the identity of the firm in the mind of the customers and made real to employees, it becomes a powerful governance mechanism to shape how people in platforms, business teams, and even partner organizations think and behave. Through the right culture all in the ecosystem share the priorities (e.g., Amazon's and Huawei's customer-centric approach, Alibaba's mission-driven focus, and Tencent's user experience). Because of the complexity of human thought and behavior, culture has many facets. We can, however, group these numerous elements into three large categories of culture.

Stories and Other Organizational Customs

Symbols, rituals, stories, and other organizational events are the first cultural artifacts we experience when we join or visit an organization, because they are the most visible. Market-oriented ecosystems need to tell stories and embed rituals that support their culture. During your onboarding as a new employee at Huawei, for example, you will be told many stories about how the company lives out its customer-centric focus. One favorite story is about the 2011 Japanese earthquake, which led to a tsunami and major problems at the Fukushima nuclear power plant. Because of the disaster, many transmission towers were knocked down and communication was interrupted. Instead of running away for the sake of safety, Huawei decided to send even more people to help a customer, Tokyo-based communications company SoftBank, restore telecom services. Such a response immediately earned the trust of Masayoshi Son, the CEO of SoftBank, and helped the Japanese company build an even closer partnership with Huawei in the years to come.

Internally Defined Criteria

A subtler but more powerful part of culture is how people in an organization think, behave, and feel, according to internally defined criteria. Culture shows up in people's values, norms, and unwritten rules and their emotional responses to how things are done in a company. Market-oriented ecosystems need to make as explicit as possible what matters to the culture and should provide feedback loops to help people learn. For example, at Amazon, people know that CEO Jeff Bezos is serious about customer focus rather than competitor focus. As a former vice president recalled in an interview with us, he once joined a meeting with several senior vice presidents and Bezos. During the meeting, one participant mentioned something about what Walmart had recently done to gain market share. When Bezos heard this comment, he immediately stood up, interrupted the meeting, and reinstated Amazon's belief of customer focus, not competitor focus. Although the executive we spoke with was amazed by Bezos's reaction, the other participants were not, because they had worked at the company for many years and had already seen similar responses time after time. But Bezos never missed any opportunity to reinforce his core belief underlying all decision making.[6]

External Reputation

A company's market reputation is its external identity as perceived by its best customers. Amazon wants to be known for its customer obsession, Google for its technological innovation, Facebook for its product, and Supercell for its outstanding games that endure over time. For these reputations to become real, every member of the ecosystem needs to think, act, and feel in ways that broadcast the desired culture. Culture is the greatest brand carrier, and it plays out in every customer interaction.

With this last category of culture in mind, you can begin to define your firm's ideal, or right, culture by asking, "What is the short list of what we want to be known for by our best customers?" This question balances both your firm's internal values or behaviors and its external promises and identity. Make sure that customers outside and employees inside have a shared mindset about this desired aspect of your culture. As already stated, Tencent wants to be known for great user experiences in its products. Huawei wants to be known for amazing customer focus and customer service. Amazon wants to be known as "the most customer-centric company in the world" for selling virtually anything online (and recently offline) and delivering lightning fast. When these external aspirations become embedded in employee behaviors and organization actions, culture has real business impact.

How Market-Oriented Ecosystems Live the Right Culture

Once the right culture is articulated, it plays a significant role in the consistent governance of the market-oriented ecosystem. With its mission to "make it easy to do business anywhere," Alibaba has kept one eye on the outside—evolving technological development and unserved customer needs or "pain points"—and another eye on identifying new business opportunities to make its mission actionable. The company first worked with a B2B model that connected Chinese businesses with overseas buyers. Then it developed

Taobao, which connects small and medium-sized businesses inside China with Chinese buyers, and Alipay to solve the payment problem. Then came Alimama to create user traffic through targeted social advertisement and Cainiao to support logistic flow.[7] Alibaba's culture is to perpetually scan the external world to find out who the firm can connect with and what their unserved needs are and to make the right choice to enrich the Alibaba ecosystem. In short, culture guides its key business decisions.

Amazon believes that it owes much of its success to the entire organization's being tapped into customer possibilities. This customer-oriented culture allows Amazon to quickly and continuously evolve throughout the organization in the service of the customer. Says Bezos: "We've had three big ideas at Amazon that we've stuck with for 18 years, and they are the reason we're successful: Put the customer first. Invent. And be patient."[8] And he makes this point continuously.

Huawei further illustrates a customer-obsessed culture. When employees join the company, they know they are signing up for customer focus at an Olympic level. Customer needs are more important than any other need, even that of major investors or government officials, who are critical stakeholders in China. For example, CEO Ren Zhengfei only spends time with customers, employees, and partners, not investors or government officials. In one story well known internally in Huawei, Ren refused to see an investment team headed by Stephen Roach at Morgan Stanley, which manages a total worth of US$3 trillion, as investing in this relationship was not his priority.[9] While that story is telling indeed, Huawei's response in the aftermath of the 2011 Japanese earthquake, as mentioned earlier, is impressive. The customer loyalty dividend that this action created was tremendous, especially with SoftBank, a major Japanese telecommunications company.

Supercell focuses its culture on innovation. In addition to its five top-ranking innovative mobile games, Supercell also innovates in many other areas. In 2015, its Clash of Clans games placed a big bet on Super Bowl advertising. The ad shows the *Taken* and *Star Wars* star Liam Neeson (as "AngryNeeson52") threatening to go after

"BigBuffetBoy85," who is trying to take his gold in a battle waged online in a coffee shop (over scones). Supercell decided to pay for a full minute of play, which cost about $9 million for the airtime alone during the big game. The first gaming product to be advertised during the Super Bowl, it became the most popular advertisement on YouTube of the Super Bowl 2015 advertisements (measured by view count). Indeed, it was so successful that Supercell's example was soon followed by California-based tech company Machine Zone.[10]

Facebook keeps its systemwide innovation-culture juices flowing through its strong preference for action over perfection. The company attributes much of its success to a clear capability around innovation because of Facebook's cultural strengths in trying out new ideas, testing, and improving in the service of innovation. "Action is better than perfection," said one executive on the topic of innovation. The hackathon culture encourages employees to move fast, break things, and make impact. The cultural norm means easy iteration, fast failure, and quick learning. It is *not* about seeking your own advantage or micromanaging potential opportunities into a state of inertia.

DiDi understands that all parts of the ecosystem should operate with equal quickness because just as a chain is only as strong as its weakest link, an ecosystem is only as agile as its slowest part. DiDi's core management team has an off-site meeting with staff every month (it is livecast online). Here, the CEO and other executives communicate their thoughts, progress, and positions on key issues. They go as far as taking online votes as they openly discuss the ten major issues of the day. In their matching of passengers and drivers, DiDi also exploits big data and AI not only to respond quickly to customer demands but also to anticipate where the peak demand of cars will be so that the wait time of passengers will be minimized.[11]

Google establishes its ideal culture of agility by turning its values into the right behaviors for customers and employees. The value of respect for the individual translates into a great transparency among employees about what is going on: what decisions are being made and what actions are being taken to serve customers. Because Google believes in the individual's right to know, it shares

what is happening in the company as much as feasible. This openness encourages a common, widespread ground of understanding
and a climate of cooperation. From this fertile ground has developed a culture marked by high energy and a willingness to go above
and beyond the job description in pursuit of a common good.[12]

To reinvent your organization around a set of critical capabilities, ask yourself if you have the right culture to shape people's
priorities and behaviors in your ecosystem. What would someone
write or say about your culture? Does your culture bridge internal
values and your external brand? Does it turn the purpose, mission,
vision, or strategy into concrete actions? Does it evolve to focus on
the right issues that matter to future customers?

Managerial Implications

Getting the right culture in each of the market-oriented ecosystems
entails anything but luck; it requires deliberate tools and practices.
We have identified several approaches that the eight ecosystems we
studied use to succeed. You might consider how the following approaches could be used in your organization to clarify the right culture and make it real to all stakeholders.

Process Tools

Process tools help shape a winning culture by ensuring that people
feel, think, and act consistently with the promises they made to customers and other key stakeholders. The strongest cultures, therefore, are not inwardly focused on who they are and who they want
to be but are outwardly focused on who needs them and who they
need to be to meet others' needs and expectations.

Translate the Culture into Behaviors for Employees. Define your principles, and
make them known. Consider the words on the Amazon jobs website:
"If you love to build, to invent, to pioneer, on a high-performance
team that's passionate about operational excellence—you'll love it

here."[13] How better to signal to potential employees and customers alike what to expect from Amazon? A recent survey of 350 Amazon customers revealed that none cared about their emotional experience nearly as much as they cared about the timely execution of their orders. These customer expectations (brand promises) shape employee behavior around operational excellence. To be the most customer-centric company in the world, Amazon also translates this vision into fourteen core leadership principles that guide how people should think, decide, and behave. Ask yourself, How does what our brand promises translate into actions and behaviors on the part of my employees? Are the employees defining and initiating these culture-related actions?

Design Ways to Support These Employee Behaviors. We will get into these approaches in much greater detail in later chapters. For now, we will briefly outline what is required for culture to be institutionalized.

- Make sure that the top leaders walk the talk. Culture is alive when leaders live out their beliefs and signal these beliefs clearly to everyone in the organization through their business decisions, their use of time, and their decisions about people. For example, Amazon decides to invest in new businesses or service offerings only if the new investment serves clear customer needs. From the online retail selling of books, CDs, DVDs, fashion, and appliances to Amazon Marketplace, AWS, Amazon Prime, Amazon Go, and other offerings, all ecosystem decisions are based on one simple criterion: is it what customers need? Amazon institutionalizes such thinking into its PR&FAQ exercise. People develop a business proposal by thinking backward from how a product or service could be of value to the customer. They summarize this thinking in a mock press release, ideally less than six pages long, followed by critical FAQs like whether the product or service can be sustainable, how it differentiates itself from competitors, and how it fits into Amazon offerings.[14] Business leaders also build the company culture not only through

different communication forms but also in their business and
management decisions.

- Ensure that management and organizational processes
  instill the desired culture. These elements include staff-
  ing, training, promotions, performance measurement, all
  rewards, organizational structure, work design, information management, physical arrangements, and leadership
  development. Through these processes, managers reinforce
  any employee actions that align with customer expectations.
  Even more, customers may participate in these traditionally
  internal practices; for example, customers may have a voice
  in setting criteria for hiring, participate in training activities as attendees or participants, and help allocate rewards.
  When customers advise or participate in these practices, they
  are more engaged with the company.

- At all levels in your organization, choose, develop, and promote leaders who reflect your desired culture. For example,
  without defining the right culture, leaders cannot advance at
  Amazon or Alibaba, because 50 percent of a leader's performance assessment is tied to core values. As a leader, you are
  a culture carrier who exemplifies and reinforces the culture
  inside and out. You tell the stories and reinforce the rituals
  that make the culture tangible to others. You also reinforce
  the behaviors that express the culture in more practical
  ways: how you and the rest of the ecosystem treat each other
  as colleagues and customers.

Practices or Rituals

Effective rituals enact the culture needed for the type of success that
the ecosystem seeks and what the leader is good at. Ren at Huawei
is gifted at writing letters and telling stories. For example, he uses
evocative language to describe his company's marketing challenges
(e.g., "The coldest winter Huawei is facing") and to build a sense of
urgency and constant dedication to hard work. He also wrote pub-

lic letters to certain employees to amplify the positive or negative behaviors he wanted to convey within Huawei. All leaders need to be great communicators and must find what works for them. Maybe your style is more about interactive webinars, a podcast series, or a lightning round of interactive town halls. The key is to realize that any culture requires care and feeding, and a deliberate use of rituals that work for the leader and the larger ecosystem is essential.

Consider the following list of some practices we found particularly compelling. Table III-1, in the introduction of part III, is filled with many more suggestions. We offer these to you in the hope that some ideas may be worth adapting to your unique situation. We also hope that the sheer number of successful rituals that others have found effective inspires creative thought. Ask yourself, what can I do on an hourly, daily, weekly, or longer basis to embed and support the culture we need?

- **Storytelling:** At Huawei, CEO Ren writes letters, tells stories, and shares photos. To drive home the message of pleasing customers, not the boss, Ren shares a photo of himself waiting in line for a taxi at Shanghai Hongqiao Airport. The message? At Huawei, employees should waste no energy or effort to serve their bosses, including himself.

- **Use of time:** Amazon's Bezos allocates 70 percent of his time to new businesses.[15] Facebook's Zuckerberg primarily focuses on new products while leaving all operational, commercial, and management matters to Sheryl Sandberg (chief operating officer). Ren only spends time with customers, employees, and partners.

- **Naming of facilities or building:** How you name a building, a room, or another structure at your organization conveys who or what will be heralded inside the company. While some companies name their meeting rooms after different famous scientists or accomplished actors, Bezos has named his brand-new headquarters Day 1, for a term he often uses to mean that Amazon is still a startup with tremendous opportunities for growth.[16] (There is also a Day 1 Building on the south campus and another Day 1 Building on the north campus.)

- **Physical setting of offices:** What do the offices of senior executives look like? For some companies, the execs may have corner offices on the top floor. For other companies, the CEOs or senior executives might just sit with employees in an open space, with no private offices. All these arrangements convey the kind of culture you want to create in the company. The physical setting of offices always conveys the extent to which a company values transparency, equality, and collaboration.

- **Frugality:** At Amazon, resource constraint is seen as a source of creativity. To quote a senior executive: "I think frugality drives innovation, just like other constraints. One of the only ways out of a tight box is to invent your way out."[17]

- **Setting high standards:** At Supercell, the development team decides in advance what rates of player retention and participation its new product must pass to reach the next development gate. These benchmarks are announced throughout the company, and games not meeting the standards are abandoned in full view of the entire company—to no one's shame.[18]

- **Taking the long view:** Google is famous for practicing this long-view philosophy day in, day out. This perspective creates a culture of ownership in which people act not so much for the quarterly return but more for the long-term health of the company.[19] Google believes that this cultural mechanism encourages wiser decision making and gives leaders and employees the license to abandon a bad idea.

- **Daily meetings:** At JD.com, almost every team holds a meeting every morning to discuss what decisions need to be made that day and what decisions were made the day before (or recently) and the known outcomes. This level of transparency, combined with accountability, keeps everyone honest and helps the group learn together. It also provides meaningful feedback while decisions are being made, and not after the fact.[20]

Which of the above process tools, practices, or rituals can you adapt to make culture real in your company? How can you make sure everyone in your organization and ecosystem really cares about customers, is excited about innovation, and acts with agility? Reinventing the organization is a wasted exercise if you and your employees cannot think, feel, and act differently.

Conclusion

We cannot overstate the importance of culture in creating the common expectations for the entire ecosystem and the means to achieve those expectations. Culture is a part of the air that we breathe and is reinforced or diminished by innumerable decisions, practices, and systems put in place. Above all else, leaders need to define the right culture, which connects external promises with internal employee actions. The right culture consciously supports the four core capabilities of the market-oriented ecosystem: external sensing, customer obsession, innovation throughout, and agility everywhere. Culture also governs personal behavior and employee practices when practice rituals are implemented.

CHAPTER 7

Performance Accountability

How Can You Make People Accountable for Results and Motivated to Produce Them?

Expectations without accountability are false promises. Accountability matters at a personal level. Personal desires to lose weight, exercise more, save money, get more sleep, read more, make new friends, or learn a new skill become false hopes and discarded New Year's resolutions without accountability.[1] Even politicians who make election promises but do not honor them are unlikely to be reelected.

Countries that progress economically, socially, or politically instill a spirit of accountability among citizens. Lee Kuan Yew's thirty-one-year tenure as prime minister of Singapore has been characterized as an economic miracle. As the leader of an island with no natural resources, he helped turn Singapore into a leading global economy with a world-class airport, skyscrapers, and a favorable business climate.[2] Much of Singapore's success can be attributed to a spirit of accountability he instilled throughout the country. Prom-ises made by government leaders were fulfilled. Business regulations were followed. Citizens were expected to live up to cultural norms.[3]

Likewise, organizations have to ensure a spirit of accountabil-ity if they are to fulfill their purposes, live their values, establish a culture, and instill their brand (see chapter 6). Market-oriented ecosystems govern with clear accountabilities. In this chapter, we examine three aspects of accountability: what makes it work, how it works in the ecosystems we studied, and the tools you can apply to ensure accountability.

How Positive Conversations Create Accountability

Over the last few years, virtually everything about performance management systems has been criticized. Both leaders and employ-ees dislike the awkward infrequency of the feedback, the numerical reductionism, and the competitiveness and defensiveness it provokes among employees as it ranks them out of a seemingly black box. Other problems include the lack of connection to company results and the stultifying burden of paperwork for both managers and HR. The list of companies that have disbanded traditional performance reviews continues to grow. As long ago as 2015, fully 6 percent of *Fortune* 500 companies had scrapped competitive performance rank-ings, 95 percent of managers were dissatisfied with the way their companies conducted performance reviews, and nearly 90 percent of HR leaders said the process failed to yield accurate information. Minneapolis-based Medtronic "completely ditched the old style of performance management," in the blunt words of Caroline Stockdale, a former chief talent officer for the $29 billion medical technology company. Medtronic ditched all parts of the unpopular process: the numerical ratings, the forced bell curves, the Kilimanjaro of paper-work. "Ratings detract from the conversation," Stockdale said. "If an employee is sitting there waiting for the number to drop, they're not engaged in the conversation, at best. At worst, it can actually make them angry and disaffected for a period of up to a year."[4]

But listen closely to what is also being said. In the criticism of the current systems, we still hear loud and clear that accountability matters. It is human nature; we need to be answerable, or we just don't . . . fill in the blank—make a bed, show up to class, get a job, meet a deadline. Why do car rental agencies charge such outlandish premiums to top up your gas tank? They don't want to be in the business of filling gas tanks. They need to hold *you* responsible for doing the job for them. Who willingly vacuums a rental car before returning it? Almost no one, because there is little accountability for doing so. Would you work to improve your bowling if no pins ever fell and no one kept score? Unlikely. In thirty years of teaching, we have never seen a student complete an audited course. No matter how heartfelt the original intent, students don't put in the work of learning if they don't have assignments and grades. At a minimum, these accountability mechanisms focus time and attention, placing some reasonable degree of priority on the work. Performance accountability and reward remain very powerful tools for shaping people's behavior and decisions. The question is not in getting rid of accountability and rewards but in designing them appropriately to build in the best possible way the capabilities a company or an ecosystem needs.

Traditional appraisal systems often fail because they mistakenly focus on rigid processes (e.g., setting goals, measuring accomplishments, and allocating rewards) rather than on positive conversations. The type of appraisal system is much less relevant than the ability to have a positive conversation. Affirmative conversations are not just a calendared event; they work best as an ongoing process when leaders interact regularly with employees. Imagine having only an annual review with your children instead of daily (and sometimes hourly) conversations about their behavior. With a focus on positive conversations, almost any performance system can work effectively. The most important thing that managers and other leaders can do to improve performance accountability is to have candid dialogue between themselves and their employees.[5] By having these conversations, leaders model how to be transparent about accountability issues without being burdened with complex processes.

These positive conversations help people gain what is called a growth mindset, concentrating on what can be improved.[6] By focusing on the future, they encourage resilience and perseverance. They address the behavior problem without judging the person and thus validate people and their potential. When leaders focus on helping people learn from both successes and failures rather than only criticizing the failures, they can offer career opportunities that match the employees' skills and commitments. The locus of control for improvement shifts from the leader to the employee. The resulting conversation is not about the forms, tools, or processes but about creating a positive relationship between leader and employee.

If you want to lead, you have to hold those you lead accountable for their actions. Avoiding or delegating accountability (for example, to someone in HR) undermines your leadership credibility and hampers employee performance.

Concrete Examples of Accountability from Several Firms

Google often uses what it calls objectives and key results (OKRs) to encourage breakthrough innovation by setting ambitious goals and tracking progress.[7] It defines OKRs very specifically:

- Objectives are ambitious and may feel somewhat uncomfortable.

- Key results are measurable and should be easy to grade with a number (Google uses a scale of 0 to 1.0).

- OKRs are public so that everyone in the organization can see what others are working on.

- The sweet spot for an OKR grade is 60 to 70 percent; if someone consistently fully attains his or her objectives, the OKRs aren't ambitious enough and the person needs to think bigger.

- Low grades should be viewed as data to help refine the next OKRs.

- OKRs are not synonymous with employee evaluations.

- OKRs are not a shared to-do list.

In practice, using OKRs is different from other goal-setting techniques like key performance indicators or balanced scorecards because of the very ambitious goals of OKRs. When used this way, OKRs can enable teams to focus on the big bets and accomplish more than the team thought was possible, even if they don't fully attain the stated goal. OKRs can help teams and individuals get outside their comfort zones, prioritize work, and learn from both success and failure.

Google's annual OKR typically includes a "moonshot project," or what it calls a 10X opportunity.[8] Employees are required to think about *moonshots*, that is, breakthrough opportunities that can lead to a tenfold difference in business growth. To capture such huge opportunities, people are forced to think out of the box rather than about incremental improvement. New ideas like Google Fiber, self-driving cars, smart eyeglasses, and Project Loon (internet-transmitting balloons) were moonshot projects.[9]

Alibaba holds employees accountable for demonstrating six core values in their day-to-day job and performance, and "customer first" is number one among all core values.[10] Alibaba's accountability for customer success prompted successful new business models one after another.

Huawei's fundamental incentive performance system is designed to keep employees looking up and out: Huawei is not a public company and is in fact owned by the employees. This internal ownership naturally keeps employees focused on the larger picture. In fact, CEO Ren's shares constitute only 1.2 percent of the company's total, and 140,000-plus employees hold the rest. This employee shareholding system is referred to within Huawei as the "silver handcuff." In addition, Ren has relentlessly signaled his deep belief in customer obsession as the key to the survival of the company. Business teams that fail to serve customers well will be quickly reorganized and the business leaders replaced.[11] Executives who fail to serve the customers or grow the business have been quickly demoted or deployed to other positions at Huawei. Amazon, Google, Facebook, Tencent, Alibaba, DiDi, Huawei, and Supercell all relied heavily on customer metrics as a core part of accountability. They look intently at growth in terms of user numbers (e.g., daily active users or monthly active users), the time customers spend with the products, the money customers spend (e.g., average revenue per user), their attrition rate, and their conversion rate. The conversion rate is especially important, as it indicates the ratio of effective sales leads and revenue growth that follow from marketing campaigns. This ratio measures the company's success in finding new customers and refreshing existing customer relationships.

Other than results, market-oriented companies hold people accountable for how their behavior affects the overall ecosystem. At Amazon, another key principle after customer obsession is to think and act like owners: "Leaders are owners," proclaims Amazon's job site. "They think long term and don't sacrifice long-term value for short-term results. They act on behalf of the entire company, beyond just their own team. They never say 'that's not my job.'"[12] Behaviors specified in leadership principles are periodically measured and account for 50 percent of employee performance.

At Facebook, employees are expected to build community inside and outside work using their own tools. They are expected to take initiative and "personalize their community at scale." This aspect of accountability for the service that Facebook provides is considered key to employee engagement.[13]

How well do you hold your people accountable for the right results and behavior? Do you set stretch goals, track data metrics, or measure behavior, of use some combination of these methods? Do your employees accept their personal accountability for achieving the company goals?

Managerial Implications

The process for setting expectations is as important as, or even more important than, the criteria being set. Leaders who imposes strict standards encourage conformance, which reduces employee effort, flexibility, and engagement. Having a positive conversation by actively involving employees in defining expectations helps commit them to the outcomes. The more ownership that employees feel, the more creative and energized they will be. When the situation changes—a common occurrence these days—committed employees more readily adapt. The tools and practices below reinforce this foundational notion. Adapting these tools into a positive accountability conversation ensure that promises are kept.

Understanding Human Motivation

Much has been learned in recent years about how to improve on existing accountability practices, even incrementally, to make a big change in expectations. Using a more current understanding of human motivation to hold better conversations will help shift your and your employees' energy and behavior toward the positive. Table 7-1 shares some of the emerging best practices we've seen.

TABLE 7-1

Emerging practices for performance and development dialogue

Current practice	Emerging practice
Have the conversation about performance occur at one point in time.	Have performance conversations in real time (ongoing) around events (annual celebration, promotion, salary).
Focus on ability ("You are smart") that creates a fixed mindset.	Focus on effort ("You work hard") to create a growth mindset. Praise efforts as well as results.
Look back to emphasize performance ("You are good at . . .").	Look forward to see opportunity and create learning ("What did you learn that you can apply in the future?").
Emphasize what is wrong.	Focus on what is right (keep a five-to-one positive-to-negative ratio).
Leader's role is to command and control, and leader is not close to the change process.	Leader's role is to coach and communicate by modeling both change and personal improvement.
Focus on action.	Focus on the sustainability of actions.
Talk about what has happened and what should happen.	Listen and engage in affirmative conversation about what could happen next.
Prepare for a performance review by doing paperwork and filling out forms.	Prepare for a performance review by thinking about how to help the individual person.

Additional Managerial Suggestions

We can expand on table 7-1 with the following more-detailed suggestions for encouraging accountability in the most effective way:

- **Focus on the employee in his or her own role.** Do not try to rank your employees against one another or compare the performance with that of other employees, but consider each employee according to his or her own progress.

- **Provide feedback more often.** Rather than conduct a single review once a year, the new systems tend to provide feedback more often, perhaps at the end of each major project or every quarter. For example, Deloitte has also implemented weekly check-ins with team leaders to help fuel performance. Conversations occur in real time, not during prescribed times.

- **Make your reviews, whenever they are conducted, shorter.** Simplicity of the review is critical. The more complicated the process, the more it distracts from the personal conversation. In its reviews, for example, Deloitte uses only four questions, two of which require yes or no answers.

- **Move from focusing on the past to focusing on the future.** Rather than review an entire year's performance at one go, these shorter, more frequent reviews are designed to help employees move forward with their careers rather than look back on past accomplishments or failures.

- **Take some of the subjectivity out of the process.** One major problem with standard performance reviews is that a reviewer's assessment of an employee's skills says more about the reviewer than about the employee. To combat this tendency, Deloitte has changed its questions to ask what a manager would *do* with a person (promote him or her, incentivize the person, etc.) rather than what the leader *thinks* of that person.

- **Shift from a focus on employee management to a focus on fueling employee performance.** More-frequent check-ins and reviews mean that a manager has more opportunities to steer an employee toward his or her best performance.

- **Shift from trying for the simplest view of performance to the most impact.** Many review systems in the past were designed to distill employee performance down to a single number—a rating or ranking. This new breed of review is more about generating a richer, nuanced view of every employee to facilitate better performance. The few questions we suggested earlier may evoke a rich conversation about many key topics.

Outcome versus Behavior

In any positive conversation, you need to be clear about expectations in terms of both the outcomes (what is accomplished) and the behaviors (how work is done). Figure 7-1 presents an outcome-behavior matrix to help you look at both these considerations at once. Clarity about these issues encourages innovation at firms like Alibaba, Amazon, Facebook, and Google. Let's examine each quadrant in the figure.

- **Quadrant 4, good outcome, right behavior:** This is the ideal quadrant. When good outcomes are accomplished in the right way, employees should be rewarded generously.

FIGURE 7-1

Outcome–behavior matrix

| | | Outcomes (what is accomplished) | |
		Bad	Good
Behavior (how work is done)	Right	2 Bad outcome but the right behavior	4 Good outcome and the right behavior
	Wrong	1 Bad outcome and the wrong behavior	3 Good outcome but the wrong behavior

- **Quadrant 3, good outcome, wrong behavior:** These outcomes are isolated events that are not sustainable or predictable. Although rewards are often based more on outcomes than on how they are created, a leader should also give serious consideration to employees' behavior for the sake of their future development. If their behavior is so bad that it hurts the company culture, the problem needs to be addressed quickly through remedial action, warnings, or, in extreme cases, dismissal.

- **Quadrant 2, bad outcome, right behavior:** This is the take-a-risk quadrant. Employees are engaging in the right behavior even if they don't immediately achieve the right outcomes. Failure must be tolerated and treated as an opportunity to learn. At Facebook, for example, people can be promoted if they fail convincingly and help people learn from it.

- **Quadrant 1, bad outcome, bad behavior:** Accountability in this quadrant requires that employees either change their work patterns or leave the firm. Candid conversations help employees know how they are doing before their behavior hits this low bar.

At Facebook, such outcome and behavior metrics are captured through peer reviews and are transparently translated into their bonus through an agreed-upon formula. Even line managers cannot change the bonuses of their subordinates, because it is determined by a formula.[14]

Reinforcement versus Consequences

How extra hard would you work to receive a 1 percent salary increase over the company average? If you underperformed, how motivated would you be to improve if you were only penalized 1 percent for missing your goals? Suppose the penalty for your organization's completely missing all its goals was a scolding letter from senior management, all compensation left intact? We have seen all these

FIGURE 7-2

Reinforcement–consequences matrix

		Consequences	
		Financial	Nonfinancial*
Reinforcements	Positive	Salary increase, bonus, equity	• Recognition • Work itself • Work/career opportunity
	Negative	Limited or no salary increase, bonus, or equity	• Reprimand • Negative review • Diminished work/ career opportunity • Fewer work choices

*There are several wonderful lists of nonfinancial rewards. See, for example, Bob Nelson, *1501 Ways to Reward Employees* (New York: Workman Publishing, 2012); and Bob Nelson and Barton Morris, *1001 Ways to Energize Employees* (New York: Workman Publishing, 1997).

situations, and they never lead to success. One newly appointed CEO asked the existing executive team to self-rate their success. They all gave themselves full marks. In the next team meeting, the CEO shared their self-ratings and asked the obvious question: "If all of you are meeting your goals, why did we lose a billion dollars last year?" Either the goals were wrong or misleading, they were not really met, or they were not tied to organizational outcomes. Consensus and transparency in setting and reporting goals—and linking them to consequences—is what accountability is all about.[15]

Different performance requires different consequences. They can be positive or negative, financial or nonfinancial (figure 7-2). Companies with high-performance accountability use all four quadrants in the figure, depending on how well the employees meet the company standards.

In managing a positive conversation, focus more on positive reinforcement than on negative. Research suggests that there should be a five-to-one ratio of positive to negative reinforcement to get the right accountability.[16] Positive financial results have the benefit of being precise, measurable, and comparable across positions and people. Some organizations publish their salary increases to signal employee performance in the past year. Employees may observe which employees receive the largest increases and can discern the financial relevance of good performance. That said, nonfinancial reinforcement sometimes matters even more. Recognition, interesting work, and unique work opportunities send even louder and often more public signals of how well an employee performed.

At Tencent, the bonus awarded each game studio varies because the bonus is tied to a preset formula of game revenue, profit, and growth. This connection makes each studio work very hard to launch successful games such as Honor of Kings because the year-end bonus for the game producers or game developers can vary substantially across studios.[17]

Platform teams also need the right incentives. It may be a revenue-sharing model (such as when a platform serves as distribution channel for games) or a form of bonus allocation determined by the dedicated business teams the platform supported in the front end. This positive reinforcement ensures that platform teams can strive to support business teams to win in the marketplace.

Conclusion

When you make best use of performance accountability (outcomes and behaviors) and consequence management (reinforcements and consequences), you can improve ecosystem governance by ensuring the right behavior, the commitment, and the desired outcomes from people across different units in the ecosystem. No matter how many tools and practices we share, accountability is an art as well as a science. It must be practiced with courage, consideration, creativity, and an eye toward both human motivation and the business outcome desired. Leaders who instill effective accountability in their ecosystems understand the human heart, the mind, and the pocketbook. Therefore, they need great skill and discernment to find the right forms of accountability in situations in which so much is being demanded of highly educated and highly skilled people under great stress. There are many levers to pull: salary, bonus, profit sharing, promotion, special assignment, education, and job rotation. Great companies and leaders take all these options into account, blending the accountability and incentives into the lives of the individual and the larger culture of the enterprise in ways that multiply the effects of each.

CHAPTER 8

Idea Generation

How Can You Generate and Generalize Ideas That Will Have an Impact on the Ecosystem?

Sir James Dyson worked his way through 5,126 failed prototypes before coming up with a design that ultimately transformed household cleaning (a bagless vacuum cleaner).[1] Pixar's teams create, on average, 125,000 storyboards to make a ninety-minute feature film, winnowing them to the 12,000 that constitute the actual feature. Edwin Catmull, president of Pixar sums it up: "Early on, all of our movies suck . . . [O]ur job is to make them go . . . from suck to non-suck. We are true believers in the iterative process—reworking, reworking and reworking again, until a flawed story finds its throughline or a hollow character finds its soul."[2]

The fact is that creativity in any endeavor is seldom a bolt of lightning. Much more often, it is the result of a lot of work—a mountain of discovering and discarding—within a process that delivers what is needed for the end in mind. An artist who is curious can turn that inquisitiveness into the creation of artistic outcomes (music, painting, writing, or other outlets). An organization filled with inquisitive people whose curiosity helps them probe, poke, and question can create the iPad, AWS, and Honor of Kings.

Idea generation requires both personal curiosity and organizational creativity. Curiosity is an event; creativity is a sustained pattern. While curiosity provides the fuel, creativity is the engine that turns the fuel into power. Curiosity comes from people's interests, and creativity is embedded in organizational processes. The more replicable the process and the structures supporting the keen interest, the greater the expectation that new ideas will be generated and will take the organization forward. In an organization, creativity requires organizational patterns that encourage people to keep on trying, year in and year out, product after product and service after service. Without a steady stream of new ideas, organizations languish by solving today's and tomorrow's problems with yesterday's solutions. Your job as a leader is to turn personal curiosity into sustained organizational creativity.

Concrete Examples of Idea Generation from Several Firms

Amazon's legacy of idea generation encompasses three cardinal rules—put the customer first, invent, and be patient. It includes the following cascade of creative triumphs (not an exhaustive list):

1994: Amazon—a self-operated online bookstore that capitalizes on the long-tail strengths of carrying huge numbers of SKUs—is founded.

1998: Amazon expands beyond books (its first move into an adjacency strategy), moving into CDs, shoes, fashion, housewares, and other consumer products, becoming the so-called Everything Store.

2001: Amazon Marketplace invites third-party sellers to enlarge the category and quantity for the sake of better prices and better selection for customers, even at the risk of cannibalizing its own direct-retail business with customers.

2002: Super Saver shipping is introduced, making buying easier for customers.

2003: Amazon acquires CDNow, an online music store.

2005: Amazon Prime is introduced, tying in the company's best customers by anticipating their needs and offering discounts.

2006: AWS is launched, empowering third-party sellers to operate more efficiently online and offline.

2006: Fulfillment by Amazon is introduced; it enables third-party sellers to use Amazon's fulfillment network.

2007: Kindle is introduced, moving Amazon from physical products to digital products and content like e-books. Kindle and other smart devices make such digital content easily accessible.

2007: Amazon Music is launched. Amazon continues to offer more digital content by launching this online music store.

2008: Amazon acquires Zappos, an online shoe seller, and creates an immediate adjacency.

2010: Amazon Studios is launched, offering more digital content in the form of television series and movies; some content, including comics, is derived from online submissions and crowdsourced feedback. These products are distributed through Amazon Video.

2011: Amazon Video, Amazon's digital video streaming service, is launched as a competitor to Netflix and Hulu.

2011: Amazon Appstore for Android is launched to sell apps for Android operating systems.

2011: Yap, a voice-recognition technology firm, is acquired.

2012: Amazon acquires Kiva Systems (which is then renamed Amazon Robotics) to support mobile robotic fulfillment for Amazon warehouses.

2012: Amazon Game Studios is launched as Amazon starts developing games on its own.

2013: Amazon begins selling in India by reinventing its approach to succeed in the Indian ecosystem. After an initial failure, the company tuned in better to the realities of the Indian infrastructure and succeeded.

2013: Amazon Fire is launched. This tablet computer (a competitor to the Apple iPad) includes access to the Amazon Appstore for Android, streaming movies and TV shows, and the Kindle Store for e-books.

2014: Amazon Echo voice-command device is launched. It is followed by the cheaper Echo Dot, touchscreen-enabled Echo Show, and the fashion-forward Echo Look.

2014: Amazon introduces Alexa, the cloud-based voice service available on devices from Amazon and third-party device manufacturers.

2014: Twitch is acquired. The service enables gamers to stream their video game play (Xbox, PlayStation, PCs, and mobile gaming platforms) for others to watch online.

2014: Amazon Dash is launched. This consumer goods ordering service uses a proprietary device for ordering goods online.

2014: Amazon Fresh, an online grocery-ordering and delivery service available in some US and European cities, is launched.

2014: Amazon introduces Prime Now, a one-hour delivery service on daily essentials. The service is exclusively for Amazon Prime members.

2015: StoryWriter, a free, cloud-based screenwriting app that supports independent screenwriters, is launched.

2016: Lumberyard, a free, cross-platform, exceptional game engine developed by Amazon, is integrated with AWS to allow developers to build or host their games on Amazon's servers and to support livestreaming of their games via Twitch.

2016: Amazon introduces BLU G mobile phones—well-priced phone to compete with others (including the iPhone).

2017: The acquisition of Whole Foods Market catapults Amazon into hundreds of physical stores and provides the parent company with enormous amounts of customer data. Amazon starts to integrate online retail business with offline retail business to improve customer experience and operation efficiency.

2017: Amazon acquires Souq.com, a Middle Eastern e-commerce firm.

2018: Amazon acquires Ring, a smart-home security firm.

2018: Amazon Go is launched. The first automated grocery store, it promises "no lines, no checkouts, no registers" and aims to be a game-changer for the grocery and retail industry.

Figure 8-1 depicts the growth blueprint of Amazon into adjacencies over the years. This growth is based on the company's passion for generating new ideas to fulfill the unserved customer needs for lower costs, better selection, and more convenience.

Amazon's sustainable innovation over two decades resulted not from luck but from design. The company has refined its innovation engine over years and turns personal curiosity into sustained creativity by creating a pipeline of ideas. Using Amazon's well-established PR&FAQ idea-proposal tools and its "two-pizza teams" (to keep problem-solving teams light and agile), the employees who win an approved proposal are empowered to work on a product or service prototype with a singular focus in a six-month period. Plugging in an Amazon platform armed with data and tools, the small teams operate with great autonomy. As the six-month

FIGURE 8-1

Amazon's new business innovation to meet customer needs

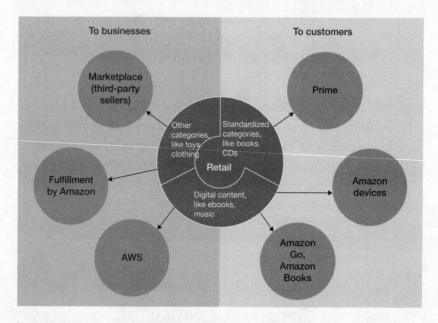

Source: Arthur Yeung and Tencent market-oriented ecosystem research team (Tencent Research Team), case study of Amazon; employees and former employees of Amazon, interview with Tencent Research Team.

deadline nears, the teams need to present their prototypes and customer-feedback data for review. In light of the data and results, the teams can either scale up their innovation for additional resources or dissolve it and move on to other projects. Figure 8-2 captures Amazon's innovation pipeline. Every year, Amazon bets on about fifty big ideas. Of these ideas, only some fifteen to twenty become projects. Then perhaps four of five of these projects make it to the product stage. Ultimately, only two or three innovative projects grow into big businesses like Prime, Echo, and AWS. Extensive experimentation is going on, and only the best ideas emerge as businesses.[3]

The idea-generation model of Amazon truly follows the principles of think big, test small, fail fast, and learn always, with the following characteristics embedded in the process:[4]

FIGURE 8-2

Amazon's innovation pipeline of ideas

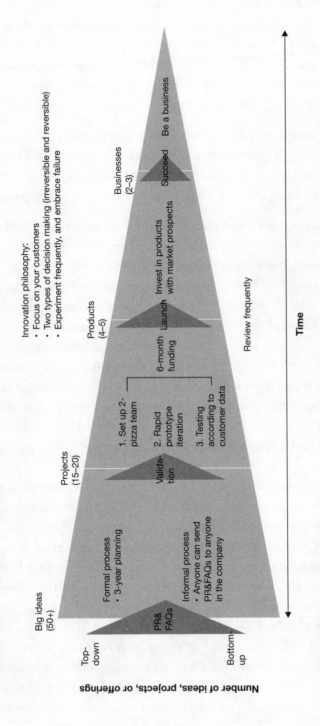

Source: Arthur Yeung and Tencent Research Team, Amazon case study.

- **Creative abrasion:** the ability to generate ideas through discourse and debate. Amazon encourages creative abrasion through its PR&FAQ tool. The person who comes up with an idea needs to debate with other colleagues how this innovation serves customers and differs from existing services or products. The discussion is intense and fact based.

- **Creative agility:** the ability to experiment through quick pursuit, reflection, and adjustment. Once a PR&FAQ is approved, a two-pizza team can be formed to build a prototype and test the idea internally within a six-month period.

- **Creative resolution:** the ability to make integrated decisions that combine disparate or even opposing ideas. Along the process, innovation needs to satisfy and test competing demands, for example, functionality vs. user-friendliness. The development of Echo is a classic example. Originated as a home music player based on voice recognition, Echo was also tested for its functionality as a tool for shopping. The voice-recognition function ended up being too clumsy for this function, because shopping presents vastly more decisions than does simply asking for a song. Nevertheless, the growth of Echo did stem from its ability to provide simple searches (like weather, location, stock price) and its access to connected home appliances.

As these characteristics show, Amazon clearly generates ideas to anticipate customers, create innovation, and change quickly.

The Google model for idea generation accomplishes the company's goal of exploring cutting-edge technology to solve complex human problems through advancing the fields of deep learning and AI. Google received its start through funding from the National Science Foundation and has maintained closely collaborative (ecosystem) ties with academia and the larger scientific community as well as the ever-changing world of technology startups through its venture capital arm. Google funds over 250 academic projects a year, publishes the results on public databases as well as its own research site, and invites top scholars to spend sabbaticals at Google every year. And these top researchers often stay, submitting to the lure of Google's unique research environment, unparalleled data sets, and some of the best research colleagues they could ask for.

At Google, idea generation for innovation works as a loop, with researchers and product teams working closely together to create new products and to continuously identify new areas of investigation and study. "Getting close to data and the real needs of users gives you the opportunity to innovate further," says Greg Corrado, director of augmented intelligence research at Google. He and his team work actively not only on product groups but also with other Googlers working on their 20 percent projects (Google encourages employees to spend 20 percent of their time on projects that interest them). "Rather than a group of mad scientists working on Frankenstein's monster deep in the bowels of the organization, they are active collaborators."[5]

Figure 8-3 summarizes Google's innovation mechanism. The firm uses both bottom-up approaches (e.g., the 20 percent projects) and top-down ones (e.g., Google's moonshot projects, which can lead to tenfold increases in growth, and its semisecret R&D facility, Google X) to generate ideas for innovation. By facilitating cross-discipline teams through the internal posting of ideas and by providing the strong support of its IT infrastructure, Google makes it easy to experiment with new ideas. Google practices the innovation mantra of thinking big (its 10X opportunities), testing small, failing fast, and learning always.

Business writer Greg Satell describes the success of Google's integration efforts:

What makes Google special is the way that it's been able to integrate an entire portfolio of innovation strategies into a seamless whole. Product managers focus on customer needs. Researchers go where the science takes them. Engineers working on 20% time projects follow their passions. Anybody who wants to can adopt one or more of these approaches.

That takes more than a management philosophy or a streamlined operation—it requires a true spirit of discovery deeply embedded into the organization's DNA.[6]

FIGURE 8-3

Google's innovation mechanism

	Technology insight Solving serious issues with innovative methods based on technological insights		10X opportunity: think big Moonshot: creativity and the courage to explore
	1998–2010	**2011–2015**	**2015–present**
Innovation concept			
Innovation management	"20% time" mechanism to encourage staff to make more bottom-up innovation	Streamlined products, investing more resources in important directions; turning a democratic, bottom-up process into top-down focused strategies	Controlled expenditure; keeping the long-term view and supporting subversive style of innovation while emphasizing return
Innovation results	Bottom-up innovative products that enhance product richness and variety as well as creativity and a sense of initiative in employees. Example results: Gmail, Google Adsense, Google News	Top-down, focused investments driving the rapid development of new products in strategic directions and product solutions with heavy investment of resources Example results: Google Plus, Google Cloud	Google: development of the company is driven by top-down decisions on product innovation in strategic business fields as well as bottom-up innovation that optimizes performance. All are equally important. Other bets: the development and incubation of bottom-up, revolutionary, innovative businesses or technologies. Example results: Waymo, Calico, Verily

Source: Arthur Yeung and Tencent Research Team, Google case study.

Like Amazon and Google, which have inquisitive people who work with established creative processes to generate ideas, other market-oriented companies focus on creativity and speed. For example, Facebook has a rapidly moving pipeline that depends on frequent reviews with quick go/no-go decisions and a "swarm the problem" practice of hackathons (figure 8-4). Alibaba draws on integrated customer profiles that develop tools to offer focused information (advertisement) to targeted users in a fraction of second. DiDi has developed new tools and applications to anticipate and match user traffic with drivers using the best routes. The goal is to have a car arrived at your place within three minutes, which is usually faster than the time it takes to reach your own car. And from its daily user feedback and suggestions, WeChat can release new versions almost weekly in its early days rather than monthly or yearly.

While the phases presented in the idea pipelines of market-oriented ecosystems look familiar to many firms, in practice the pipeline is radically different in energy and outcome from the typical stage-gate process in traditional companies. In our own work, when we talk with a firm about building a modern organization that fosters innovation, the leaders too often say, "We have done this." When we probe, we discover that the firm has a series of stage-gates that allow it to create a pipeline of ideas. This stage-gate process is like a funnel in which thousands of ideas are generated and then winnowed down through iterative testing. Such an approach works in pharmaceuticals, where the testing validates the efficacy of the drug and enables approval. It does not work for market-oriented ecosystems. Instead of taking about an eighteen- to twenty-four-month process from ideas to commercialization, a market-oriented ecosystem's idea pipeline needs to have much quicker iterations. The pipeline *can* move faster, partly thanks to the quick availability of feedback, and it *must* move faster, partly because of the competitive time pressure to win in an accelerated time frame.

FIGURE 8-4

Facebook's idea pipeline

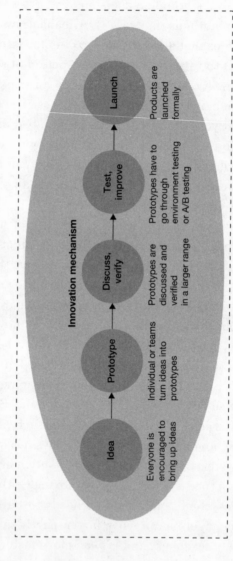

Innovation mechanism

Idea → Prototype → Discuss, verify → Test, improve → Launch

Everyone is encouraged to bring up ideas

Individual or teams turn ideas into prototypes

Prototypes are discussed and verified in a larger range

Prototypes have to go through environment testing or A/B testing

Products are launched formally

Hackathon

- Held every quarter (or more frequently)
- People build up teams and propose their ideas within 24 hours
- The proposal will be reviewed by a committee; winning teams have a chance to present their ideas to Zuckerberg
- Output from hackathon: instant messaging, video, mobile development architecture, HipHop compiler, Timeline, etc.

XX Review (quick review by executives)

- Zuckerberg review, Boz review, etc.
- Frequency: monthly
- Everyone has a chance to propose ideas to senior manager
- Purpose of review: constructive feedback and resource support
- Managers take responsibility to help their staff to modify plans and coordinate resources

Source: Arthur Yeung and Tencent Research team, Facebook case study.

Managerial Implications

Being curious means having a growth mindset instead of a fixed one. Creativity occurs when individuals turn their personal curiosity into something new. An artist who is curious can turn that curiosity into an artistic creation (music, painting, writing, or other outlets). As we observed at the beginning of this chapter, curiosity is an event and creativity is a sustained process. Curiosity leads to creativity, which leads to innovation. With this observation in mind, let us now look at how you can enhance your employees' personal curiosity and encourage creativity in your organization.

Enhancing Personal Curiosity

We have identified six steps you can take to increase your personal curiosity. Market-oriented ecosystems find employees who can quickly go through these steps (see chapter 9).

First, start with the phenomenon. Curiosity begins by observing ideas, experiences, or customer problems. Employees become anthropologists who constantly scan the environment (chapter 2) and listen closely to problems that customers cannot easily solve. Often, unorganized thoughts or challenges become the foundation of curiosity.

Second, name the dimensions and elements of the phenomenon. Words matter, and by naming what you observe, you make your observations become real and take shape. Random ideas become more ordered when they are named and defined.

Third, align how the parts fit into a system. With the ideas defined with words, you can align related ideas into a system. When curious employees see replicable patterns, a single observation is less an isolated event and is combined with other observations to form sustained organizational creativity.

Fourth, experiment. In figuring out what works and what does not, you need to start small and learn always. Experimental incubators exist to see which ideas work and which do not.

Fifth, expand the experiments to more complex settings. As results accumulate, teams should expand their experimentation and test the results in increasingly complex situations. Learning from experiments increases creativity. Experimentation ultimately allows external information to be accessed, analyzed, and acted on so that key capabilities are institutionalized.

Sixth, scale and replicate so that the ideas can be self-sustaining. Ultimately, curiosity becomes self-sustaining when a second generation takes ownership of the ideas. Letting the next generation take over the creative process enables the process to grow and evolve past the founder. The real power of ideas comes when they empower others.

Employees who follow these six steps will increase their personal curiosity and become more fully engaged in working within market-oriented ecosystems. They will also find meaning from the opportunities to explore new ideas.

Embedding Organizational Creativity

Market-oriented ecosystems encourage personal curiosity, which leads to organization creativity and a constant pipeline of ideas. You can encourage bottom-up idea generation many ways. In our work with market-oriented ecosystems and other companies, we have seen three major approaches for generating new ideas:

- **Build:** In this first approach, companies find ways to encourage employees to generate new ideas on a voluntary versus mandatory basis, on a scheduled versus ad hoc basis. The examples in table 8-1 illustrate how the market-oriented ecosystems we studied encourage and capture new ideas from

TABLE 8-1

Different approaches to encourage idea generation by employees

	Scheduled efforts	Ad hoc efforts
Voluntary	Facebook: hackathon (quarterly)	Amazon: PR&FAQ
	Google: product-area strategy summit	Google: 20 percent rule
	Alibaba: product meeting	Facebook: flash team
		Supercell: game concept
Mandatory	Amazon: new idea based on three-year strategic plan	
	Google: moonshot target	

Note: PR&FAQ is Amazon's exercise of having employees write simulated press releases and FAQ documents to help the team be clear on the customer value in any innovation.

Source: Compiled by Arthur Yeung and Tencent Research Team, case study and Alibaba, Amazon, Facebook, Google, and Supercell.

their employees. Once an idea is generated, companies use an innovation pipeline like the one in figure 8-2 to find the resources to build a prototype and experiment on it quickly. Either scale up or die fast.

- **Buy:** Companies, especially big established companies, can complement idea generation by acquiring companies with innovative talent and products. For example, Google acquired YouTube and Android. Facebook acquired WhatsApp, Instagram, and Oculus in virtual reality. AWS acquired many startups that were deep into technology. In these acquisitions, the purchase is not just about a product, service, or technology, but is often also about talent. Retaining employees who are curious becomes a major contributor to organizational creativity. The market-oriented ecosystem structure allows acquired employees to work in cells where their ideas can turn into business opportunities.

- **Borrow:** Companies can also work with alliances to generate new ideas. You can invest in innovative companies in different areas like biomedical technology, satellite imaging, the internet of things, and financial technology to supplement and complement your service offerings. You can partner

with leaders in specific domains to come up innovative applications for different industries. Both Alibaba and Tencent have
recently become very active in partnering with retail companies in fashion, fresh food, appliances, and other offerings so
that, using AI and big data, they can cocreate new solutions
for these traditional industries. Finally, you can form joint labs
or projects with academic institutions to explore cutting-edge
technology like AI, biotech, and material sciences—that is,
disciplines still in the early exploratory stages.

As the above suggestions show, ideas are generated and generalized by turning personal curiosity into organization creativity.

Conclusion

There is a tension between endless creation and disciplined focus.
As Apple's Steve Jobs famously advised Google cofounder Larry
Page about the benefits of focus: "The main thing that I stressed
was focus," Jobs said. "Figure out what Google wants to be when it
grows up. It's now all over the map. What are the five products you
want to focus on? Get rid of the rest because they are dragging you
down. They're turning you into Microsoft. They're causing you to
turn out products that are adequate but not great."[7]

Michael Schrage, innovation expert and research fellow at Massachusetts Institute of Technology, also points out how Apple used
a top-down approach to spur innovation: "Apple's clarity of vision
and relentless dedication to the user experience and design assured
that the company's talent would overwhelmingly focus their efforts
on delivery, not novelty. Apple innovation culture was more top-
down alignment of talent than facilitation of bottom-up empowerment. But successfully delivering that vision to overwhelming
market approval proved intoxicating and addictive for much of the
company's top technical talent."[8]

However, innovation can also arise from various places throughout the organization, for instance, from people in customer-facing

teams, platforms, or business allies. It can be top-down, bottom-up, or outside-in through buying or borrowing talents. Many market-oriented ecosystems use a combination of all these approaches to keep their new ideas flowing.

To keep your organization innovative, you need to assess how effective your organization is in generating, capturing, testing, screening out, and scaling up new ideas. Without a well-tuned innovation pipeline in place, your organization may not be able to keep up with the fast-changing needs of your customers or the radical disruption created by technological advancement.

CHAPTER 9

The Talent Pipeline

How Can You Bring In the Right Talent and Move It throughout the Ecosystem?

The following account is an American story, but it has played out and repeated itself in many cultures and countries around the world. Why do we say this? Adventurous, curious, smart, and forward-thinking people of high energy and an enterprising nature can be found anywhere. This account just happens to be a well-documented one that many Americans know well:

When [Thomas] Jefferson took office in 1801, most of the United States population lived within 50 miles of the Atlantic Ocean. Knowledge of the western part of the continent was limited to what had been learned from French traders and fur trappers and Spanish and British explorers . . .

He hoped to establish trade with the Native American people of the West and find a water route to the Pacific. Jefferson (an incredible learner) also was fascinated by the prospect of what could be learned about the geography of the West, the lives and languages of the Native Americans, the plants and animals, the soil, the rocks, the weather, and how they differed from those in the East . . .

President Jefferson's choice to lead an expedition was Meriwether Lewis, his former secretary and a fellow native of Albemarle County, Virginia. Having reached the rank of captain in the U.S. Army, Lewis possessed military discipline and experience that would prove invaluable. While in the Army, Lewis had served in a rifle company commanded by William Clark. It was Clark whom Lewis chose to assist him in leading this U.S. Army expedition, commonly known today as the "Corps of Discovery." On February 28, 1803, Congress appropriated funds for the Expedition, and Jefferson's dream came closer to becoming a reality.

It was important for Lewis to gain certain scientific skills and to buy equipment that would be needed on the journey. In the spring of 1803, Lewis traveled to Philadelphia to study with the leading scientists of the day. Andrew Ellicott taught Lewis map making and surveying. Benjamin Smith Barton tutored Lewis in botany, Robert Patterson in mathematics, Caspar Wistar in anatomy and fossils, and Benjamin Rush in medicine . . .

While in Philadelphia Lewis purchased many of the items required for the journey. His shopping list included scientific instruments such as a chronometer and a sextant, an air rifle, arms and ammunition, medicines, ink and other materials for journal keeping, and a large array of other items, including 193 pounds of portable soup, a corn mill, mosquito netting, blankets, oiled linen for making tents, candles, tools, and reference books.[1]

Try to imagine sending someone into a vast, unknown wilderness— someone who lacked the experience, knowledge, skills, behaviors, and basic courage to survive. Who did not know how to create a team out of a random group of strangers. And who was not willing to learn constantly to stay ahead of danger and to capitalize on unexpected opportunities. When Thomas Jefferson selected Meriwether Lewis to lead the Corps of Discovery, the president made the most important decision of the entire undertaking. Without Lewis, the expedition would never have taken place. Jefferson saw in this young man the rare talent that could lead a team across a continent filled with unexpected mysteries, wonders, and dangers—and return with his troops to tell the tale. The Lewis and Clark Expedition, as it became known, was America's moonshot of 1803, and Lewis was Houston, the Kennedy Space Center, and Neil Armstrong rolled into one. He was talent extraordinaire.

Competence, Commitment, and Contribution

Every day, market-oriented ecosystems operate at the edge of the known world. They strive to push into the unfamiliar. Their mission is to create new ideas, new technologies, new customer experiences, new designs, and new ways of solving problems. Not only do they think through opportunities, but they also rethink possibilities. Keeping this passionate, inquisitive outlook requires having extraordinary people at the helm and on the team to push forward into the unknown. There is no question that organizations with better overall talent are more likely to succeed than those with inferior talent. Why? Organizations don't think, but the people do.

But individual talent alone is not the full story. Organizations shape how people think, act, and feel. *Managing* talent is about making sure that the right people in the right places think and act in the right way. The buzz about "winning the war for talent" implies that it is talent alone that enables organizations to win. But talent is only part of the story. The right talent needs to be in the right place at the right time, must fully understand the mission, and must be armed with the best tools—that is what helps market-oriented organizations succeed. These requirements for optimizing the talent in your organization are so fundamental that we even have a joke about it:

> **Question:** What is the most important strategic action a leader can make?

Answer: Place your lowest-performing employees with your competitor, and encourage them to keep doing exactly what they are doing . . . for a long time.

Talent has many definitions and foci. For the very top leaders of a company, talent focuses on their visionary skills, succession planning, and performance as a team. For the next generation of leaders (often the square root of the number of employees), talent requires a leadership brand that connects leader actions to customer expectations (see chapter 6 on culture). For the high-potential employees (often 5 to 15 percent of the workforce), leaders manage talent by defining who has high potential and then investing in them to prepare them for the future. These selected high potentials often spend 5 to 15 percent of their time engaged in learning opportunities. And managing talent for all your employees means helping them be competent in, and committed to, their work and find meaning from it.

In response to these talent demands, companies have tried a multitude of programs and investments to attract, retain, and upgrade talent. Yet, sometimes after stipulating that talent matters, companies can get lost in the myriad of efforts and lose sight of the basics. At the risk of grossly oversimplifying, we propose a deceptively simple formula for talent:

$$\text{Talent} = \text{Competence} \times \text{Commitment} \times \text{Contribution}$$

Competence means the knowledge, skills, and values required for today's and tomorrow's jobs. This means bringing the right people into the organization, moving them through it, and, depending on their performance, either removing or retaining them over time. In today's world of free-agent work, competence may be accessed without ownership, because contingent workers might make up a significant part of the total workforce. Competence also refers to how the connections between people, robotics, and other technology will be a source of future talent. Competence inside the organization is also tied to customer expectations outside the organization. It is not enough to be the employer of choice, but the employer of choice for *employees whom our customers would choose.* Hiring, training, and paying employees should increase their ability to serve customers. Sometimes, you need to involve your customers in these traditional people practices. Customers can help set hiring criteria, attend and deliver training, and collaborate in determining performance and compensation.

Competence clearly matters, but without commitment, competence loses its impact. Committed or engaged employees work hard, put in their time, and do what they are asked to do. Commitment shows up in an employee value proposition: employees who give value to their organization (through insight, hard work, and performance) get personal value back. Employee commitment, or engagement, has been linked to delivering strategic goals and to customer commitment. In the last decade, commitment and competence have been the expected components of talent.

But despite the competence and commitment of the next generation of employees, we have found that unless they are making a real contribution through their work (finding meaning and purpose in it), their interest in the work will diminish and their talent will wane. Contribution comes when employees move from behavioral commitment to emotional connection because they believe that the organization's purpose will help them fulfill their personal values. When this connection is made, employees become better by acquiring new skills from their work and by belonging to a group of like-minded individuals.

Simply stated, competence relates to the head (being able), commitment relates to the hands and feet (being there), and contribution to the heart (simply being). In this talent equation, the three terms are multiplicative, not additive. As a governance mechanism, the right talent reduces risk and increases your ecosystem's chances of success. A CEO once told us that his primary strategy was talent. If he put the right person in the right job with the right skills and commitment at the right time, the executive did not have to worry about strategy, because it would take care of itself. Once Jefferson picked the right people to run his expedition, he could have confidence that the expedition would succeed. Likewise, talent (competent, committed, and contributing employees) is the fuel that runs market-oriented ecosystems.

How Several Market-Oriented Ecosystems Deploy and Upgrade Talent

At Tencent, all talent and leaders are selected and assessed according to the company's leadership model, particularly the focus on user experience. In the company's lexicon, *customer-centric* means constantly paying attention to the details of products and services from a user or customer perspective. Everyone in the company strives to understand the most critical needs and concerns of the user. They do this through observation, review of user feedbacks, intuition, and systematic data analysis to identify the underlying problems in products that meet their core customers' everyday needs. Only by focusing there can Tencent people create exemplary products like WeChat Pay, which, as described earlier, builds on the Chinese custom of exchanging red packets during Chinese New Year; Honor of Kings, an immensely popular interactive mobile game; and WeSing, which offers customers the karaoke experience anytime, anywhere. A person's user-centric orientation is one of the most important qualities assessed when Tencent is reviewing, training, and promoting talent, and customer focus has become the dominant attitude for all Tencent business teams.

The QQ Mail team at Tencent is an excellent case study of customer focus in talent choices. QQ Mail, the number one email product in China, outperforms many other email platforms in this country. How does the team achieve this level of success? Table 9-1 outlines the key principles that drive the team's actions and decisions. The team's focus on making sure that everyone's time and attention is completely dedicated to customer understanding and service can only be described as world-class.[2]

When Amazon hires people, it uses its fourteen leadership principles as a basis for evaluating them. First among these principles is customer obsession. As people cycle through the rigorous loop of three to five interviews at Amazon, half of the interview centers around cultural fit, in particular, customer focus. Amazon bases all its decisions primarily on facts and data from customers. Within

TABLE 9-1

Tencent's QQ mail team and customer obsession

Key principles	Implications
Demand comes from users	The "1000-100-10 principle": • Underlying this principle is the admonition not to ignore customer feedback. Team members must always work hard and smart to meet the users' fundamental needs for each process. To be better means to innovate. • All the staff must study the users. For example, every month, the team members must reply to one thousand messages in the user forum, review a hundred articles from network comments, and talk with or interview ten external users. • As a result, the QQ Mail team has made more than a thousand improvements in the application's features or functions.
Be a user first	For half an hour every day, each team member must pretend to be a fresh user and use his or her own mailbox to experience the details of the application and to discover the users' needs.
Do not resist changes	The team actively adapts to new changes in users' demand or other changes in the external environment and develops the product with flexibility.

Amazon, the saying goes, "If you have data to support your case, you win. Otherwise, Jeff Bezos wins."[3]

Alibaba also hires people by looking for evidence of their customer focus. And again, the customer is first among equals in Alibaba's core six values. Alibaba's chief strategy officer, Zeng Ming, has focused talent on a customer cocreation process.[4] The company follows four steps to create customers. First, it makes sure the right people (who have customer-focused predispositions) are assigned to cocreation projects. Second, it works with targeted customers to know both what they want and what they need. Third, it builds action plans to deliver customer value. Finally, it continually improves its customer interactions over time. The famous Single's Day (celebrated on November 11, because of the four ones in the date 11/11) shopping festival is a highly successful output of such processes.

Huawei is unusually intense about training people in customer focus after they are hired. New hires are immersed in a week-long orientation program, with paramilitary exercises in the morning and then deep sessions on company culture in the afternoon. The newcomers hear story after story, such as the one about the Huawei engineers who rushed to help Japanese telecom clients after the 2011 earthquake and tsunami that caused the nuclear power plant disaster. Stories like these make "putting customers first" come alive.

Facebook's cultural values emphasize the individual impact of employees, and its efforts to recruit and retain talent encourage this impact. Facebook hires builders and entrepreneurs who can hack prototypes, test them quickly, and build businesses through cross-functional project or flash teams. Newly hired Facebook engineers are not pigeonholed into roles or even departments. They join Facebook, period. From the start, they operate in the larger Facebook playing field: the onboarding process exposes them to Facebook's overall technical framework, tools, and work patterns. After this initial boot camp, they move into any number of opportunities, depending on their interests and the opportunities then available. Figure 9-1 profiles the work experiences of a typical engineer at Facebook.

This attitude of flexibility is expressed most strongly in the quarterly (or more often) hackathons in which engineers tackle new challenges in highly concentrated forty-eight-hour working sessions, teaming up freely with anyone in Facebook with the specific aim of coming up with breakthrough ideas. An amazing number of winning products—including chat, video, and mobile development architecture; the HipHop compiler; and Timeline—have come out of this process. CEO Zuckerberg reviews the winning products and ideas personally.

A variation on this theme is Facebook's practice called Hack-a-Month. The practice allows engineers to participate in other teams' projects for an entire month. At the end of the month, engineers and leaders of both sides can negotiate for changing groups. This model is so fundamental to both the engineer's growth and the organization's innovation that every leader helps subordinates find hacking opportunities and supports the move as part of a leader's responsibility.[5]

Further supporting these efforts is a dedicated internal home page in which everyone in the company can see vacancies and Hack-a-Month opportunities. To be eligible, a person simply needs at least one year of tenure and must be well qualified in his or her current position. Because many employees participate in Hack-a-

FIGURE 9-1

Glimpse into work experience of project engineer at Facebook

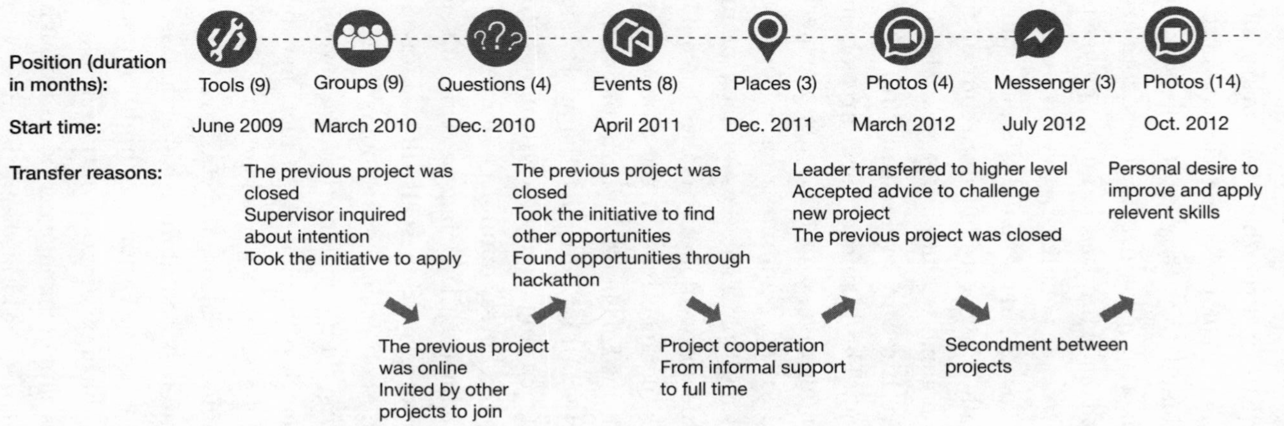

Position (duration in months):	Tools (9)	Groups (9)	Questions (4)	Events (8)	Places (3)	Photos (4)	Messenger (3)	Photos (14)
Start time:	June 2009	March 2010	Dec. 2010	April 2011	Dec. 2011	March 2012	July 2012	Oct. 2012

Transfer reasons:

The previous project was closed
Supervisor inquired about intention
Took the initiative to apply

The previous project was online
Invited by other projects to join

The previous project was closed
Took the initiative to find other opportunities
Found opportunities through hackathon

Project cooperation
From informal support to full time

Leader transferred to higher level
Accepted advice to challenge new project
The previous project was closed

Secondment between projects

Personal desire to improve and apply relevent skills

Month to increase their personal experience (especially teamwork experience related to their own work), they will often return to their original team after their temporary situation. This mechanism encourages employees to participate in the exchange program, but it is not mandatory. Staying in one position for continuous accumulation is also recognized. Supervisors are obliged to support Hack-a-Month opportunities, but no employee is required to participate. Nor are people penalized, overtly or covertly, for not doing so.

Supercell, for its part, expands its personnel cautiously because very few people of great talent are required for outsized business success in the game business. Remarkably, only twenty new staff members were hired in Finland in 2016 (out of about four thousand résumés). The hiring criteria are, obviously, rigorous: new staff have, on average, over ten years of experience in the gaming industry and an outstanding track record. Many staff members can work in multiple modes as artists, planners, programmers, and more. This ability not only makes them flexible, but also gives them multiple perspectives on the games they are creating. Like the philosophy at Facebook, cultural fit at Supercell is an absolute must on such small and creative teams. Passion for making great games (versus making money), a willingness to accept responsibility, keenness to express opinions and exert influence, and compatibility with team are all key factors. Once an employee is hired and the work is under way, Supercell allows individuals and even whole teams to join another game-development team if their work seems more promising than the game they are developing. Internal mobility is a hallmark of Supercell. In fact, new projects emerge from the groups themselves as game leads attract internal and external people through their ideas, and staff are free to choose projects according to interest and ability. Nevertheless, even though teams' establishment and operations are highly autonomous, all decisions are based on the maximization of the company's interests.[6]

Companies cannot manage new ideas through the innovation pipeline if teams cannot be formed and dissolved with little friction. There are two reasons for this caveat. First, with rigid teams, the right talent cannot be sourced easily from different units in the organization or ecosystem once the idea proposal is accepted. Second, if the idea proves to be unfeasible, teams that cannot find job opportunities inside the organization will have a harder time dissolving themselves and failing forward. Idea pipelines and talent pipelines need to work hand in hand, as witnessed in innovative market-oriented ecosystems like Amazon, Supercell, Facebook, and Google.

Managerial Implications

To reinvent your organization, ask yourself how effectively you source, develop, move, retain, and remove your talent. Given the market-oriented ecosystem's aforementioned experiences with talent and our summary of talent research, we offer you a checklist in table 9-2 to audit your talent practices and identify areas for improvement. The checklist suggests actions you can take to improve the quality of your talent.

Conclusion

Undeniably, having top talent ultimately creates winning organizations. The best talent has plenty of professional choices. While talented employees don't work for free, they do need to be treated like volunteers—with care and gratitude—because they could work in almost any organization they choose. Organizations that are successful at managing talent continue to give employees three important emotional benefits:

- **Believing:** An employee finds personal meaning from organizations because of the realization that his or her personal values derive from, and align with, the organizations' purpose and values.

- **Becoming:** An employee learns and grows by participating in an organization's activities because they enable the person to pursue new talents through opportunities.

TABLE 9-2

Talent checklist

How well does my organization engage in the following practices?   **Assessment***

Make sure that the job requirements for hiring are from the outside in (are driven by customer promises and investor expectations).

Set cultural standards (values, style, personality) for whom we hire.

Encourage diversity of background and thinking as we seek new employees.

Seek referrals from our best employees for whom we might hire.

Create a social media presence to build our employer brand.

Target promising sources of talent (e.g., universities, search firms, downsized firms) to attract top candidates from these locations.

Use contingent workers (consultants, outsource providers, temps, etc.), as appropriate.

Ask about specific behaviors (behavioral event interviewing) to screen candidates.

Involve multiple screeners, including peers and line managers, in candidate screening.

Create a customized value proposition (including salary, work opportunity, autonomy, and career progression) for top candidates so that the best people are attracted to the firm.

Offer a mentoring program for key employees.

Have a workforce plan that links strategic goals with important positions and skill requirements for those positions.

Encourage our better employees to move around to support the quick formation and dissolution of teams.

Allow employees to learn from experience by having them take on stretch assignments or be a part of a project team.

Invest in a personalized development program so that our valued employees are aware of their developmental opportunities.

Make sure that formal training programs focus on skills that can quickly be applied to work improvement.

Encourage employees to learn from situations outside their work experiences (e.g., volunteer groups and corporate philanthropy).

Give employees a career roadmap that helps them see what they can become.

Make employees primarily responsible for their personal career journey.

Start succession planning with a focus on the requirements of the position more than the traits of the individuals.

Find creative ways to retain valuable employees.

Quickly and fairly, remove employees who don't fit the business requirements.

Help employees find a way to realize personal meaning from their participation at work.

Create a growth mindset with which employees continually learn and grow from work.

Ensure that line managers are ultimately responsible and held accountable for talent.

Total _____

Scoring key

100 to 125:
• Great news. Your company is a talent magnet, and you have people who can help you win in the future.
• The risky news is that others may come after your people.

75 to 99:
• You follow good talent practices that will help you accomplish goals.
• But you might not accomplish them as quickly as you would like.

50 to 74:
• Beware of the risks you face with second-tier talent.
• Focus on a few areas to improve your talent processes.

Under 50
• Yikes! You are in a talent deficit and need to upgrade your talent processes quickly to avoid falling further behind.

*On a scale of 1 to 5, where 1 = very poorly and 5 = very well, how are we doing?

• **Belonging:** An employee has a personal identity and develops new relationships because the organization puts the employee in contact with others.

The market-oriented organizations we studied meet their employees' needs to believe, become, and belong. By enhancing these sentiments in their employees, the organizations deliver better value to customers and investors. Market-oriented ecosystems create an environment that not only attracts and retains top talent, but also allows people to grow and easily move around in their organizations to take on new challenges.

If you focus on talent, as Jefferson did with Lewis and Clark, you will find enormous success as your people explore new opportunities. Successful talent leaders spend between 20 and 30 percent of their time on talent-related activities. They surround themselves with others who complement them.

Managing talent is not happenstance or easy. When the talent practices described in this chapter are implemented, your organization will have the key ingredients for success.

CHAPTER 10

Information Sharing

How Can You Share Information, Data, and Tools within the Ecosystem?

One of the ironies of living in our age of hyperconnectedness and extreme "self-divulgence" through blogs, tweets, WeChat, WhatsApp, Instagram, Pinterest, and, yes, Facebook posts is that all this transparency and self-expression 24-7 has done little to change some fundamental aspects of corporate culture. In the era of #SayHerName, #MeToo, #BlackLivesMatter, #LoveWins, #Muslim AmericanFaces, and #codeofsilence, most corporate cultures remain places of careful disclosure, of cautious positioning and highly political consideration. Information is not transparently shared upward, downward, or sideways; nor is data or tools.

The mindset of not sharing information for the sake of safety or power still prevails. Too often, too many people in too many organizations fail to speak up to tell the truth to their peers, their leaders, and, sometimes, even themselves. They are afraid to propose new ideas, and they never admit a mistake. For various reasons—fear chief among them—they avoid the perceived risk of openly challenging authority or defying convention, out of concern of being seen as offensive, incompetent, or simply different or challenging.

Psychologists would say that fear of being separated shuts us up. Or maybe it is fear of being separated by a pink slip. Whatever the cause, many people venture from their cubicles only to conform as team players who do not rock the boat. At some level, their behavior is quite rational. History is bloodied with people who spoke truth to power: William Tyndale, Sir Thomas More, Martin Luther King, Gandhi, Joan of Arc, and any number of journalists and judges in troubled parts of the world. Because in any society—a country, a city, a corporation, or a family—when the power structure is not ready for change, speaking up can truly be a dangerous occupation.

Fragmented technological infrastructures can also impede information sharing. In many companies, different business units may have developed their own sets of customer databases or technical tools (like payment, security, and search) to support their own needs, regardless of the units' similar customer bases and technical functionality. While such self-sufficiency allows different business units to seize market opportunities and respond to customer needs faster than their competitors can, it creates the problems of isolated silos as these companies grow more complex. Besides redundant functions in multiple systems and low resource utilization, valuable information is scattered across different systems and databases. Everyone sees a piece of the puzzle, but no one sees the whole picture. And when a new business requires data across multiple systems and platforms, efficiency and responsiveness is low if not difficult.

Fortunately, in organizations that truly thrive on meeting external challenges, delighting customers, innovating relentlessly, and performing with extreme agility, the opposite is true. Information access is a key to having ideas with impact. But this advantage doesn't come from a tsunami of unfiltered information but from accessing the information that leads to better decisions. People are pressured not to shut up but to speak up, speak out, take a chance, and challenge existing orthodoxies in public, not just in private or anonymous internet conversations. They are encouraged to use every social and technical means available to investigate a thought, follow a hunch, generate an insight, test an idea, and create a team. They announce their mistakes and fail out loud (as we've said, sometimes with champagne, if they work at Supercell). When a leader posts his or her 360-degree assessment, the probability of improvement goes up. When employees share their objectives and key results (OKR) goals, the action builds accountability.

Information transparency does not stop with a willingness to share both good and bad news. Market-oriented firms build transparency by sharing data, tools, and coding across teams, platforms, and strategic partners within the ecosystem. They break down the silos and dismantle the walls between different systems and databases, sometimes at the cost of slower business growth in the short term, to enhance the long-term competitiveness of the ecosystem.

Once market-oriented ecosystems make their data transparent, the members can quickly generate insights from one part of the ecosystem and share with others elsewhere in the ecosystem. Information transparency elevates the value of the platform and makes it more strategic. By capturing data and tools from different parts of the ecosystem, the platform offers a more integrated view of customer preferences, the competitive situation, and any market changes. Information sharing also obviates the need to reinvent the wheel in different teams and allies that are doing something similar to another group's work but not as well.

Concrete Examples of Information Sharing from Several Firms: How Market-Oriented Ecosystems Increase Information Sharing

Google launched a search engine to organize the chaotic mass of material on the web. The company tamed the tangle simply by ranking search results according to their popularity. Scale then begat scale, and algorithms begat information that could be turned into so much more, and Google has never lost its focus on external research and external engagement in learning.

The logic of the Google search engine also applies to its internal information transparency. Google's unified database, technical codes, tools, and other components are shared without reservation to allow for experimentation. Every Google employee has open access to the Google code base (source code that builds the software or application). The only internal information not shared is that which cannot be shared according to the law or protection of user privacy. Anything else, ranging from the outcomes of corporate performance goals to individual metrics and results, is fair game for anyone to look at and learn from. Staff members have direct access to the founders on a weekly basis to ask any questions and to hear corporate news, including recent decisions and concerns.[1]

In 2004, Facebook launched an externally facing social network to connect college students with each other before it turned itself into an open-source platform that became the most sophisticated platform in the world by operationalizing information transparency. Within Facebook, there is a very strong culture of open sharing. Any working methodology, process, or tools that are repeatedly used by many people should be automated and uploaded to the tool platform. Various well-known tool platforms in Facebook have helped speed up internal development processes.[2] This relentless engagement with the outside world is an open and social act—an exercise in transparency while the organization and ecosystem learn together.

Amazon focuses on the opportunities that digitalization and other new technologies present not only because technology provides new offerings, but also because it allows companies to scale, and scale is what enables exponential growth. Who among you has not received suggestions from Amazon that you have not gone ahead and purchased? Probably everyone reading this book has made such a recommended purchase; we certainly have. This amazing deep knowledge of the customer preferences and behaviors is not owned by the sales or marketing teams exclusively, as in so many other companies, but permeates the company and the rest of the ecosystem. The reason for the ubiquity of the knowledge is information sharing, thanks to extreme data collection about the customer at multiple touchpoints that are combined and made accessible through the platform. Anyone in the ecosystem, including engineers, can access the information that they need in minutes to test ideas and come up with new products and services in open collaboration with others.

We have already discussed Amazon's famous two-pizza teams and the access that they have to data, information, and the tools on the platform. Because of the self-service nature of the platform, these shared resources and capabilities are readily available to all innovation teams and to anyone with a new idea within Amazon. Bezos explains why: "I am emphasizing the self-service nature of these platforms because it's important for a reason I think is somewhat non-obvious: even well-meaning gatekeepers slow innovation. When a platform is self-service, even the improbable ideas can get tried, because there's no expert gatekeeper ready to say 'that will never work!' And guess what—many of those improbable ideas do work, and society is the beneficiary of that diversity."[3]

Alibaba organized a highly fragmented Chinese market composed of millions of consumers and a huge number of small businesses and created interconnections through its platform. Although the firm did not invent online retail in China, Alibaba succeeded beyond any expectations because it built a data-driven platform with the ability to sense and respond quickly to what the external market was facing and what small Chinese businesses and consumers truly needed and would value (i.e., trustworthy credit and reliable logistics). Alibaba created its own success by enabling the success of others through data and tool sharing.

Since 2016, the company started to build a strong midplatform, a technology service platform that integrated data and technology capabilities to enable its front-end businesses to respond to market changes. Four units make up Alibaba's midplatform: (1) a shared business platform that builds the common modules for Alibaba's e-commerce business such as merchandise, marketing, transaction, and settlement; (2) a search unit that offers algorithms and data applications to support Alibaba's e-commerce businesses and personalized recommendation; (3) a data technology and product unit that focuses on using AI and big data in e-commerce, advertising, delivery, and other areas to achieve digital operation; and (4) an innovation community to prioritize resource allocation for new business incubation.

Alibaba uses data integration and transparency to empower its customers' (or members') services throughout its ecosystem. In the creation of the Alibaba middle platform, the integration of user data from many systems is one of the most difficult challenges. This integration is also regarded as Alibaba's top-priority project. The membership project focuses not only on the integration of user information at a technical and data level but also on the coordination and cross-selling opportunities of each business unit when it is interacting with Alibaba users. After ten months of effort, Alibaba Group launched 88VIP, a super-membership program covering almost all of Alibaba's core services. Perks of 88VIP members include shopping discounts for eighty-eight selected brands, Tmall Supermarket and Tmall International, and membership benefits in a wide range of services such as Youku VIP (video hosting), Eleme (food delivery), TaoPiaoPiao (movie ticketing), national shopping card, and Xiami Music. This super-membership program identifies the core active users and encourages them to experience and purchase a wide range of product and service offerings in Alibaba's ecosystem (including, of course, Alibaba's strategic partners).[4] More importantly, by sharing and integrating its membership data and systems, Alibaba can deepen the overall understanding of its users, their needs, and their preferences and can provide critical insights for business innovation and optimization.

As a new business at Alibaba, Hema Fresh uses a new retail business model that integrates online and offline products and services. The business requires a combination of fresh-grocery, restaurant, online retail, and delivery services. As a result, the integrated requirements of e-commerce, grocery store management, and logistic services are huge. Thanks to the support of Alibaba's strong midplatform in membership management, merchandise display, shopping cart management, e-payment, and personalized recommendations, Hema Fresh did not need to reinvent everything but only had to utilize the service modules offered by the shared platform. Yi Hou, CEO of Hema Fresh, describes the effect of the platform: "Without the strong platform enabled by Alibaba, Hema would take at least twenty-four months to build up its operational and service capabilities. Now, they can get it done in nine months."[5] Similarly, to penetrate new markets like Indonesia, Alibaba's midplatform offers plug-and-play systems and services to local e-commerce firms (including the acquired company Lazada). Shared technical ability and the replication of expertise like the capabilities and resources that rocketed the Single's Day shopping festival into the stratosphere of consumer purchases can also ramp up Alibaba's e-commerce business in Indonesia much faster than would normally be expected.[6]

Supercell also makes its knowledge of the outside world transparent to its inside workforce. While its business is simpler than that of Facebook, Google, Alibaba, or Amazon, the company provides daily companywide updates on how the world is reacting to its offerings: how many new users have been acquired, the total number of active daily users, player spending, and player return rates. Such total transparency gives everyone in the company a common understanding of the world in which Supercell is competing together.

Game development at Supercell is not the work of an isolated genius but the joint work of a broad collective. Nothing could be more open or transparent than game development at this company. At Supercell, any staff member can propose ideas for new games, and any employee can be asked to help create new ideas. Half or more of the development team is also active in creating new ideas for new games. People at Supercell understand very well that the goal is to create games that will satisfy a mass audience and that have the potential to continue to change to satisfy the players for years to come. Because these standards are so high, many more potential games are eliminated than are developed to the point of launch. A great example of this selectivity is a game called Smash Land, which survived the development process for nine months before being shut down. While people enjoyed playing the game, the game team did not believe that it had the potential to sustain player interest for years. That weakness was a deal breaker. The decision to pull the plug on a game is noncontroversial because the success criteria are very clear and because feedback on the game's development has been transparent throughout the entire process. Significantly, stopping the development of a game is viewed not as a failure, but as a learning experience to be celebrated. Shutting down a game generally entails a companywide postmortem presentation with shared lessons and a toast of champagne because *not* launching a product that would fail is cause for celebration indeed![7]

To reinvent your organization, ask yourself how transparently your information is shared downward, upward, and sideways in your company. How openly do different units in your organization or ecosystem share data, tools, codes, or new knowledge?

Managerial Implications

You can enhance information sharing as a governance mechanism for your organization and employees.

Transparency and Information Sharing at an Organizational Level

Different companies use different vehicles to share information for business alignment and to share tools and data for business operations. Table 10-1 shows examples of how the eight companies we studied shared information and tools in their ecosystems. You can adapt these practices to increase information transparency and sharing in your own company.[9]

To share information between teams, platforms, and business partners, everyone in the ecosystem needs a spirit of openness, trust, and reciprocal contribution. Organizations also need to avoid the not-invented-here syndrome that plagues many groups. We have seen this called "legalized plagiarism," where employees are encouraged to "steal" ideas from one unit or team and move them to another. People quickly recognize who idea generators are, because these creatives are at the heart of the organization network analysis, which tracks who influences whom in the organization.

TABLE 10-1

How market-oriented ecosystems share information, tools, and data

Company	Sharing information upward, downward, and sideways for transparency	Sharing data, tools, and knowledge for operational effectiveness
Alibaba	• Quarterly business meetings to solicit new ideas from front line and to prioritize and make them action items • Active inclusion of customers in co-creation of new products or services	• Midplatform with integrated data and technology within business teams
Amazon	• PR&FAQs to share innovative ideas from all levels • Posting of internal job opportunities to facilitate talent movement in delivering strategy • Broadcase, the internal video-sharing site that presents all Jeff Bezos's internal speeches; "Principal Talk" (knowledge sharing by principal engineers); or some system training	• Through AWS, various services and tools that support each of the Amazon businesses • Internal knowledge-sharing platforms like WIKI and Community
DiDi	• "On the Road": monthly meeting for all employees • Quarterly meetings for business leaders	• Technology platform that integrates data and tools
Facebook	• All-hands meetings (called "Work@FB") for shaping and sharing strategic direction	• Open access to unified code base, data, and tools • Broad sharing of technical information and support • Facebook Learner Flow, the platform for AI to be more easily applied to Facebook's products and software
Google	• Weekly TGIF meetings (Thank God It's Friday meetings, now, ironically, held on Thursdays) for sharing direction • Quarterly product meetings for soliciting and prioritizing ideas for improvement • Transparent sharing of projects and positions through an online platform	• Sharing of strong IT infrastructure support and tools headed by best technical leaders • Sharing of coding from different units to avoid reinventing the wheel • For each product area, its own infrastructure team, which not only supports the internal business but also provides cross-product-area support in technical resources, according to demand
Huawei	• Frequent communication of key issues and challenges faced by Huawei through letters and emails by CEO Ren Zhengfei • Active use of cross-business or cross-functional committees for information sharing and making decisions from multiple perspectives	• Shared customer teams to enable cross-selling opportunities across different product lines to customers in a region. • Regional platforms that also share deep expertise and knowledge on key customers in a region

(continued)

TABLE 10-1 (*continued*)

How market-oriented ecosystems share information, tools, and data

Company	Sharing information upward, downward, and sideways for transparency	Sharing data, tools, and knowledge for operational effectiveness
Supercell	• Celebrating with a bottle of champagne the lessons learned from both successes and failures	• Daily releases of market and user information of different games to all employees
Tencent	• Semiweekly executive meetings, monthly strategy meetings, and bi-annual strategy conference to share information, knowledge, discuss priorities, and align actions • Online platform to enable employees to ask questions, share information, and express viewpoints	• Technology and Engineering Group, which gives business teams back-end technical support in big data, security, and AI • For each business group, its own platforms to share technical support and data unique to the group

Note: PR&FAQs are sessions in which Amazon team members write simulated press releases and FAQs.

Source: Compiled by Arthur Yeung and Tencent Research Team, case studies of the companies listed here.

Transparency and Information Sharing at a Personal Leadership Level

In our coaching work, we have shown many leaders ways to better share information to help them motivate employees and make people accountable for their contributions. Use table 10-2, which summarizes many of the insights we have found, to assess the transparency of your leadership and how well you share information. When you or your team master these information-sharing skills, you communicate more clearly what is expected of your employees, partners, and allies.

Conclusion

We have sat in meetings in which executive teams needed to have difficult conversations about strategy, technology, structure, people, and performance. Often, in traditional firms, people showed respect by phrasing the information to soften it, to make sure it was palatable to those who needed to hear the message. Sometimes,

TABLE 10-2

Assessment of leadership transparency and information sharing

Principle	How well does our senior leader or our leadership team engage in the following practices?	Assessment*
Drive simplicity.	Simplify a message and put it into terms or frameworks that people can understand and relate to (prioritize ideas).	
Focus on why.	Instead of simply saying what should be done, help employees see why it should be done.	
Be persistent and consistent.	Stick with the same basic message until it is understood by others. On average, the message must be repeated ten times before a person truly understands it.	
Be curious and open-minded.	Seek out new ideas by asking questions and being open to new alternatives; seek feedback on the impact of behavior.	
Focus information on impact.	Focus information on solving problems or resolving challenges more than merely sharing insights.	
Use structured data.	Use empirical (structured) data to diagnose problems and offer solutions (e.g., rely on statistics to inform decisions).	
Use unstructured data.	Be willing to observe situations, see patterns, and trust instincts to spot circumstances that might not show up in spreadsheets.	
Focus on what is right more than on what is wrong.	Be willing to celebrate good news and learn from bad news in a timely way.	
Turn ideas into actions.	Ensure that the insights lead to decisions that affect personal and organizational actions.	
Recognize signals of personal behavior.	Model by your behavior (what you say, how you say it, when you say it, and where you share it) what matters the most.	
	Total	_____

Scoring key

43 to 50: Outstanding information sharer; others can observe and learn from this individual or group.

35 to 42: Good information sharer.

27 to 34: Adequate information sharer; find one or two areas to start to improve.

Under 26: Watch out. Think about ways you can improve your information sharing.

*On a scale of 1 to 5, where 1 = very poorly and 5 = very well, how are we doing?

people spend more time before a meeting to ensure that the information is packaged just right than they spend in the meeting. Then, after the meeting, some of the participants continue to discuss what should have been said. Too often, the message is so massaged that it is never really delivered at all. In other cases, business unit or department heads hold on to their systems and databases, their territory and source of power. They try to outspeak one another, ignoring the increasing cost of information silos to the whole company.

In high-performing market-oriented ecosystems, management ensures that information, data, and tools are shared with radical openness, overcoming psychological, cultural, and technological barriers to align business priorities. These ecosystems design unified code bases, tools, and platforms at the outset for the easy sharing of data and tools across internal teams and external partners and customers. And when the original structure and systems become barriers to information transparency, managers have the determination and wisdom to enforce changes. In high-performing ecosystems, people speak up, share their ideas and reactions, and readily dismantle the information silos. Only when information is easily shared inside and outside the ecosystem can a company become truly customer-centric, innovative, and agile.

CHAPTER 11

Collaboration

How Can You Work Together to Get Things Done in the Ecosystem?

Collaboration surrounds us. In nature, bees form a hive, ants form a colony, birds fly in formation—all these forms of collaboration make the whole tribe more than the individual members. Systems theory teaches us that individual parts do not operate as well independently as they do through interdependence or collaboration. The parts of a car do not make the car until they come together; a steering wheel or wheel axle is useless without the other parts working as a system. In political systems, a federation combines individual states or provinces into a more viable nation, or group of "united" states.

And for human beings, collaboration is pervasive. The strangers in chapter 1 collaborated to save the swimmers caught in a riptide. Teams consistently outperform individual talent. Organizations exist to turn individual competencies into organization capabilities. At its heart, the market-oriented ecosystem is an extension of these collaborative systems. The famous inventor Alexander

Graham Bell legendarily attributed most great discoveries to the cooperation of many minds.

Attempts to collaborate are not new. The successfully collaborative nature of the business ecosystem is, in many ways, its secret sauce. And that sauce is *hot*. The world has long had business communities, supply chains, industry groups, and guilds. Prato, Italy, had its legendary woolen textile cluster in the fourteenth century; Japan has its zaibatsus and then its keiretsus. The big three automakers in Detroit built a gigantic original equipment manufacturer system to supply their components. Large conglomerates in Germany, South Korea, India, Malaysia, Brazil, and Russia have survived in hot and cold economies. Developing countries have government-linked companies that provide capital, talent, and, sometimes, interconnection platforms.

To some extent or another, these systems are always filled with diverse companies with their own specialties, expertise, and offerings, but these collaboratives are not agile, efficient ecosystems. Sometimes, companies try to fill the gaps by making tighter connections: mergers, acquisitions, joint ventures, and alliances. These organizational moves almost always promise more than they can deliver, and they typically reduce the value of the constituent parts in the process. The relationships are slow, inefficient, hard to manage, and generally transactional, with a strong dose of "what's in it for me?" because every company has different objectives, metrics, costs, risks, cultures, values, hurdle rates, and time horizons for returns on investment. Typically, in any of these situations, "might makes right" and bargaining is very win-lose (who wants to sell to Walmart with death-grip squeezes on margins, but who could turn down the volume?). Thus, decision makers try hard to keep all the resources needed for success inside the company, where the resources can be controlled. But in a world of great speed and complexity, it is simply impossible to have everything you need in-house when you need it.

What makes a modern business ecosystem different—a true ecosystem, like that of Facebook, Google, Supercell, Alibaba, and the rest—is its ability to truly collaborate. As a governance mechanism, true collaboration is the ability to coordinate separate external and internal resources, activities, roles, focus, and investments in ways that anticipate and meet the needs of customers, generalize innovation, and move quickly to create a win-win arrangement. We know the ecosystem truly collaborates when we see the following:

- Increased profitability for all members of the system

- More-integrated customer solutions

- Expanded market access

- Significantly shorter time to market than what could have been accomplished otherwise (through any of the other organizational or environmental solutions described above)

- Enhanced learning and growth (in strength and capabilities) among all the participants in the system

The preceding advantages are made possible by the intelligence and power of big data, technology, and the skills and insights of the people who understand how to bring everything together around the customer need: two-pizza teams with a Cray supercomputer, so to speak. An ecosystem in nature consists of two basic parts: the biotics (the living plants and animals, including the bacteria in the soil, the birds, and the bees) and the abiotics (the nonliving factors such as water, rocks, sunlight, salinity, and even wind and shade). The parallel is obvious: it takes both spirit and digital prowess—the very human and the very technical—to create the collaboration that is needed to turn complexity into outstanding customer offerings. When it works—and it does work in these global giants—the external and internal elements move with great agility to innovate and meet customers' needs better than anyone could ever have imagined even just a few short years ago.

How do the platforms and teams work together to make the whole more than the parts?

- Platforms provide principles and define standards, and teams enact practices and win in the marketplace. The platform does not prescribe what the teams should do but instead provides principles and standards that others can follow and collaborate on.

- Platforms generate user traffic or sales leads, and teams convert this traffic into business opportunities.

- When platforms share data, technology, tools, and competencies, teams can adapt and apply these resources to their own unique situations.

- Through this sharing, platforms help teams build the four essential capabilities of market-oriented ecosystems: external sensing (information), customer obsession, innovation, and agility. Teams provide the forums for experimentation on new ideas (see chapter 10).

- Platforms share learning across teams, recognizing good ideas and moving them around quickly.

- Performance and incentive schemes ensure that the platform is responsive to the needs of the teams and strategic partners.

The preceding benefits of platforms and cells can be summarized as synergistic interaction. The collaboration between platforms and teams and among teams creates a learning community where ideas and data with impact are generalized to make the whole more than the parts.

In an ecosystem, the lead firm's job is to promote a rich collaboration that combines a set of niches (specialized teams or cells), each of which makes a different contribution to customer value, and this richness creates a virtuous cycle by generating new knowledge or additional demand as the teams interact. The lead firm creates a structure and incentives for attracting partners, manages the overlapping functions, and reduces conflicts. It focuses everyone in the ecosystem on the customer and the need to continuously and flexibly innovate for the customer. In the ecosystem, the partners' and teams' roles are many and varied: market intelligence, components suppliers, operational capacity, sales channels, and complementary products and services. Lead firms like Amazon, Google (Alphabet), Tencent, and Alibaba can also create markets for the ecosystem because of their reputation. They help a product, service, or technology gain market acceptance, and they build an ecosystem (e.g., as Tencent did for WeChat, as Google did for Google Maps, and as Amazon did for AWS). Map services provide a good example of the synergistic effect of collaboration. For map-providing services like Google, Tencent, and Alibaba, the ability to collaborate with business partners such as public transportation firms, Uber, DiDi, and Meituan is important. The user's decision to use these maps is critical to their usefulness. The more that cars or public transportation (or even people) use the maps, the better the maps' ability to help drivers avoid traffic jams and find the best possible routes. In this case, collaboration in sensing real-time data on traffic from as many strategic partners as possible is critical to make the service smarter.

Concrete Examples of Collaboration from Several Firms

Google embeds collaboration across its unique businesses and partners. Google Maps and the associated infrastructure act as an innovation hub where potential partners can create new applications that incorporate elements of Google functionality. Partners can easily test and launch applications and have them hosted in the Google world, which has 150 million customers globally.

Business professors Peter James Williamson, of the University of Cambridge, and Arnoud De Meyer, of Singapore Management University, describe the collaboration in Google's Open Handset Alliance: "By 2011, [Google] brought together 84 technology and mobile telephony companies working with the open 'Android' operating system to 'offer consumers a richer, less expensive, and better mobile experience by accelerating innovation.' By sharing a common platform, partners in the Android ecosystem could launch a wider variety of new applications (such as games and mobile services) more quickly and cheaply."[1]

Contrast Google's approach with that of Apple. Apple holds tight control of its design process because its design capability is unique, and the company views the process as the most precious part of Apple's brand identity. However, a huge amount of the company's value has been created through its open-sourced approach to apps development. Those apps, after all, sold a lot of iPhones. To date, Apple has paid over $10 billion in fees to apps engineers for their content or applications.

Jeff Wilke, CEO of Amazon's consumer business, shed some light on the company's collaboration philosophy at *Fortune* magazine's Brainstorm Tech conference.[2] When he was asked how Amazon could possibly go after so many different opportunities at once, Wilke described Amazon's "separable single-threaded teams." The term *single thread* means that the team is only required to focus on one product or service—no distractions. "Separable means almost as separable organizationally as APIs are for software," he explained. In software, an application program interface (API) is a set of routines, protocols, and tools for building software applications. Basically, an API specifies how software components should interact. So single-threaded teams don't work on anything else; they are just making sure that the subroutine works flawlessly.

Clearly, single-threaded teams (usually in the form of two-pizza teams) are only possible with the strong support of powerful data and technology from AWS. These teams can focus on their own mission and experiments without having to worry about other required support. As a result, Amazon can conduct numerous experiments with few resources and amazing agility.

For example, Amazon online shopping identifies sales by zip code in the United States, identifying both high-income and high-revenue-producing zip codes. Since a large portion of product sales are made during the Christmas season, the company could thus open pop-up stores in key zip code areas. The information from online sales informed which products would be offered in these small, focused retail fronts. These pop-ups' share of targeted customers increased because of various Amazon teams' ability to reach out to targeted customers with physical stores during a high purpose season.

Likewise, Amazon's acquisition of Whole Foods Market offers a great example of collaboration. The supermarket's retail footprint complements Amazon's online sales. The fresh-grocery business is a large, mostly untapped market for Amazon, given the frequency of purchases and the potential to drive more shopping in other categories. Amazon moved quickly to integrate the two companies through several collaborative steps: It made two announced price cuts on select Whole Foods Market items, to be consistent with Amazon's reputation for low prices. It made select Whole Foods Market private-label items available through Amazon's existing online-distribution footprint. Amazon also offered Whole Foods Market delivery and pickup through Amazon Prime in targeted cities. And the company introduced lockers and pop-up stores in select locations.

Amazon will likely continue to collaborate through the Whole Foods Market acquisition. The collaborative efforts will likely include a version of Amazon Prime that includes a customer reward program for Whole Foods Market; tighter integration between Whole Foods Markets, Prime Now, and online grocery service Amazon Fresh; and more price cuts. Through these experiments, Amazon will continue to innovate unique ideas and collaborate to transform the physical retail experience over time.

In a similar vein, Tencent WeChat offers an open platform for different companies and partners to offer their products or services through WeChat. This customer focus turns WeChat into a mega-app that integrates a wide variety of services in people's daily lives (including e-payment, transportation, bike rentals, dining, movies, internet games, music, shopping, news, utility payments, investments, lottery tickets, insurance, and hotel reservations).

The Alibaba platform has recently become very powerful because of its ability to quickly launch new businesses that take advantage of the shared resources and capabilities offered by the platform. For example, Alibaba quickly developed Hema Fresh, a complex, innovative retailer that combines online and offline business in fresh-grocery and restaurant services, in nine months (instead of the more typical twenty-four) through the close collaboration between Hema Fresh and the midplatform, which provides interfaces for customer

FIGURE 11-1

Alibaba case study: the rapid launch of Hema Fresh with the help of platforms

September launch of the "New Retail Project 1," which fully utilized Alibaba's middle-platform technologies

We spent 9 months working on this. Although it is very crude, the full process is functioning. This is rather shocking, because a system like this would otherwise take at least 2 years to complete.

—Hou Yi, CEO, Hema Xiansheng

■ **All-in-one online/offline supermarket supported by big data:** Founded by Hou Yi, a former leader of JD Logistics, this service is an all-in-one "supermarket + restaurant + logistics + app."

■ **The system is much more complicated than offline supermarkets and pure e-commerce:** The system combines online and offline services, including warehouse management system logistics, enterprise resource planning and finance, store point of sale, distribution logistics, apps, membership, payments, marketing, etc. There is no mature model for this technology.

■ **Alibaba's middle-end technology was fully utilized to accelerate the product launch:** Alibaba's technological prowess and development capabilities were vital to building Hema. Hema Xiansheng directly used Alibaba's underlying technological structure, payment system, and membership system, shortening the development period to only 9 months.

■ **The system is synced with Alibaba's latest technology through the middle-platform interface:** The Hema app has been integrated with Alibaba's personalized recommendation technology, and is able to achieve personalization quality comparable to that of apps like Mobile Taobao or Tmall.

Source: Alibaba case study from Tencent MOE research project led by Arthur Yeung.

membership, point-of-sale payment, logistics, and targeted marketing. Figure 11-1 provides details on the successful collaboration between this brand-new business and the powerful midplatform.[3]

Managerial Implications

In market-oriented ecosystems, four types of collaboration need to be managed seamlessly to deliver on the four critical capabilities of external sensing or information gathering, customer obsession, innovation, and agility:

1. Collaboration between the platform and business teams (like the collaboration between Alibaba's midplatform and Hema Fresh)

2. Collaboration between the platform and strategic partners (like the collaboration between WeChat and strategic partners in dining, transportation, etc.)

3. Collaboration between business teams (like the collaboration between Amazon online retail, Amazon Prime, and Whole Foods Market)

4. Collaboration between business teams and strategic partners (like the collaboration between Google Android and mobile phone companies)

Unfortunately, in too many cases, collaboration fails. Information is hoarded, not shared. Internal politics, not customer service, drives decisions. Innovation is hampered by limited risk taking or sharing of ideas. And agility is impaired by a slow decision making and a not-invented-here mindset.

In the ecosystem, each business team may generate innovative ideas. The systemwide collaboration challenge is to capitalize on the platform's support and each other's capabilities so that you can conduct rapid experiments and, once an idea is proven successful, systematically share it with other business teams. For example, one of Arthur's responsibilities at Tencent is to create forums and other occasions to share ideas, innovations, and best practices with, and among, strategic partners. Closer collaboration, including business collaboration, knowledge sharing, consulting support, and financial investment, is pursued at all levels between Tencent and its strategic partners and among these strategic partners. To increase your chances of successful collaboration, you can apply five principles we have identified as ways to collaborate either between the platform and teams, between the platform and your partners, or among the teams in the ecosystem (table 11-1). Let's look at these ways in detail.

Define Your Overarching Goals

These central aspirations create focus for the collaboration effort. Many collaboration efforts involve bringing people together from

TABLE 11-1

Key principles and actions for collaboration

Principle	Actions
Overarching goal	• Define vision, mission, or strategy that encompasses and is larger than the individual parts and that drives unity and alignment.
Information	• Create disciplined processes or infrastructure to share information, data, and insight across businesses.
Competence	• Ensure that employees or partners have collaboration skills.
	• Move people across units, platform, and even strategic partners.
Authority	• Clarify decision rights and roles for platforms, cells, and allies.
	• Create cross-unit business teams, and give them authority to make decisions.
Rewards	• Establish both financial and nonfinancial incentives for collaboration.

TABLE 11-2

The ABC's of overarching goals

Criterion	Definition
Aspirational	Defines a state that is a stretch, where desired outcome exceeds the resources at hand
Behavioral	Focuses on people's day-to-day behaviors in relation to the strategy
Customer focused	Emphasizes value added to external stakeholders, particularly customers of the unit
Disciplined	Woven into the fabric of the firm, e.g., hiring, training, resource allocation, compensation, decision making, technology
Energizing	Inspires and excites, creating emotional energy and passion for the goals
Future oriented	Focuses on the future, creating a forward-looking point of view

different parts of the organization and with different agendas and competing goals. Taking the time to identify a goal that is bigger and has more impact than what the individual parts can accomplish on their own is a key starting point. These goals build the case for collaboration and cannot be accomplished without it. They override competing local units' goals and meet a set of criteria that we call the ABC's of overarching goals, as laid out in table 11-2.

Prioritize Information Sharing

Ideas, expertise, data, or tools from any single unit can be easily shared and accessible to other units when collaboration is successful. We have seen this systemwide sharing of ideas work well when organizations complete what is called a learning matrix (table 11-3). For this model, we thank Steve Kerr formerly at General Electric and Goldman Sachs. There are five steps to completing the matrix:

1. Fill in the blank in the statement "To be world-class at X, we must ___." The X can be anything the ecosystem is committed to doing well, for example, service, quality, customer focus, cycle time, or training. The outcome of this step would be the identification of eight to twelve requirements for an ecosystem initiative to succeed. You might need a small research team, a task

TABLE 11-3

Learning matrix for sharing innovation throughout the ecosystem

The X represents the ecosystem's commitment to a goal (e.g., excellent customer service, effective employee training). The A, B, C columns, or critical success factors, represent the actions or mindsets that are required to reach the goal. In each box, rate how you are doing on a scale of 1 to 5, where 1 = very poorly and 5 = very well.

| Businesses (teams or allies) where work is done | To be world class at *X*, we must____ | | | | | | | |
| | Critical success factors for *X* | | | | | | | |
	A	B	C	D	E	F	G	H
1								
2								
3								
4								
5								
6								
7								
8								
Etc.								

force, or another group to define these eight to twelve
critical success factors. These answers become the
table's columns labeled A through H.

2. Then answer the question "Which business teams or cells
    would demonstrate these requirements?" These business
    teams become the rows labeled 1 through 8, etc., in the
    table.

3. Now, for each square, rate the team on a scale of 1 to 5,
    where 1 is "not good at all"; 2 is "sort of good"; 3 is aver-
    age; 4 is "good"; and 5 is "others think we are good" (cer-
    tified by someone outside the business). This rating is
    given either by an organizational unit leader or a rating
    team external to the unit (e.g., an ecosystem group that
    inspects the unit or an outside rating agency). Scores
    of 0 to 4 can be provided by the members of the orga-
    nizational unit; a score of 5 must come from someone
    outside the unit.

4. When each square is filled, you have an overall learning
    matrix for a particular initiative (X). This matrix helps
    pinpoint pockets of excellence and an overall ecosys-
    tem score on any initiative. This overall score may be
    a scorecard for an ecosystem leader assigned to pursue
    initiative X. This matrix provides a baseline for sharing
    ideas across these different units.

5. Create processes for sharing with the teams in the
    lower-scoring squares the ideas and knowledge from the
    higher-score squares in each column.

A number of mechanisms can help spread knowledge and experience from one high-scoring square to another square:

•   Make the higher-score squares the best-practice sites where
    others can visit and learn from.

•   Create cases from the higher-score squares for others to
    draw on.

- Move talent from teams in higher-score squares to teams in lower-score squares.

- Create incentive system for those in higher-score cells to create and share knowledge; for example, give bonuses to teams in higher-score squares.

- Assign someone from the ecosystem to oversee the entire matrix process and ensure that a larger percentage of squares rate 5 in each successive year.

Seek and Support Competence

Employees who are competent and have personal expertise work to make the whole more than the parts. Not all soloists make great contributors in a choir. With our colleagues, we have identified a set of personal collaboration skills (table 11-4).[4] You can identify and assess these skills in people when hiring new employees, managing rotational assignments, considering promotions, or training existing employees.

TABLE 11-4

Personal skills for collaboration

Collaboration skill	Definition
Fosters trust	Lives up to commitments, respects others' opinions, considers the well-being of others, and keeps confidences
Acts with flexibility	Easily moves between required roles: leader and follower, expert thought sponsor and thought supporter, social connector and task manager
Is open	Willingly shares idea and information and participates in group problem solving with an open mind, sharing thoughts and ideas without inhibiting the contributions of others
Focuses on team more than self	Emphasizes overall team goals and works to make the team successful by being an active participant in team undertakings and by caring for teammates
Delights in others' success	Willingly shares credit and celebrates others' success; talks positively about others
Manages differences	Is able to disagree without being disagreeable; willing to have difficult conversations when there is disagreement; seeks common ground; focuses on ideas, not people; and asks questions to probe new ideas

Distribute Authority

Authority relates to decision rights and people's roles. Leaders often delegate authority by defining what tasks need to be done and then who has the decision rights for these tasks. Decision rights include answers to questions such as these: What decision needs to be made? Who is primarily accountable for the decision? When will the decision be made? How will it be made? How will the quality of the decision be tracked and improved?

In collaborative work, authority is often distributed across cross-unit teams. Because these teams are likely to have representatives from the platform and multiple cells, decisions are made with input from several stakeholders. With clear authority comes accountability so that collaborative efforts can respond as quickly as the situation requires.

Offer Rewards

There are costs to collaboration. They include people's time and attention, opportunity costs, and the political cost of trying to avoid conveying a sense of winners and losers. Collaboration between teams, and between teams and platforms, increases when there is a credit-allocation system like internal pricing or bonus sharing to recognize extra efforts provided by the platform or other teams. Ultimately, collaboration often means extra work and inconvenience; it might even not be part of the day-to-day demands of the platform.

Financial rewards may encourage collaboration. In one business, 10 percent of the bonus money allocated to each unit had to go to individuals who were not in that unit. This financial incentive signaled the importance of collaboration. Nonfinancial rewards also encourage collaboration by celebrating individuals and teams that collaborate. Instead of honoring those who hoard information and practice not-invented-here pathologies, successful market-oriented ecosystems celebrate—in videos, newscasts, executive speeches, and other forums—those who collaborate.

In Tencent, Alibaba, and Huawei, collaboration between business teams (e.g., game-development studios, business teams, customer-facing project teams) and platforms (e.g., for distribution, cloud services, or regional expertise) is conducted through internal pricing mechanisms. Business teams are treated like internal customers rather than people waiting in line for support. Market-oriented collaboration is fostered between teams, platforms, and partners to ensure efficiency and the best use of resources.

Conclusion

By definition, market-oriented ecosystems make the whole better than the parts. Examples include teams that make individual skills better when they work together, cross-silo activities that connect functional expertise within a platform, the sharing of resources between a platform and individual cells, and collaboration among cells. When people or groups collaborate, the ecosystem excels in the four required capabilities radical reinvention: external sensing, customer obsession, innovation throughout, and agility everywhere.

PART IV

TURNING IDEAS INTO IMPACT

HOW TO LEAD A MARKET-ORIENTED ECOSYSTEM

From previous chapters, you should be able to explain *why* environment and strategy create a need for organization reinvention (part I), *what* reinvention looks like in terms of capabilities and morphology (part II), and *how* iconic market-oriented ecosystems embed the new organizational logic through governance of day-to-day operations (part III). Now, in part IV, we want to focus on *who*, or the leadership that is required to sustain the new organizational form and thus complete the organization reinvention process (figure IV-1).

By answering why, what, how, and who; by using diagnostic tools; and by drawing from the menu of managerial actions, you should be able to turn the ideas drawn from the ecosystems we studied into impact for your organization.

This part of the book has two chapters. Chapter 12 reviews the leadership role in making the market-oriented ecosystem happen. In all the companies we studied, leaders have a profound impact on ecosystem sustainability. This impact happens when leaders personally own, model, and advocate the market-oriented ecosystem logic as part of their competitive agenda. Individual leaders magnify their impact when their personal ideas become others' insights. In this chapter, we share what constitutes effective leadership and how leaders can create next-generation leadership.

Chapter 13 shows how the principles and practices of the market-oriented ecosystems adapt to any setting. To make this point, we describe how three organizations from diverse industries reinvented

FIGURE IV-1

A six-part framework for reinventing the organization as a market-oriented ecosystem (MOE)

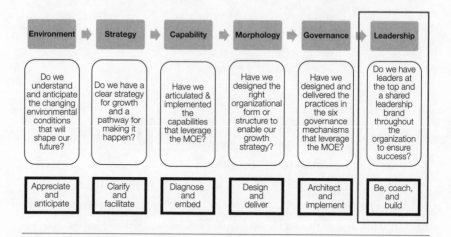

themselves. In the previous chapters, we suggested many tools, guidelines, and actions that you could adapt to your organization. Now, we illustrate how to turn these independent ideas into a systemic approach to reinventing your organization. Any organization (public or private sector, big or small, old or young, domestic or global, high-tech or not) wanting to create external information sensing, customer obsession, innovation throughout, and agility everywhere requires reinvention. With the ideas in this book, we want to enable you to create ideas (about ecosystems, organizational forms, and governance) that have impact through leadership and the dissemination of ideas to other settings.

CHAPTER 12

Leadership

What Can Leaders Do throughout an Organization to Make the Right Things Happen?

How many of the ten most-admired companies on *Fortune*'s 2018 list can you match with their founders or top leaders? See if you can fill in the blanks in table 12-1. Table 12-2 presents the most-admired firms in China in 2018 and their leaders. Can you match up any of these companies and leaders?

We find that people can usually match most of the top leaders (at least in their home countries) to the most-admired companies. Why? The company takes on the personality of the leader, who is also often the founder. Leaders become the face of the companies they create or manage. As a matter of fact, in the eight successful market-oriented ecosystems we studied, the current top leaders are the founders and their companies reflect their personal values and leadership style.

We want to understand what ecosystem leaders do to ensure the sustainable success of their organizations and how they lead their organizations even though the leaders have different styles and

TABLE 12-1

Fortune's ten most-admired companies and their leaders or founders, 2018

How many leaders can you match with their companies?

Company	Answer	Leaders and founders
1. Apple		A. Kevin Johnson and Howard Schultz
2. Amazon		B. Satya Nadella and Bill Gates
3. Alphabet		C. Jamie Dimon
4. Berkshire Hathaway		D. Gary Kelly and Herb Kelleher
5. Starbucks		E. Jeff Bezos
6. Walt Disney		F. Fred Smith
7. Microsoft		G. Warren Buffett
8. Southwest Airlines		H. Larry Page and Sergey Brin
9. FedEx		I. Tim Cook and Steve Jobs
10. J.P. Morgan		J. Robert Iger and Walt Disney (you should not miss this one!)

TABLE 12-2

China's ten most-admired companies and their leaders or founders

How many leaders can you match with their companies?

Company	Answer	Leaders and founders
1. Huawei		A. Lei Jun
2. Zhuhai Gree Group		B. Li Baofang
3. Haier Group		C. Wang Wei
4. Xiaomi Corporation		D. Jack Ma
4. Alibaba Group		E. Liang Wengen
6. Kewichow Moutai		F. Dong Mingzhu
7. SF Express		G. Pony Ma
8. CRRC Corporation		H. Zhang Ruimin
9. Sany Heavy Industry		I. Ren Zhengfei
10. Tencent		J. Liu Hualong

Source: "Top 10 Most Admired Companies in China for 2018," *China Daily*, October 18, 2018, http://www.chinadaily.com.cn/a/201810/18/WS5bc7bdc1a310eff303282fc6.html.

approaches to leadership. By learning what these outstanding leaders do, you can reflect on and apply these insights to enhance your own effectiveness as a leader and to build leadership at multiple levels throughout your organization.

Roles and Responsibilities of Ecosystem Leaders

The overall responsibility of leaders is to ensure the sustainable success of their organizations. To do so, leaders link their personal attributes and stakeholder results (figure 12-1).

In 2009, one of us (Dave) and his colleagues conducted a meta-analysis of the views of leadership experts to define what effective leaders know and do. This research, summarized in his and his colleagues' book *The Leadership Code*, found five roles or domains that effective leaders need to master: strategist, executor, talent manager, human capital developer, and personal proficiency.[1] As we examine what the top leaders of market-oriented ecosystems focus on, we identify similar (but somewhat different) areas of leadership priorities, as summarized in figure 12-2.

All the leaders in the ecosystems we studied invest tremendous time and energy on these five roles or domains:

- Business strategist:

  - Anticipate and imagine the future.

  - Create new market opportunities and products or services from a deep understanding of key trends (especially technological developments and unmet customer needs).

  - Build consensus on where to grow (customers, products, or regions) and how to grow (buy, build, or borrow).

- Organizational architect:

  - Replace bureaucracy's focus on internal rules and routines with customer-centric information and innovation.

FIGURE 12-1

The virtuous cycle of leadership attributes and results

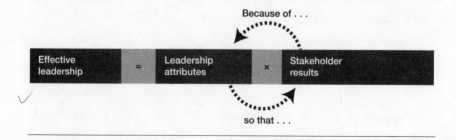

FIGURE 12-2

Leadership domains or roles that market-oriented ecosystem leaders focus on

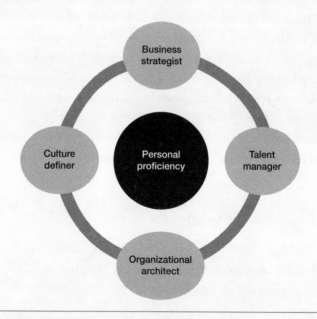

- Establish autonomous teams or cells that draw on platform resources and connect to each other in an ecosystem.

- Ensure employee accountability and tie employee rewards to the customer, innovation, and agility capabilities.

- Instill collaboration that is based on common values and governance mechanisms.

- Culture definer:

  - Define the right culture as one that is based on purpose, brand, and values by being clear what the company wants to be known for.

  - Embed culture by constantly communicating the why, what, and how of culture.

  - Personally model the culture in your daily actions.

  - Embed the culture through your choices of governance mechanisms.

- Talent manager:

  - Commit to the strategic importance of talent and people.

  - Set rigorous standards to select high-caliber employees who fit the desired culture.

  - Inspire people with meaning and purpose (meeting their need to believe).

  - Help your people develop new competencies, for example, by moving them across units (meeting their need to become).

  - Help them create positive relationships with each other (meeting their need to belong).

- Personal proficiency:

  - Demonstrate personal competencies for growth, including energy and passion, empathy for others, the ability to learn fast, a mission-driven outlook, resilience, and an entrepreneurial spirit.

  - Help other leaders acquire these personal competencies.

Let's now look at a few examples of each of the five areas to see them in practice.

Business Strategist

Leaders who are business strategists answer the question "Where are we going?" and make sure that those around them understand and act on the answer to that question. They not only envision a future but also convey it with simplicity and clarity.

Since Amazon's inception, Jeff Bezos has been extremely clear what the company should focus on and how it should move forward to build a customer-centric company: large selection, low prices, and convenience. To achieve this goal, he spends 70 percent of his time on new businesses and new products rather than getting bogged down in operational details. He also forces the whole organization to think forward, especially seven or eight years ahead, through the annual strategic planning process that sets a general direction and at the same time he makes daily choices to fold this future strategic direction into the present.

Jack Ma deeply believes in his company's mission "to make it easy to do business anywhere." Excited about the breakthrough in internet technologies and driven by the company mission, he commissions his chief strategy officer and a task force to envision how business will be conducted thirty years later and what Alibaba can do to make it happen. The result was five new strategies in retail, technology, finance, manufacturing, and energy.

Pony Ma positions Tencent as a social network platform that connects people, things (i.e., internet of things), services, and companies and as an entertainment platform that offers digital and cultural content like games, music, literature, and movies. He also counts on strategic partners like JD.com and Meituan to offer other products and services. To stay strategically agile, Ma undertook a major strategic evolution for the company in 2018. Tencent began using internet and ABC technology (AI, big data, and cloud computing) to enhance operational efficiency and customer experience across industries (B2B internet services) on top of its traditional focus on user experiences (B2C internet services).[2]

Mark Zuckerberg has very clear priorities about how to use his time, primarily in strategic direction and product innovation. He spends significant time thinking about new business opportunities fueled by new applications (like Instagram and WhatsApp) and new technologies (like augmented reality and AI) and how Facebook utilizes these opportunities by building internal teams or acquiring new capabilities from the outside. As the best product manager in Facebook, he regularly reviews new products and features. Winning teams from hackathons will get feedback and advice from him for further development. He also sends strong, direct messages to his engineers about the new products he wants the company to invest in. When the wave of mobile tech flooded the internet years ago, Zuckerberg made it clear to all engineers that he would stop reviewing any new products or features that were not available on the mobile platform. His passionate sharing of company priorities is a highly effective way to steer the strategic direction of the company.[3]

Cheng Wei at DiDi strives to provide people with smart transportation today, envisioning a time when cars are designed for sharing and autonomous driving substantially improve safety, experience, and efficiency. Using real time big data, DiDi collects information from millions of its networked vehicles on the road. The company is also experimenting with municipal governments to make their cities smarter with the ability to better manage traffic flow.

All market-oriented leaders allocate time and energy to zoom out to envision the future and at the same time zoom in to focus on daily operations. These leaders are clear on where to grow their businesses and how to go about doing it (see chapter 3).

Organizational Architect

Organizational architects answer the question "How can we redefine our concept of the organization and redesign its key building blocks to better deliver employee, customer, and investor value?" They redefine the logic of the organization from hierarchy to system to capability to ecosystem and then develop greater capabilities through the collective strengths of different units within the ecosystem (refer to figure 1-2). Many companies already have some parts of an ecosystem structure, but a true market-oriented ecosystem requires the concerted integration of these parts if it is going to deliver radically greater value in this ever-changing world.

Pony Ma formally announced Tencent's ecosystem strategy in 2012. The approach was based on the evolution of an open-platform strategy and the divestiture of its search business to Sogou and its e-commerce business to JD.com. These strategic partners represent "half of Tencent," as Ma redefines which business activities Tencent should focus on in the entire ecosystem, not just in the company itself. Allies and partners become important components of Tencent through business collaboration, reciprocal supports, and equity participation. In late September 2018, Tencent also formally announced the formation of a technology committee to unlock synergies embedded in its various technical teams across business groups.[4]

In 2015, Alibaba's Jack Ma decided to adopt an organizational model of small autonomous teams and a strong midplatform. More than twenty agile business teams are run by young business managers who are fully empowered to base their decisions on market needs. To further empower these agile teams to win, Jack Ma decided to integrate user data and ABC technological support at the midplatform level, so that the platform offers plug-and-play services to the agile customer-facing businesses.[5] As a result, Alibaba's profit and revenue grew rapidly again after 2015.

As these examples show, successful leaders can reframe their organization's design through market-oriented ecosystem principles and practices. In the era of fast-changing markets, the importance of organizational architecture cannot be overemphasized.

Culture Definer

People who define culture address the question "What do we want to be known for not only by our employees but also, more importantly, by the customers we are serving today and tomorrow?" All market-oriented ecosystem leaders have the primary responsibility of articulating the right company culture. They cannot leave this important charge to HR. Leaders need to communicate the right culture widely and consistently, use it to influence all kinds of business decisions, and weave it throughout their talent-management systems.

Ren Zhengfei at Huawei is passionate about building the right culture and instilling accountability to drive people to prioritize the customer. Customer first, employee dedication, and self-criticism for continuous improvement are three overriding values. He reinforces the culture by telling stories and writing letters to employees, shrewdly using his time only with customers, employees, and partners (not investors or government officials), generously investing in technology and people for long-term success, and basing personnel decisions on the articulated values and culture.[6]

Jeff Bezos is obsessed with building the most customer-centric company in the world by offering low prices, wide selection, and the most convenience. He articulates fourteen leadership principles and weaves them in all Amazon's business decisions (including which business adjacencies to move into and which innovative products and services to offer) and personnel decisions (selection, review, promotion, and separation). As he and many other Amazon executives assert, good intentions are not enough. A successful ecosystem needs good mechanisms to make things happen.[7]

Market-oriented ecosystem leaders believe that culture is real, not for decoration. Defining the right culture turns embedded company values into marketplace value for customers and investors.

Talent Manager

Talent managers answer the question "Who goes and stays with us on our business journey, and how can we help talented people reach their goals?" These leaders know how to identify, build, and inspire talent from both inside their home country and outside. Employees today require skills and behavioral commitment to do their work, but increasingly they also seek emotional commitment that comes from having a higher purpose: to go beyond making money and to make a difference in society.

Talent managers especially need to identify and nurture high potentials who meet future business requirements. Market-oriented ecosystem leaders realize that the best way to grow emerging leaders who explore unknown territories is to empower them with bigger job responsibilities, quick feedback, and the right blend of accountability and reward. Let high-potential employees learn fast, fail quick, and grow forward.

Bezos insists on setting high standards for talent. Using the fourteen leadership principles and multiple interviews for rigorous screening, Amazon purposely assigns respected executives who know Amazon culture very well as "bar raisers" to ensure that the new hires will rank above average in their teams.[8] Demanding standards apply to everyday decisions and work behavior. People are expected to work extremely hard (work-life balance is not a priority at Amazon) and to be ready to take on new roles and responsibilities when needed.

Starting from its early stage as a small firm in the early 1990s, Huawei has been aggressively targeting the best universities (like Tsinghua University) in China to attract their graduates with generous packages. Ren believes the best way to develop talent is through job rotation across functions and countries. Meritocracy is strongly advocated. Talent can be promoted or demoted quickly, according to performance. For example, a senior executive overseeing Huawei's smartphones and other devices has been demoted several times in his career.

With his company's increasingly diverse and global business operations, DiDi's founder Cheng Wei is striving to make DiDi embrace diversity in many forms. Diversity may include traditional aspects like gender and race, but also diverse skill sets (e.g., people good at conquering new markets and those good at running existing markets), nationalities, ages, and backgrounds.

Through these activities, leaders engage not only the hands (competence) and brains (commitment) of their employees, but also their hearts (contribution) to perform tasks that are meaningful to the employees. Successful leaders ensure that talent delivers results today, and they develop the human capital to support business environments for the future.

Personal Proficiency

Effective leaders cannot simply be reduced to what they know and do. Who they are as human beings has everything to do with how much they can accomplish with and through other people. Being personally proficient is not a role, but a set of leadership actions, beliefs, and values that enable the above roles. Personally proficient leaders have strong convictions and believe in their mission or purpose. This mission, coupled with a set of strong values, propels them to move forward in spite of repeated setbacks and other challenges. Proficient leaders also learn fast from both success and failure.

We also discovered that the ability to navigate paradoxes has become another crucial personal skill in a rapidly changing world. Leaders need to cope with the paradoxes of both top-down and bottom-up work, both customer focus and employee focus, both long-term and short-term actions, both divergence to get new ideas and convergence to focus attention, and so forth. To navigate these apparently opposing requirements, proficient leaders also need to be learners who act with courage and can move quickly while constantly adjusting. Paradoxes are not managed, or solved, but navigated to encourage dialogue and flexibility.

Bezos, Pony Ma, Jack Ma, and Ren are leaders with clear missions and strong values. They turn personal values into company purpose. They are authentic leaders who walk their talk. Their values give them emotional energy and resilience through tough business downturns. For Bezos, the bursting of the dot-com bubble in late 2000 was a life-or-death challenge for the company. For Pony Ma, the 3Q battle with Qihoo 360 in 2010 challenged his leadership abilities. Without a clear mission and strong values, leaders can either give up or make the wrong business decisions.

Leaders of all market-oriented ecosystems are amazingly quick learners. Compare all these leaders now to themselves three or five years ago to see their incredible growth. In his mid-thirties, Cheng at DiDi has shown extremely sophisticated strategic thinking, organizational architecture abilities, and personal leadership. Starting out as an English teacher, Jack Ma has transformed into a well-respected business visionary and leader around the world. In face of setbacks, Pony Ma has learned to reflect objectively on what's going on, face reality, and explore a better future. The Qihoo 360 battle in 2010 led him to Tencent's open-platform strategy and, eventually, its ecosystem strategy in 2012. Clearly, as a leader, who you are personally will speak volumes about what you know and how you do your work.

Styles of Market-Oriented Ecosystem Leadership

It is a daunting task to assume all the preceding leadership roles. Market-oriented ecosystems use different leadership styles at the top to handle these complex and challenging roles. There are at least three types of leadership styles—distributed, pairs, and solo.

Distributed Leadership

At Supercell, Ilkka Paananen is the former president of US video game company Digital Chocolate, with fourteen years of operations experience in gaming before he cofounded Supercell. The other leaders on his team bring equally deep experience in game development, synchronous and asynchronous system development, graphics optimization, and artistic game design. In interviewer Sonali De Rycker's words, Paananen believes that "the less the leaders control, the more powerful they become."[9] Paananen explains this idea: "My goal is to be the world's least powerful CEO. What I mean by this is that the fewer decisions I make, the more the teams are making. In a dream scenario that means the team is making all the decisions. A couple of years ago, we were working on something called Smash Land. Everyone in the company loved it, and it was so close to meeting its targets but didn't quite make them. So the team went to a cabin together, talked it out and took the decision to pull the plug. I was travelling at the time, so they didn't bother to consult me—they just emailed the decision to let me know. That's just how Supercell should work."[10]

Leading in Pairs

Business heads who lead in pairs provide support for each other while managing the diversity of requirements in a complex environment.

DiDi: Cheng Wei and Liu Qing. With eight years of experience at Alibaba before building DiDi, Cheng Wei was thus very experienced in internet and domestic operations. Cheng is focused on two things: the future and business operation. He is both analytical and optimistic, working not only to build what is needed today but to project into the future. As he says: "I believe that what I've been doing stands for the future. The future is on our side . . . DiDi is fortunate to have started building online platforms before it was too late. In the second round of the Internet Revolution, we hope to build a super transportation AI and gradually transition into an AI company."[11]

Liu Qing (or Jean Liu), Cheng's counterpart, was a managing director at Goldman Sachs Asia before joining DiDi. She has strong experience in finance and development, with a global perspective and vision. Liu is known for her cool head and focus on the long game. She is said to have great deal-making acumen and approaches competition collaboratively.[12] Apple's Tim Cook says that Liu does not view DiDi as simply a ride-sharing company:

> Jean Liu is a disrupter, and not only through her ambitious effort to change the way people in China commute, travel and connect with one another. With DiDi Chuxing, the ride-sharing, taxi-hailing startup she leads alongside Cheng Wei— its name means "Beep Mobility" in Chinese—Jean has built a transportation platform that offers convenience and flexibility to tens of millions of commuters.
>
> She and her team are succeeding with innovative, big-data algorithms that aim both to improve the efficiency of DiDi's service and to ease the congestion on roadways. By analyzing commuter patterns the way oceanographers track the tides, DiDi may help traffic jams go the way of the flip phone.[13]

As Cheng Wei puts it: "Two people lead to the best decision-making mechanism because one person makes mistakes and three people are too inefficient. Someone needs to be the brake on your decision making, and this person's fundamental values should align with your own so you can cover each other's faults."[14] Combining these strengths, DiDi has enjoyed enormous results: buying Uber's China operations; becoming the biggest on-demand transportation platform on the planet; raising the valuation of the company to more than US$80 billion; expanding its reach into Europe, the Middle East, Africa, and Brazil; and forming a new AI lab in Mountain View, California, its self-driving competitor's backyard.

Google (Alphabet): Larry Page, Sergey Brin, and Eric Schmidt. Page is the guy who famously defines success as improving things tenfold, not just 10 percent. *Shy, introverted, intelligent, ambitious, collaborative,* and *creative* are words often associated with Page. His work philosophy is "We should be building great things that don't exist." He calls these ambitions "moonshots" and encourages people to take giant leaps in thinking and acting.[15]

Brin, Page's other half, provides the extroversion. Brin created or sanctioned the cultural attributes that have also made Google famous because he understood that talent was the key differentiator—in fact, the only differentiator—for Google. The company lives in the land of plenty when it comes to technical talent (Silicon Valley), and Brin wanted Google to have its pick of the best people. It has a policy of recruiting only class A employees and giving them the freedom to exercise their creativity while they are fully supported by free everything (meals, coffee, snacks, fitness facilities, day care, massages, laundry services, and medical care). In return, employees are expected to have great ideas.[16]

As a team, Page and Brin created a culture in which people's ideas must compete on their own merits, in a Darwinian environment of survival of the fittest. Many of Google's popular products and strategies came on the market through this process, as exemplified by the creation of Gmail by Paul Buchheit and the informal company motto, "Don't be evil," which was coined by Buchheit and Amit Patel.

When they added software engineer Schmidt, Page and Brin considered top-level teamwork so important, they hired a coach to help them successfully integrate the mild-mannered, but driven Schmidt, with his patient, unobtrusive style of management. Schmidt is largely credited with Google's ability to scale.

Facebook: Mark Zuckerberg and Sheryl Sandberg. We can't think of a leadership duo in the field of technology or elsewhere better known than Zuckerberg and Sandberg. Part of their renown comes from the recent highly publicized controversies over Facebook's identity (Is it a giant platform or a social media giant?) and Sandberg's high profile around women and leadership. As Facebook's founder and number one product manager and strategist, Zuckerberg seized the opportunity for Facebook to be mobile. His leadership is almost uniformly described as challenging, pushing people to perform beyond what they had previously seen as their limits. At the same time, he greatly values the creative outputs of teams, as clearly shown by Facebook's two-pizza-team approach to innovation, and he understands that innovation arrives hand in hand with ongoing failure.

As chief operating officer, Sandberg brought to Facebook her ability to scale by focusing on revenue and operations. She brings her professionalism, honed in her stints at the World Bank and in Washington, D.C., to the jobs of creating the business model and running the operations. She also brings a high awareness of the value of diversity on teams. Like Zuckerberg, she is inclined to "lean in" to very big ideas and plans—to create a movement.[17]

Zuckerberg and Sandberg work well as a team. Observers credit their constant communication, trust, and transparency for the success of their professional relationship. While Facebook's goals, priorities, and challenges are constantly changing, the two executives manage to stay on track with each other through twice-weekly meetings in which they give each other honest feedback and work through their disagreements. Their focus on feedback and open dialogue is reflected throughout the organization.

Tencent: Pony Ma and Martin Lau. Ma is Tencent's chief visionary and product manager, having founded the company with some college friends in a cramped Shenzhen office. They launched an instant-messaging service called QQ for the Chinese market, and never looked back.

While Ma is Tencent's chief visionary, Martin Lau, two years younger than Ma, strengthens the company's strategic and operational capabilities—playing to his background with McKinsey and Goldman Sachs. Lau plays critical roles in the growth of Tencent since 2005, and his international and financial chops are helping the company grow beyond its Chinese borders.[18]

Individual Leaders

These leaders were the primary movers in the founding of their businesses, and they remain firmly at the helm. Nevertheless, every one of them is surrounded by a strong team.

Huawei: Ren Zhengfei. Huawei today follows a system of rotating the senior leadership every six months, at which time another board member becomes the acting CEO. Still, Ren has created the leadership culture and maintains a strong personal impact. As the chief management architect and thought leader, he is responsible for building the Huawei culture of "customer first, dedication and long-term hard work." He takes the long view, having a time horizon of ten to twenty years. This long view is reinforced by a decision to stay privately held and is fueled by a commitment to invest in R&D. He describes his leadership style as having seven parts:

1. **Purpose-driven ambition:** Helping customers realize their dreams by providing them the best service and solution possible.

2. **Adaptive vision:** Continuously focused on the future and seldom ruminating about the past, he is always thinking about the kind of company he wants Huawei to be in the next ten years.

3. **Inspiration:** Ren uses storytelling to passionately deliver his ideas to employees.

4. **Humble dedication:** Very careful not to feed the myth of his leadership, Ren emphasizes the importance of working hard and sharing responsibility and rewards.

5. **Directive style:** Ren's army background is revealed in his intensity and toughness. He shares without losing control.

6. **Winning by cooperating:** Ren has shifted over time to embrace the idea that you can win and still be cooperative.

7. **The power of learning:** In Ren's view, thinking enables you to connect the dots needed to work with an agile vision and strategy.[19]

Alibaba: Jack Ma. Jack Ma is a vision-driven top leader whose main strength is his ability to inspire others through his passion. He constantly talks about his vision and endlessly reiterates Alibaba's values, mission, and culture. He works hard to embed in all Alibaba employees the Ali-style methodology and manner of thinking. He broadcasts the vision through stories and metaphors: "riding the tiger alive," "only starving the lion and not starving the ants," and "the sense of mission can go 102 years." Very self-deprecating, Ma is the first to volunteer that he received bad grades in school and started out with no money. He has shared the following list—his assessment of the most important leadership virtues:

1. Develop one valuable skill that sets you apart from everyone else (in his case, English).

2. Embrace your shortcomings (Forrest Gump as role model).

3. Never give up; it's never too late to start.

4. Create a clear, lengthy, purposeful vision, and promote your values. And instill a clear set of values, as outlined in Ma's "six-vein spirit sword": customer first, teamwork, embrace change, integrity, passion, and commitment.[20]

5. Have an obsession. Develop personal mantras and heartfelt stories.[21]

Amazon: Jeff Bezos. The founder of Amazon would say that growing up on a farm was a significant influence on his leadership style as an adult: self-reliance, fixing things that are broken, doing the best with what you have—and no frills.[22] In his pursuit of the ultimate experience for the Amazon customer, he grants few luxuries to the employees who do the work. His leadership style very much obsesses about the customer: no delays, no defects, no out-of-stock products. Story after story about Bezos's style underscores this dominant trait: employees are expected to do what is necessary, no matter what the personal cost. As early as 1999, he said, "Our vision is to use this platform to build Earth's most customer-centric company, a place where customers can come to find and discover anything and everything they might want to buy online."[23] Staying simple, staying committed, knowing the market, and getting the word out: these are core to his leadership.

Differentiated Leadership among Different Units within Ecosystems

In addition to fundamental leadership skills common to all effective leaders at the top (figure 12-2), ecosystems must have differentiated leadership to ensure that leaders act consistently with their market requirements.

Differentiated Leadership between Cells and Platforms. For leaders working in cells or business teams, leadership is better for talent who competes more aggressively in the marketplace, acts bolder, and iterates products or business tactics faster. Most business leaders of Alibaba's highly autonomous business teams are in their thirties. The same holds for DiDi's leaders in different business teams. Tencent is also in the process of aggressively growing younger talent to take up leadership positions in customer-facing business units because a substantial portion of its users are millennials with unique preferences.

However, leaders working with platforms (in business, technology, or functional support) should be more professional or technological oriented, more systematic in their thinking, and more patient with the longer time horizons needed for building infrastructure and back-end functional competence. For example, technical architects who design the overall IT infrastructure and standardized service modules need to think systematically and over long term. HR leaders need to build up centers of expertise and shared services to empower HR business partners embedded in business teams or alliance partners.

Differentiated Leadership According to Life Cycle. Leaders in different stages of the business life cycle require different skills, styles, and other attributes. For business units at the experimental stage, where growth is their primary concern, the leaders need to be more creative in their thinking, courageously exploring new model or products, taking risks, and otherwise acting entrepreneurial. Successful leaders get excited by challenges that might produce high-velocity business growth. They get bored quickly once the business becomes stabilized or routine.

Leaders in the mature stage of a business, however, should focus on predictability and consistency of operations. They need to skillfully build standardized systems and processes and manage large numbers of people using clear key performance indicators to ensure predictable results. Finally, they must strive for consistent quality in their products or services to reach agreed-upon targets.

DiDi consciously distributes its leadership teams to different phases of business development, depending on the teams' areas of expertise. As the company enters a new market segment that aspires to become a market leader relatively quickly (say, three to six months), DiDi deploys leaders and talent with a "trailblazer" mindset and set of skills. Once DiDi establishes its market leadership in a certain category, the "trailblazer" team moves on and the "settlement" team takes over the operation to ensure consistency of services and steady growth of business. Using Chinese history as a reference,

Cheng at DiDi labels the two types of teams as "barbarian tribes" and "civilized dynasty."[24]

In short, there is no single leadership model that fits all leaders within market-oriented ecosystems. Specialized types of leadership are expected in different units, depending on where (cells versus platform) and when (which stage of the business life cycle) the team is operating.

How to Adapt Leadership Insights to Your Organization

You don't need to simply admire the market-oriented ecosystems' leadership we have described. You can transfer their experiences into your own organization.

Assess and Develop Yourself and Other Senior Leaders

First, audit your leadership competence model. We found that over 80 percent of organizations have a competence model that defines the key attributes (skills and behaviors) required for different leadership roles. Compare your competence model to the leadership in market-oriented ecosystems (figure 12-2). How does your definition of leadership match these five domains? If required, update your model to include these emerging skills embodied by ecosystem leaders. In addition, assess how your leadership model accommodates different kinds of leadership, depending on where and when the leader operates.

Second, compare both individual leaders and your organization's overall leadership capability with your revised leadership model. Using the transformation roadmap from chapter 1 (see table 1-3), we offer some diagnostic questions you can use to assess your own readiness and that of the next generation of your leaders to sustain and reinvent your organization (table 12-3). How well do you score yourself on these roles and tasks? This comprehensive list of questions can help you start to identify your leadership gaps and your focus of development.

TABLE 12-3

Diagnostic questions for effective leadership in market-oriented ecosystems

Dimension	How well do potential next-generation leaders engage in the following practices?

Part I: Understand context (business strategists)

Environment	• Anticipate and acknowledge external changes that will shape the industry. • Have a deep sense of how technology will shape the future of the industry. • Understand future customer expectations by forming relationships with future customers. • Communicate to investors (debt or equity) confidence about how intangibles will create future value.
Strategy	• Articulate the organization's purpose (mission, vision, or strategy). • Encourage strategic agility to enable the organization to create and shape future opportunities. • Make strategy happen by turning strategic aspirations into organizational processes and individual behavior.

Part II: Recognize new organizational forms (organizational architect)

Ecosystem capabilities	• Recognize the importance of ecosystem capabilities for delivering key employee, customer, and investor outcomes. • Articulate the capabilities required for success. • Become the primary spokesperson who is accountable and responsible for delivering critical organization capabilities. • Establish the ecosystem outcomes of external sensing, customer obsession, innovation throughout, and agility everywhere.
Morphology	• Establish organizational roles with clear accountabilities for platforms, cells, and allies. • Help each of the organizational elements demonstrate excellence in its area: platforms as shared resources; cells or teams as market-oriented businesses; and allies as partners. • Create connections between the platform and cells and among the cells so that the ecosystem is stronger than any individual cell.

Part III: Design and deliver governance (culture definer and talent manager)

Culture	• Realize the impact of culture on delivering sustainable success. • Articulate the right culture in light of how key customers and investors should view the organization. • Establish the value of your company's values by turning those internal core values into value created in the marketplace. • Embed the right culture by creating an intellectual, behavioral, and process agenda. • Model the desired culture in one's personal behavior.
Performance accountability	• Articulate clear short- and long-term expectations for behavior and other outcomes for employees. • Encourage positive accountability by focusing on what is right more than on what is wrong. • Coach and communicate with employees (more than commanding and controlling them) to help them meet expectations.

(continued)

TABLE 12-3 *(continued)*

Diagnostic questions for effective leadership in market-oriented ecosystems

Dimension	How well do potential next-generation leaders engage in the following practices?
Idea generation	• Generate new ideas for how to improve through benchmarking, experimentation, continuous improvement, and acquiring talent. • Demonstrate curiosity by asking questions, spending time observing, exploring options, seeing patterns, and experimenting. • Instill a disciplined process for filtering ideas into actions. • Ensure organizational creativity through build, buy, and borrow efforts.
Talent pipeline	• Appreciate and define the right competencies required for business success (i.e., those that build external sensing, customer-focus, innovation, and agility capabilities). • Bring the right people into the organization, move them throughout the organization (mobility), and retain (and remove) people, as appropriate. • Help employees have a positive work experience by encouraging them to find meaning in their work activities. • Create talent management practices that help employees with productivity and personal well-being.
Information sharing	• Encourage employees to speak up and share ideas openly. • Respect ideas from all employees (encourage diversity of thinking), and focus on ideas that will have the most impact (encourage convergence of action). • Use both structured and unstructured information to set business direction and to operate the business. • Share data, tools, and insights with leaders in other units.
Collaboration	• See how the pieces fit together into systems so that the whole is more than the parts. • Encourage people to turn personal competencies into collective or shared capabilities. • Instill cooperation between the platform and cells and among cells. • Generalize good ideas from one cell to other cells.

Third, invest in upgrading yourself and your leadership team. In most market-oriented ecosystems, the key leaders are the founders. But leadership throughout the organizations is hired and developed according to preferred criteria. Investments to upgrade leadership might include job experiences, task assignments, training and development, and personal coaching.

Finally, measure the improvement in leadership by monitoring how your leaders demonstrate the key attributes and actions and deliver the anticipated stakeholder results. Leaders are not just born but are bred. You can, therefore, adapt these leadership principles in your organization.

Develop Leadership for the Future

Looking ahead, leaders and leadership will continue to shape market-oriented ecosystems' and other companies' success. Let us consider some of the challenges for ensuring next-generation leadership.

Creating Leadership Brand. Individual leaders matter, as evidenced by the examples of the founders and CEOs who created the ecosystems we studied. These exemplary leaders anticipate environmental opportunities to create new industries. They redefine business models for strategic success, deliver ecosystem capabilities with new organizational forms, and capitalize on governance mechanisms to ensure their organizational and personal success.

But collective leadership matters more. None of these individual leaders acted alone; they instilled leadership throughout their organizations. At all levels in these ecosystems, individuals demonstrated the five leadership roles depicted in figure 12-2 and turned strategic goals into daily actions. These companies all invested in developing a unique leadership brand, where the cadre of leaders represents the unique identity of the firm. Amazon leaders look, act, think, and feel different from those at Google or Facebook.

Managing Leadership Succession. A frequent challenge of notable leaders who are also their companies' founders is to create the next generation of leadership. Leaders who replace themselves with future leaders ensure the continuity of their organizations. Sometimes, dynamic leaders have their personal identity and ego so linked to their organization that they cannot readily transfer their leadership equity to the next generation. Ultimately, a leader's success rests with the future leaders who enhance and build on the current leaders' accomplishments. The ability to transfer leadership equity from the founder or another strong individual leader to a broader leadership team ensures sustained success.

We have coached incredibly successful leaders who have created billion-dollar or billion-yuan companies and who are aging.
We often ask them if they have qualified successors in place. They
usually say yes. Then, we ask them if they are willing to relinquish
their titles, power, and positions to these next-generation leaders.
Are they willing to step aside so that the future leaders can prepare their company for the future? The yeses to this question are
a little more hesitant. These exceptional leaders often have a hard
time disconnecting their identity from the firms they created and
are leading. They may have invested so much in their professional
pursuits that they have little personal identity left to give meaning
to their outside lives.

So, what advice can we give current leaders who want to prepare the next generation of leadership? First, are you intellectually
and emotionally prepared for your own succession? Intellectually,
are market conditions and firm responses starting to pass you by?
Do you find yourself missing some key triggers in the environment?
Are you perhaps responding to others more than you are blazing
a trail to new agendas? Even more importantly, are you emotionally able to deal with the enormous demands of leadership, taking
risks; making difficult decisions that shape many lives; staying energized with investors, customers, and employees; and curious to
discover new ideas? It is better for leaders to leave at the peak of
their careers rather than to leave on the downside, but this timing
requires serious self-awareness.

Second, succession is not a single event but a long-term process.
The pool of potential successors should be given opportunities to
lead in a host of settings and be exposed to key internal and external stakeholders. Once a successor is selected, the parting leader
needs to transfer leadership equity. He or she moves this transfer
along by publicly encouraging all stakeholders to turn to the new
leaders for direction. It means sharing decision making and giving
credit, publicly acknowledging the new leaders' readiness for the
new business requirements. It means letting go when it is time to go.

Third, do let go. Once a successor is identified and in place, the
previous leader needs to let go. Do not cast a lingering shadow over

your successor's choices. To relinquish their position, dynamic leaders often need to find new vistas for their skills and passions. Think of Bill Gates, who founded and built Microsoft and precipitated the information age and then, when he left, shifted his attention to philanthropy and solving health challenges for the world's poorest. His passion for, and commitment to, helping people lead healthy and productive lives keeps him from meddling with Microsoft when new leaders embark on new directions. You do not have to become a world-leading philanthropist to let go and move on; you might shift to family, hobbies, or service, but good leaders let others lead.

Conclusion

From our studies of the eight market-oriented ecosystems in this book and from our previous research, we identify five critical roles or domains that effective leaders need to master: business strategy, organizational architecture, culture, talent, and personal proficiency. Successful leaders exhibit and model these dimensions in building highly successful organizations. These leaders should be honored, and their practices studied as models.

But leadership matters more. To create a sustainable impact, the organization should outlive any individual leader, whether the person is the founder or a strong, visible leader. Creating leadership requires that you invest in the next generation by creating a leadership brand consistent with future market opportunities and by managing the art of succession and letting go.

CHAPTER 13

Transforming Your Organization

How Can You Adapt the Principles and Practices of Market-Oriented Ecosystems to Your Organization?

Very few companies can weather extreme change; most successful companies flourish under certain circumstances and leadership and then fade from view. Of the original *Fortune* 500 in 1955, only 12 percent (sixty companies) are on the list in 2018. In 1965, firms in the Standard & Poor's 500 stayed in the index for an average of thirty-three years. By 1990, the average tenure in the S&P 500 had narrowed to twenty years. That time is forecast to shrink to fourteen years by 2026. The market-oriented ecosystem principles and practices enable firms to adapt, change, and survive.

The ecosystems we have studied are relatively young (see table 1-1), with an average age of nineteen years in 2019. Being founded in the digital or information era, these organizations were founded in a "green" field, that is, they had no legacy encumbrances to overcome. When they were created, the ability to adapt to change was simply part of their DNA. They are never stuck in a single way of viewing the world or operating in it; these very smart companies make the most of the intelligence embedded in their platform-team-ecosystem advantage.

But what about companies that are older—those founded in other eras or settings where the environment has been relatively stable? Digital technology is something new to these companies; they were not born with these tools. In today's and tomorrow's work world, a great majority of these companies are facing enormous industry transformation fueled by new technologies, unconventional competitors, and new consumer preferences.

Siwei-Johnson Industrial, a member of Arthur's Organizational Capability Learning Association, is the global market leader in the production of the special armored vehicles that escort money between banks. For years, the company grew by innovating new designs and by acquiring smaller players around the world. But in the face of disruptive technologies like WeChat Pay and Alipay, the founder suddenly realized that the company was in trouble because paper money is decreasingly used in China nowadays. For many legacy companies like Siwei-Johnson, leaders realize that you have no choice—change or die! But how?

In this chapter, you will learn four useful questions that help you diagnose your readiness and ability to transform your legacy company. Then, we provide detailed information about how three companies in industries as varied as pharmaceutical distribution (WBA [formerly named Walgreens Boots Alliance], founded in 1901), retail (JD.com, founded in 1998), and supermarkets (Yonghui, founded in 1995) are aggressively reinventing their organizations, using the six-part framework, or roadmap (figure 13-1).

FIGURE 13-1

A six-part framework for reinventing the organization as a market-oriented ecosystem (MOE)

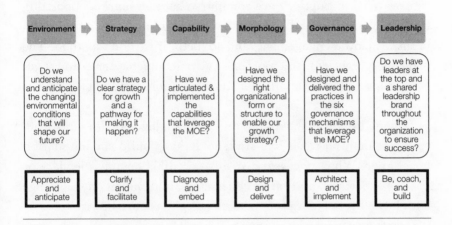

Serious Questions to Ask Yourself and Your Team When You Embark on Reinvention

All legacy companies face change and have often responded with at least some of the ideas embedded in market-oriented companies. But without a complete and integrated model, these piecemeal efforts often fail to fully deliver change. The six steps in figure 13-1 represent a systematic and practical guide to reinventing your organization so that it delivers greater value, regardless of your organization's industry, age, or size.

From our research and extensive consulting experience, we have found that for any major organizational transformations to succeed, the top leaders need to have deep conviction, consensus, and clarity on four basic questions that can make or break your journey of reinvention. Use these questions to diagnose your company's readiness. By honestly and systematically answering these four questions and using the six-step process, you can transform your organization, regardless of its industry, size, or organizational age.

Do We Really Need to Change?

Start by building a strong consensus on your three- to five-year future: What disruptions are coming? What new market opportunities can be created and captured? What will happen to our growth, profit, employee engagement, and so forth, if we don't change? The principles, practices, and tools on environment (chapter 2) and strategy (chapter 3) help you answer these questions individually and as a team.

Engage in multiple, candid, and deep dialogues with your leadership team (and other key stakeholders) to build the foundation for change. When necessary, involve credible business leaders or outside experts to facilitate a consensus. Hold one-on-one meetings with key players before the team meeting to ensure buy-in.

Create a case for why change matters. Make sure to address questions like these: Why is such a strategic pathway for growth critical and feasible for the company's sustainable success, in view of the influential trends? Why is a market-oriented ecosystem a better organizational form than a hierarchy is? Why does headquarters need to empower and serve business teams and partners rather than control them? Why do we need to share data, tools, and technologies?

Do We Know Where We Are Going?

Reduce your and others' anxiety about change. Such anxiety is inevitable when habits form 80 to 90 percent of what people do and when old habits die hard. You can reduce people's concerns by clarifying information about the change, involving people in the transformation effort, and helping them see the impact of the change on them.

Learn from, benchmark, or visit companies that have successfully gone through similar transformations. To reduce skepticism among your peers, make sure the benchmarked companies are relevant in size, age, and industry.

Clarify and agree on the aspirations and pathways of your reinvented organization—your purpose (mission or vision); the pathways to growth (customers, products, or geographic regions);

options for growth (buy, build, or borrow); critical capabilities to build (external sensing, customer obsession, innovation throughout, and agility everywhere); and the best organizational form and governance choices to deliver these capabilities. Sometimes, the desired organizational outcomes are articulated as a specific destination (e.g., a particular financial return or customer share). We think that the outcome of organizational reinvention is more a direction than a destination. The direction is to create strategic agility through strategic ecosystem capabilities. These aspirational purpose statements signal to employees, customers, competitors, and investors how the organization will be known and lead to the right culture.

Design clear, specific, and actionable plans. Fold the future into the present by imagining the future and then thinking backward from there to create plans instead of building the future as an extension of the past.

Do We Know How to Get There?

Recognize and deliver relevant capabilities to shape your organization's hardware (the platform, cell, and ally morphologies described in chapter 5) and software (the six governance mechanisms outlined in part III). Remember that what works well in other organizations may not work well in yours. As a result, the market-oriented ecosystem principles and practices on both structures and governance can only offer a blueprint for your organization to customize, experiment, and iterate to best fit your unique situation. To help you increase your chances of a successful organizational reinvention, we have several suggestions:

- Make sure the right leaders are in place. As noted in chapter 12, look for leaders who are adept at and eager to change and who have a track record of successfully delivering results. If you currently don't have the right leaders in place, promote rising stars from below and hire experienced leaders from the outside.

- Start small, and find early wins. Select a pilot site that has the highest chance of success. This step means managing duality, because the legacy business may operate with traditional management processes while the pilot business embeds market-oriented ecosystem principles and practices. By running pilots that are likely to succeed, you breed confidence and a virtuous cycle of further success.

- Develop an organizational prototype that works and that you can replicate in other parts of your organization. An ideal site must have the right leaders; embrace the market disruptions that demand a company's immediate reinvention; and be able to develop a small ecosystem with platform, cells, and allies. Grant your leaders the power to change, and inspire them to be courageous. Give them leeway to innovate in both organizational form and governance mechanisms. Offer them an appropriate blend of accountability, authority, and reward for shouldering responsibility and responding with agility. Allow them to experiment, fail, learn, and move forward.

- Foster a commitment to a growth mindset as Nadella is doing at Microsoft. See failures as opportunities to learn. Keep iterating to discover tools or models that work for you. Be patient as organizational reinvention takes time to see results.

Do We Have a Reasonable Chance of Success?

To increase your chances of success, persist with confidence in your ability to reinvent your organization. Confidence comes from clarity about the why, what, and how discussed above. It also comes from making reinvention a core personal and organizational value. Confidence gives you the courage to stay the course even when speed bumps arise.

Successful ecosystems enjoy unfailing commitment from the top. Alibaba's transformation would not have been possible if Jack Ma had not believed that the midplatform strategy would lead to improved conversion rates, which would lead to business growth and profit. Tencent's transformation of the IEG game studio would not have happened without Pony Ma's and Martin Lau's conviction that the creativity business depends on superior talent that takes game-development efforts as seriously as the executives take all their businesses.

You need to distribute leadership throughout your organization. Alibaba could not have created its midplatform strategy without its chief technology officer, Xingdian. And besides needing the conviction and support of Ma and Lau, the IEG game studio's success also required the efforts of its business leader, Mark Ren. Bet on people, not strategy. The right people can make the wrong strategy right. But the wrong people will not get results, no matter how brilliant the strategy is.

Preserve a holistic blueprint to guide the transformation. Piece-meal changes will never deliver sustained impact. Table 13-1 provides a detailed guide and checklist for you to follow to deliver the outcomes you desire and the actions you can take. With this overall framework, you can start small, but you should be sure to consider the entire picture. This step-by-step guide also allows you to track and review your progress. As you succeed in any one dimension of the framework, you can move to other dimensions.

Real-Life Organizational Reinvention Examples

To inspire you and give you confidence that market-oriented ecosystems can work for more-traditional companies, we share with you now the stories of how three such companies transformed themselves. These three companies have significantly shifted their businesses from relatively traditional bureaucracies to flexible, creative ecosystems. WBA (a pharmaceutical distribution company) is currently experimenting with market-oriented ecosystem principles and practices. JD.com (an e-commerce retail firm in China) is further along the road. And Yonghui (a leading supermarket in China) has made a remarkable migration along the spectrum, with further room to move.

TABLE 13-1

Step-by-step guide for reinvention: key areas, questions, outcomes, and actions

Question: To what extent . . .	Outcome: Because of this work . . .	Organizational actions
Environment . . . do we understand and anticipate changing environmental conditions that will shape our future?	. . . employees throughout the organization will be aware of the need for change.	*Why?* • Build consensus on what the future looks like. • Create a communication plan on the need for change. • Share information throughout.
Strategy . . . does the organization have a clear strategy for growth and pathways for making it happen?	. . . the organization's stakeholders (leaders, investors, customers, employees) will be able to: • Articulate clear strategy for growth • Define and track measurable outcomes from strategy.	*What?* • Craft a clear, simple, and aspirational growth strategy with a mission, a vision, and goals.
Capability . . . have we defined and articulated the critical capabilities for executing our growth strategy throughout our firm and ecosystem?	. . . the organization's leaders will identify and agree on which capabilities must exist in their organization and ecosystem: • External sensing • Customer obsession • Innovation throughout • Agility everywhere	*What?* • Define and articulate required capabilities to execute strategy. • Conduct a capability audit for each of the businesses. • Identify measures to track and actions to improve key capabilities.
Morphology . . . have we designed the right organizational form or structure to enable our growth strategy?	. . . the organization will accomplish these two tasks: • Create an organizational design that incorporates the principles of platform, cells, and allies. • Clearly define the responsibilities, accountabilities, and rewards for each structural component.	*How?* • Clarify the new organizational structure, which may be a pivot from the existing structure. • Create a charter for how this organization operates.
Governance . . . have we designed and delivered the practices in the six governance mechanisms to ensure the effective functioning and integration of teams, platforms, and allies?	. . . the organization will design and deliver six governance mechanisms that ensure the effective functioning and integration of the new organizational form: • Culture • Performance accountability • Ideas • Talent • Information sharing • Collaboration	*How?* • Prepare a menu of specific practices or processes that can be taken to strengthen each of these six governance mechanisms. • Help each organizational unit pick the right practices to accomplish its goals.

Question: To what extent . . .	Outcome: Because of this work . . .	Organizational actions
Leadership . . . do we have individual leaders at the top and a shared leadership brand throughout the organization to ensure success?	. . . top leaders set the strategic direction and organizational context for MOEs to operate. At all levels, the organization will have leaders who demonstrate the competencies required in the new organization. The quality of leadership will inspire employees to do their best, will ensure customer commitment (NPS), and build investor confidence (an intangible value).	*How?* • Define the roles and required leadership competencies (core and differentiated leadership skills) to make this new organization work. • Assess leaders against these competencies. • Invest in developing leaders who demonstrate these competencies.

Note: MOE, market-oriented ecosystem; NPS, net promoter score.

Walgreen Boots Alliance

Walgreen Boots Alliance, or WBA, (the parent company of Walgreens) is a global leader among pharmacy-led health and wellbeing enterprises.[1] WBA is the largest retail pharmacy and health and daily living destination in the United States and Europe and employs more than 415,000 people. Together with its equity-method investments, WBA has more than 18,500 stores in eleven countries, as well as one of the largest global pharmaceutical wholesale and distribution networks with more than 390 distribution centers delivering to more than 230,000 pharmacies, doctors, health centers, and hospitals each year in more than twenty-five countries. In addition, WBA is one of the world's largest purchasers of prescription drugs and many other health and wellness products. The company's size, scale, and expertise will help to expand the supply of, and address the rising cost of, prescription drugs in the United States and worldwide. The company has:

- Unmatched pharmaceutical supply chain and procurement expertise, offering customers innovative solutions and optimal efficiencies

TABLE 13-2

WBA adaptation of market-oriented ecosystem (MOE) principles

At WBA, innovation and entrepreneurship are institutionalized into its ongoing work culture. Through this delivery and development two-engine model, the company continues to transform itself to be a customer-focused, innovative, and agile organization.

Dimension	Company concerns and responses
Environment: Do we understand and anticipate the changing environmental conditions that will shape our future?	WBA is facing a demanding and changing business environment. The entire pharmacy industry is undergoing dramatic social (lifestyle), technological (digital age), economic (new competitors like Amazon, CVS/Aetna), political (regulation), environmental (reputation), and demographic (aging population) change.
Strategy: Does the organization have a clear strategy for growth and a pathway for making it happen?	WBA's strategy emphasizes partnerships and collaboration with leading retail, health care, technology, manufacturing, supply chain, and other entities. This strategy allows WBA to bring additional scale, knowledge, experience, and resources beyond anything it could build for itself, and to do so more quickly and in areas that are important for its future. • Delivery through traditional stores will continue to focus on efficiency and access. Throughout retail, big box stores have to adapt to win and WBA is dramatically modifying its store model. • Development will work in a new way to accelerate speed to market to respond to change, personalized customer services to anticipate and meet customer requirements, and strategic partnerships that leverage technology to enable innovation and agility.
Capability: Have we articulated and implemented the capabilities that use the MOE to our advantage?	• External sensing: Because of its size and experience, WBA has a very good idea of the larger world in which it operates. It captures ideas for new business opportunities through intimate customer contacts, regular internal idea-generation activities, and emphasis on partnerships with major retail, health care, and technology providers. • Customer obsession: WBA recognizes that an aging population and greater demand and access to health care allow it to grow. With this knowledge, WBA is developing customer-focused solutions for access to its products and services. • Innovation throughout: Emphasizing the ability to continuously innovate with a spirit of "fail fast, learn faster," innovation will occur in the store delivery business with a focus on speed to market of products and services as new retail models are implemented. Even more innovation will be central to the development businesses where WBA will find ways to better meet customer needs. • Agility everywhere: Agility is a core capability for success in WBA's new approach. In the development businesses, WBA will require leaders who act like entrepreneurs, who grab the right people, provide the right incentives, and make decisions fast. The goal is to scale rapidly in ways that a traditional company cannot and, at the same time, reinvent the traditional retail businesses.

Dimension	Company concerns and responses
Morphology: Have we designed the right organizational form or structure to enable our growth strategy?	The morphology of WBA's platform and team ecosystem is followed using this scheme: • *Platform:* WBA has a platform of insights around technology, customer knowledge, finance, HR, and legal. This platform of expertise helps stores deliver more efficiently through standardized processes and discover more quickly by applying insights to new market opportunities. • *Teams:* In the development business, WBA will form market-oriented teams to better serve customers. Examples include teams working on their recent partnerships with Microsoft, Verily, Kroger, FedEx, and Humana. The critical agenda for these teams is to discover solutions for customers that may not look like traditional stores. To do this, it is critical to hire the right leader who brings the necessary entrepreneurial style and approach. This person is selected for deep domain knowledge, entrepreneurial spirit, and agility. • *Ecosystem:* The WBA ecosystem can be engaged as necessary to move quickly into new markets (development) while maintaining traditional retail distribution.
Governance: Have we designed and delivered on the six governance mechanisms that ensure the effective functioning and integration of teams, platforms, and allies?	As WBA moves into this organizational logic, they will consider the governance mechanisms: • *Culture:* Fast-moving, entrepreneurial, deeply knowledgeable (new businesses), and simultaneously having efficiency and rigor (stores). • *Performance accountability:* Compensation model common to US-listed companies (base salary, bonus, stock awards) to encourage and reward talent for driving the overall success of the enterprise. • *Ideas:* The goal is to keep ideas and actions flowing to make decisions quickly and move on. • *Talent:* The top leader must represent expectations promised to customers. These leaders in development may come from inside or outside WBA, but they have to represent the promises made to customers. • *Information sharing:* Transparent and fast-moving. • *Collaboration:* Valued and promoted both internally and externally as core to WBA's strategy.
Leadership: Do we have individual leaders at the top and a shared leadership brand throughout the organization to ensure success?	WBA has a legacy of leadership and leaders who can manage market requirements in and across the twenty-five countries in which it has a presence. Their commitment to intelligent connectivity has become an embedded part of their corporate identity. The shared leadership commitment to customer, innovation, and agility is expanding throughout their ecosystem. WBA leaders partner with companies at any stage to help solve challenges that improve quality of life through technology solutions in unimaginable ways.

- A portfolio of retail and business brands, including Walgreens, Duane Reade, Boots, and Alliance Healthcare, as well as increasingly global health and beauty product brands, such as No7, Soap & Glory, Liz Earle, Sleek MakeUP, and Botanics

- Diversified and robust profit pools across the United States, Europe, and key emerging markets

- A unique platform for growth in developed and emerging markets

The legacy of the company lies in stores where the focus is on delivery of services and products to customers. The future of the company complements this store footprint with a focus on delivery with an innovation agenda focused on development. In this two-engine model, delivery is about optimizing existing retail drugstores and development is about innovation and the future of these drugstores including digital distribution methods and innovations inside the stores.

JD.com: Customer Trust and Strategic Partnerships

JD.com, China's top supermarket chain online or offline and the country's second-largest e-retailer was the first Chinese internet company to make the *Fortune* Global 200 list.[2] The company is highly trusted; its zero-tolerance policy toward counterfeit goods has created a loyal and lucrative following of discerning customers, who have made JD.com's fashion and luxury business grow at double the rate of the fashion and luxury market. Its e-commerce logistics infrastructure covers 99 percent of China's population, and it is able to achieve rates of over 90 percent of orders being delivered same-day or next-day—an astonishing achievement in China and one of its major competitive advantages.

In 2014, JD.com formed a strategic partnership with Tencent, launching a new business model combining social networking and e-commerce. With this move, they reached more than one billion Chinese consumers. The partnership helps brand companies leverage the most comprehensive social and commerce targeted marketing program based on big data: about 80 percent of the orders are

TABLE 13-3

JD.com adaptation of market-oriented ecosystem (MOE) principles

Though JD.com started as an e-commerce company, it needs to keep reinventing itself to ensure agility and competitiveness. Since early 2016, the company has begun to elevate itself to another level of external sensing, customer focus, innovation, and agility through both organizational innovation and technological enhancement.

Dimension	Company concerns and responses
Environment: Do we understand and anticipate the changing environmental conditions that will shape our future?	JD.com is facing the following environmental challenges and opportunities: • Already deep market penetration means that growth can no longer rely on expanding the user base, but must instead increase the average revenue per user (ARPU). • Increased competitive pressure from other online competitors requires a better selection of product offerings from brand companies and a higher conversion of user traffic to actual transactions through targeted marketing and recommendations. • Users are more affluent, demanding high-quality products and good services. • Rapidly improving technology offers better capabilities in capturing, storing, and analyzing user data. Such technological advances help JD.com make precise decisions in procurement, marketing, logistics, and other services.
Strategy: Does the organization have a clear strategy for growth and a pathway for making it happen?	CEO Richard Liu and his executive team consistently communicate the importance of transforming JD.com into a technology-driven company, rich in data, organized in a platform, team and ecosystem morphology. Within this framework, in 2019, JD.com will focus on three important things:[a] • *Lower-tier cities:* It will bring more products to China's lower-tier cities to attract more customers. • *Digitalization:* It will rely on big data and digitalization to improve the efficiency of its management systems. • *New business models:* It will introduce new business models to the offline market. It will keep testing its models until they are improved, and then duplicate them as quickly as possible.
Capability: Have we articulated and implemented the capabilities that will use the MOE to our advantage?	To execute the above strategies, JD.com is further enhancing its core capabilities: • *External sensing:* JD.com will leverage big data, AI to provide sales forecast and tailored service for customers. It also will empower its IoT (internet of things) capabilities through the value chain, especially in warehousing and logistics services. • *Customer first:* Increasing the ARPU requires that JD.com understand and anticipate the needs of its users (rather than focusing on sales of products) much better than before. JD.com has made a lot of optimization and improvement in order to enhance the user experience.

a. JD.com Q4 and FY 2018 earnings call

(continued)

TABLE 13-3 *(continued)*

JD.com adaptation of market-oriented ecosystem (MOE) principles

Dimension	Company concerns and responses
	• *Innovation*: Both organizational innovation and technological upgrades are required. The platform-team-ecosystem model is adopted. The platform offers different technical modules or application tools to be adopted and adapted by different business units for faster execution. Teams need to be further empowered and self-contained in their procurement and operation capabilities. A platform with stronger technological integration in systems and data needs to be put in place. • *Agility:* With further delegation from headquarters to different business units, the teams become more agile in making business decisions to respond to user needs and competitive situations themselves.
Morphology: Have we designed the right organizational form or structure to enable our growth strategy?	The morphology of platform-team-ecosystem is being followed: • *Platform:* The major focus is to integrate the technical teams, systems, and data that used to be scattered in different business units. The strong technological platform will provide business units with service modules to build new business capabilities and to offer more complete user profiles for targeted offerings. • *Teams*: Business teams in different business units are more self-contained with functions critical to their operations (including product procurement, display, transactions, marketing, etc.). Better alignment in accountability, authority, and reward is achieved through a set of new management initiatives and incentive schemes. • *Ecosystem:* Form strategic partnerships with industry-leading companies, including Tencent, Walmart, and Google. JD.com plans to invest and partner with more brand companies in the supply chain. It hopes to form partnerships with Yonghui, VIP.com, BuBuGao, and others. It will also invest in technological and logistics firms to beef up these capabilities.
Governance: Have we designed and delivered on the six governance mechanisms that ensure the effective functioning and integration of teams, platforms, and allies?	• *Culture:* JD.com's mission is "technology shapes our lives," its vision is to "become the most trusted company in the world." JD.com puts the customer first. • *Performance accountability/reward:* A bigger portion of the motivation bonus is allocated to teams that outperform market growth. • *Idea:* Most strategic innovation and business growth ideas come from the core leadership team chaired by CEO Richard Liu. • *Talent:* More technologically savvy people in big data, AR, VR, and blockchain are being recruited to strengthen the platform capability. JD.com also cultivated technical talents who deeply understand its business. • *Information sharing:* A steering committee consisting of technical leaders is established to guide the integration and joint development of tools and data at the midplatform.

Dimension	Company concerns and responses
	• *Collaboration:* Improve collaboration between platform and business teams. Technical business partners (TBP) are assigned from platform to work at business teams. TBP's performance reviews and bonuses are also jointly determined by the business team and the platform to facilitate better collaboration between the two.
Leadership: Do we have individual leaders at the top and a shared leadership brand throughout the organization to ensure success?	CEO Richard Liu is committed to building agile business teams at the front-end, supported by a strong midplatform (supply chain, technology, marketing, and customer service) to facilitate synergy. Technology is a key area of investment.

Beginning with Liu, a strong set of values guide the decisions and behaviors of employees. For example, there is zero tolerance for counterfeit products. Liu believes there are five principles for leadership:

1. Consistent values: customer first, integrity, collaboration, all in, ownership, and gratitude
2. Fairness, justice, and openness
3. Having passion, vision, and strength
4. Exercising strict self-discipline, leading by example, and challenging oneself
5. Being ambitious, empathetic, and mission-oriented

He also believes in four abilities:

1. A sense of awareness, learning, and innovation
2. Organizational management
3. Strategic management
4. The ability to perform well enough to be a good leader

Internal encouragement and promotion is critical: for example, to better adapt to the fast-changing development of the company and meet the needs of a large number of key talents, internal employees should be promoted, especially young employees who are 70 percent capable of fulfilling higher-level positions. For vacancies at the managerial level and above in a mature business and system, adhere to the principle of internal priority and require more than 80 percent of new positions to be appointed internally, giving internal employees more opportunities to develop in the core management team.

JD.com has abundant talent training programs to meet different level positions that can cultivate leaders ahead of time, including the JD.com pilot program for training talented directors, JD MBA, the JD management trainee program, and its elite intern program.

placed through mobile devices. And the story continues: by 2016, JD.com and Walmart formed a strategic alliance that helps improve delivery efficiency for customers, optimizes delivery routes for JD, and increases Walmart's inventory turnover rate through integrated inventory. In June 2018, JD.com formally partnered with Google on a range of strategic initiatives including joint development of retail solutions in regions around the world, which explore the creation of next-generation retail infrastructure solutions.

Organization Reinvention in Action: Yonghui Supermarket

Yonghui was founded in Fuzhou, China, in 2000 as a single fresh supermarket.[3] The company then grew quickly by establishing a presence in Shanghai, Chongqing, and Beijing. By 2010, it launched its initial public offering on China's A-share market, which enabled the company to grow even faster. In 2014, Yonghui launched Bravo Supermarkets, a chain of high-end supermarkets, and started to partner aggressively with other firms to secure a high-quality supply of products in the back end of the supply chain and user traffic in the front end. Investment by Dairy International soon followed. Investments from JD.com followed a year later, enabling the launch of Yonghui Life, a chain of small fresh convenience stores, each of which serves the square kilometer around it. By 2016, Yonghui had moved down the value chain to go into the food-processing business (Caishixian). By 2017, Tencent had invested in Yonghui, and Yonghui launched Super Species (a direct competitor to Alibaba's Hema Fresh), a chain of high-end offline-online fresh food stores that also offered in-house dining and cooking services. Yonghui also invested in Daman Global Company to strengthen its technological capability.

Like the market-oriented ecosystems we have studied, this small supermarket became a large, complex business by rapidly expanding through a combination of organizational capabilities and strategies. It has combined a large platform, a network of small teams out in the field, a rich ecosystem of allies and partners from which to learn and draw resources, and a system of joint governance that provides mutual benefit and the right incentives and structures.

TABLE 13-4

Yonghui adaptation of market-oriented ecosystem (MOE) principles

Starting out as a fresh grocery store, Yonghui keeps moving into new adjacent businesses by re-architecting the company based on platform-team-ecosystem design. As a result, three horizons of businesses—Super Species, Yonghui Life, Yonghui Delivery—are created through shared platform and businesses in current core businesses. Bravo Supermarket grew by more than 30 percent in the last few years with above-industry-average profitability (net profit: 3 percent vs. 1-2 percent industry average) while its new businesses, like Super Species, grew by 10 times in the last two years.

Dimension	Company concerns and responses
Environment: Do we understand and anticipate the changing environmental conditions that will shape our future?	Yonghui is facing several challenges and opportunities: • More competitors, including Alibaba and JD.com, are entering the fresh-grocery business and are doing it with better technology and data. • Fresh-grocery businesses need to be much stronger in supply-chain and store management to reduce waste in every step because their products are perishable; many fresh products like lobsters or crabs can die during the process. • With recent investments from JD.com and Tencent, Yonghui can make use of the technology and data from these partners, especially from Tencent through Tencent Cloud and WeChat Pay. • With approximately 1,000 merchandizers around the world, Yonghui has by far the best supply-chain management capability in fresh grocery in China. This advantage allows Yonghui to compete against online competitors. Meanwhile, the company is upgrading its technology and data capability to improve customer centricity and operation efficiency.
Strategy: Does the organization have a clear strategy for growth and a pathway for making it happen?	Yonghui is launching a three-horizon strategy to grow: • Horizon 1: Core business—Bravo Supermarket is about 6,000 square meters in size. This business continues to grow by leveraging the strong platform capability with enhanced technology and data with better user experience (like automated checkout) and targeted marketing (use of electronic discount coupons to attract customers). • Horizon 2: Innovative businesses—Super Species and Yonghui Life. Super Species is about 600 square meters, offering both fresh grocery and restaurant services. It also provides fresh deliveries to online customers within a radius of 3 kilometers. Yonghui Life Convenience Store is about 100 square meters in size. A larger number of stores will be established to increase market penetration. • Horizon 3: Experimental businesses—Caishixian and Yonghui Life & Delivery. Tapping into its front-end business-extension advantage, Yonghui has been innovating new businesses like Caishixian, a B2B enterprise. To date, Yonghui has established Caishixian fresh-food central-processing factories in six provinces in China, to provide for the vast catering needs of over 300 B2B clients, including some major restaurants and hospitals. In 2018, Caishixian attracted investments from investors such as Hillhouse Capital and Sequoia Capital, and this has given greater momentum to Yonghui's transformation into a food supply chain company. Yonghui Life & Delivery is an innovative online-ordering-plus-delivery business developed by Yonghui Yunchuang. Distinct from either pure e-tailing or pure brick-and-mortar retailing, Yonghui Delivery integrates the use of satellite warehouses and Yonghui Life mini-program/app to best satisfy diverse customer needs, including high-quality fresh deliveries within 30 minutes of online ordering to customers within a 3 kilometer radius.

(continued)

TABLE 13-4 *(continued)*

Yonghui adaptation of market-oriented ecosystem (MOE) principles

Dimension	Company concerns and responses
Capability: Have we articulated and implemented the capabilities that will use the MOE to our advantage?	By combining its core strengths in supply-chain management and its new capability in technology and data, Yonghui needs to improve the following capabilities: • *External sensing:* Yonghui always focuses on serving external customers, with platforms serving front-end customer teams as internal customers. With the location-based-service technology in place, Yonghui will be better equipped to understand which potential customers are near the store and to issue discount coupons to attract those people to visit the store. • *Customer centric:* Yonghui and most other grocery stores used to be product centric, because they didn't know who their customers were. By using multichannel touch points such as Yonghui App, online stores, and the WeChat Little program, Yonghui can integrate complete user profiles. The integrated profiles are important for procuring the right product mix in stores, store management, and marketing with greater efficiency and precision. • *Innovation:* Yonghui is constantly experimenting with new business models and management techniques by benchmarking world-class competitors in the United States, Europe, and Japan and by exploiting technological breakthroughs. It also invests up to RMB 60 million annually to upgrade its systems and practices with the professional assistance of consulting firms. • *Agility:* Yonghui empowers its customer-facing business teams to make decisions in the best interest of the company through its employees' "business-partnership" scheme: Employees at Bravo Supermarkets, Super Species, and Yonghui Life are organized into teams of six people. As business partners of their responsible sections, they share the success and failure of their sections accordingly and are empowered to make decisions like pricing to optimize company profit (e.g., big discount for bananas before the products begin to rot).
Morphology: Have we designed the right organizational form or structure to enable our growth strategy?	The morphology of Yonghui's platform and team ecosystem has transformed the company into multiple businesses with multichannel capabilities: • *Platform:* A strong midplatform is being built to increase its technological applications (e.g., membership management, face recognition, shopping cart handling, automated payment), with enhanced AI and cloud computing from the Tencent partnership. This midplatform will provide integrated support to all customer-facing businesses with shared customer data. Another important platform is its procurement and value-chain capability. While each business, such as Bravo Supermarkets, Super Species, and Yonghui Life, has its own S2B2C (suppliers-businesses-consumers) capabilities to serve their stores, there are also procurement and value-chain services common to all businesses. • *Teams:* The customer-facing teams (six people each) in all Yonghui businesses are run like their own stores. The teams are accountable for monthly financial reports and shared preset profits with the company. They enjoy decision rights in daily operations (e.g., pricing, product mix, and product display). Profits are shared monthly with transparent financial information online. • *Ecosystem:* Yonghui formed partnerships with logistic firms Dairy International, JD.com, and Tencent to enhance its capabilities at both the back end (procurement and value chain) and the front end (marketing and generation of user traffic).

Dimension	Company concerns and responses
Governance: Have we designed and delivered the six governance mechanisms that ensure the effective functioning and integration of teams, platforms, and allies?	The platform-team ecosystem is empowered by the following six governance mechanisms at Yonghui: • *Culture:* Yonghui emphasizes the culture of "helping others succeed so that you can succeed." The core values are "be tolerant, open, eager to share, and win-win." As a result, the platform teams can serve the business teams like internal customers. The transparency culture also encourages the best team to share its best practices with other teams. Transparency in financial data creates trust between the business teams and the company as the teams share profit on a transparent and timely basis. • *Performance accountability:* All business teams (six people) are assessed on a simulated financial report (monthly for store people, biannually or annually for people in regional platforms or back-end platforms). The teams are then ranked with similar teams according to their performance and divided into four categories (excellent, performing, average, and lagging teams). The lagging teams (bottom 10–20 percent) need to be dissolved and replaced with members from excellent teams. The members of lagging teams will not be fired but will be redeployed into new teams with better team leaders. • *Ideas:* When Yonghui experiments with a new business model like Yonghui Chef or Super Species, it always uses two independent teams to experiment with the new business models and products. After some period of experimentation, leadership will decide which model and team has better results and incorporate the useful results from other teams into the winning team. • *Talent:* Yonghui adopts a T-shaped talent profile. Talent needs to have deeper expertise in one area (the vertical bar in the *T*) but move around constantly to different jobs and businesses. This profile broadens people's exposure and learning. The fluid movement of talent is related partly to Yonghui's constant experimentation and innovation and partly to the company's horse-racing philosophy. • *Information sharing:* Yonghui is extremely transparent in sharing the financial data of each team, its work goals, and the best practices from the excellent teams. This kind of information sharing fosters trust and constant learning at all levels. The firm also shares data and tools across businesses from the technological platform. • *Collaboration:* Yonghui adopts an internal-market mechanism to assess the value that both business teams and platform teams add. Depending on this value, the teams enjoy a preset profit-sharing scheme from the revenue generated by the business teams, the platform teams, and, finally, the company. Yonghui adopts a 50–50 profit-sharing scheme with its employees in the core business when the company is profitable. Employees in business teams (e.g., the fish section in Bravo Supermarkets), regional service platforms (e.g., the procurement and value-chain team of the fish category), and back-end platforms (e.g., IT, HR, and marketing teams) together share 50 percent of the profit while the company shares the remaining 50 percent. This distribution fosters the climate of win-win collaboration because people in teams, platforms, or elsewhere in the company share the same stake in the success and failure of customer-facing teams.

(continued)

TABLE 13-4 *(continued)*

Yonghui adaptation of market-oriented ecosystem (MOE) principles

Dimension	Company concerns and responses
Leadership: Do we have individual leaders at the top and a shared leadership brand throughout the organization to ensure success?	Founded by two brothers, Zhang Xuanning and Zhang Xuansong in 2000, Yonghui keeps reinventing both its business model and its organizational model. The top leaders play important roles in three areas: • *Innovating the new business model:* Yonghui is constantly looking for new business models to serve customers better in the fresh-grocery business. • *Shaping the company culture of "be tolerant, open, eager to share, and win-win."* This open attitude provides the basis of constant innovation. • *Talent management through a partnership culture:* Yonghui leaders believe in people potential. By being treated as true business partners, employees can think and act like business owners with a strong entrepreneurial drive.

Conclusion

Pharmacy distribution. Retail. Groceries. The principles and practices that drive market-oriented ecosystem success are popping up everywhere. Is your industry or organization next?

Our goal with this book has been to provide leaders with a comprehensive guide to taking on the challenge of reinventing an organization. The market-oriented ecosystems that we studied point to the whys and hows. It's about delivering greater value in fast-changing markets and the kind of organization that is capable of doing that.

We have tried to make sense of what this emerging organization looks like by taking a holistic, integrated view and then breaking it down into six parts, with assessments, diagnostics, and other tools to help you on your path. As we said at the outset, taking a company in a new direction is a daunting agenda for any leader in any kind of company, old or new. Executives in so-called legacy companies have to fight against long-standing assumptions to build something new, and leaders of newer companies have to ensure that even their young organizations remain relevant. But it can be done. Every day, we work with executives who are ardently working to reinvent their organizations. They start small. They build. They keep a holistic view (as espoused in our six-part framework), and they focus on the individual parts that they can improve today. One change here leads to another there. All the parts are interdependent.

You can too. We hope this book will inspire you to break conventional thinking about what your organization—young or old—can do. Like the ordinary eighty people who at the beginning of this book acted on the spot to prevail against a deadly riptide, you and your organization now have a powerful tool in your hands to win against any current in your environment.

NOTES

Chapter 1

1. Inside Edition, "80 Strangers for Human Chain to Rescue Family from Ocean Riptide," video, YouTube, July 11, 2017, www.youtube.com /watch?v=jYCWT3CU0RE.

2. Information on Supercell is from Janne Snellman, chief operating officer of Supercell and Jim Yan, general manager, China, at Supercell, interviews by Tencent's research team on market-oriented ecosystems (hereafter cited as Tencent Research Team). The interviews were conducted by Arthur Yeung (author) and other members from Tencent Research Team. Janne Snellman was interviewed on January 10, 2017 and Jim Yan was interviewed on April 13, 2017; both interviews were conducted in person in Shanghai, China. Headed by Arthur, the benchmarking task force included five additional HR directors and consultants (Devon Shu, Emily Chen, Janet Huang, Sharon Li, and Wingwing Wang) from different departments at Tencent. The research was conducted from January to June in 2017 in person in China and in the United States and by telephone.

3. McKinsey's latest systems approach to organizations is called *organizational health*. See Scott Keller and Colin Price, "Organizational Health: The Ultimate Competitive Advantage," *McKinsey Quarterly*, June 2011, www.mckinsey.it/idee/organizational-health-the-ultimate -competitive-advantage.

4. Dave Ulrich and Dale Lake, *Organization Capability: Competing from the Inside Out* (New York: Wiley, 1990).

Chapter 2

1. Amazon, "Introducing Amazon Go and the World's Most Advanced Shopping Technology," YouTube, December 5, 2016, www.youtube.com /watch?v=NrmMk1Myrxc.

2. Dave Ulrich et al., *HR from the Outside In: Six Competencies for the Future of Human Resources* (New York: McGraw-Hill, 2012).

3. Every few months, when we update this chart, the organizations change. The pattern of new companies moving onto the chart remains the same, but the relative positioning and details of these companies change rapidly. In a week, an organization may gain or lose up to 15 percent of its market value. Such fluctuations demonstrate the rapid pace of change.

4. Aon Hewitt, "2017 Trends in Global Employee Engagement Report," https://www.aon.com/engagement17/index.aspx.

5. See, for example, Brian Primack et al., "Use of Multiple Social Media Platforms and Symptoms of Depression and Anxiety: A Nationally-Representative Study Among U.S. Young Adults," *Computers in Human Behavior* 69 (April 2017): 1–9; H. B. Shakya and N. A. Christakis, "Association of Facebook Use with Compromised Well-Being: A Longitudinal Study," *American Journal of Epidemiology* 185 (February 2017): 203–211.

6. Laura Alejandra Rico-Uribe et al., January 2018. "Association of Loneliness with All-Cause Mortality: A Meta-analysis," *PLoS ONE* 13, no. 1 (2018): e0190033, https://doi.org/10.1371/journal.pone.0190033; and Julianne Holt-Lunstad, Timothy B. Smith, J. Bradley Layton, "Social Relationships and Mortality Risk: A Meta-analytic Review," *PLoS Med* 7, no. 7 (2010): e1000316, https://doi.org/10.1371/journal.pmed.1000316.

7. Vivek Murthy, "Work and the Loneliness Epidemic," *Harvard Business Review*, September 28, 2017, https://hbr.org/cover-story/2017/09/work-and-the-loneliness-epidemic

8. Jason Daley, "The U.K. Now Has a 'Minister for Loneliness': Here's Why It Matters," *SmartNews*, Smithsonian.com, January 19, 2018, www.smithsonianmag.com/smart-news/minister-loneliness-appointed-united-kingdom-180967883.

9. Dave Ulrich and Wendy Ulrich, *The Why of Work: How to Create an Abundant Organization* (New York: McGraw Hill, 2011); Dave Ulrich, "Got Meaning?," *LinkedIn Pulse*, November 28, 2017, www.linkedin.com/pulse/finding-meaning-mundane-dave-ulrich; Dave Ulrich, "Belonging: An Emerging (Next) Leadership and HR Agenda," *LinkedIn Pulse*, January 30, 2018, www.linkedin.com/pulse/belonging-emerging-next-leadership-hr-agenda-dave-ulrich.

10. These observations came from various WeChat business leaders, interview by Arthur Yeung and Tencent Research Team, conducted June 1, 2017 at WeChat Guangzhou office in China.

Chapter 3

1. Information on Alibaba is from interview with Alibaba senior managers and industry experts by Arthur Yeung and Tencent Research Team, conducted March 14–20, 2017 in person in China and in the United States and by telephone. See also Alibaba Group, "Company Overview," accessed March 15, 2019, www.alibabagroup.com/en/about/overview.

2. Mission statements of Amazon, Google, Facebook, and Huawei came from each company's official website.

3. Jeff Bezos, "Jeff Bezos Owns the Web in More Ways Than You Think," interview by Steven Levy, *Wired*, November 13, 2011, www.wired.com/2011/11/ff_bezos.

4. Satya Nadella, *Hit Refresh: The Quest to Rediscover Microsoft's Soul and Imagine a Better Future for Everyone* (New York: Harper Business, 2017).

5. Brad Stone, *The Everything Store: Jeff Bezos and the Age of Amazon* (New York: Little, Brown and Company, 2013).

6. This information is from interviews with employees and former Amazon employees by Arthur Yeung and Tencent Research Team, conducted March 1–22, 2017 in person in China and in the United States and by telephone; Brad Stone, *The Everything Store* (2013).

7. Interview with former general manager of Amazon by Arthur Yeung and Tencent Research Team, conducted March 15, 2017 in person in San Francisco, California.

8. VIPKid, "VIPKid Journey Dallas—The Presidential Election," You-Tube, August 17, 2018, https://www.youtube.com/watch?v=99xnJtRgJi4.

9. For the list of Amazon acquisitions, refer to the following link https://en.wikipedia.org/wiki/List_of_mergers_and_acquisitions_by _Amazon#Acquisitions.

10. Brad Stone, *The Everything Store* (2013).

Chapter 4

1. Ben MacIntyre, *Rogue Heroes: The History of the SAS, Britain's Secret Special Forces That Sabotaged the Nazis and Changed the Nature of War* (New York: Broadway Books, 2016), xiii.

2. The six-month process to train SAS members is regarded as the most arduous in the world. Recruits must undertake a month of running over the Welsh mountains with fifty-pound loads. The challenge culminates in a forty-mile endurance march. They then spend weeks in the jungle, suffering dehydration and deprivation, followed by another course in escape and eva- sion, finishing up with tests of resistance to interrogation. Fully 90 percent of the candidates drop out before they complete the training, and the initial candidates have already been selected for their physical and emotional toughness. In the words of former SAS instructor Peter Wright, "these men do not understand the meaning of the word 'defeat.' They are tough beyond measure. When faced with hardship, they keep going." Each team member has a specialist skill: medical expertise, sniper skills, explosives, or commu- nications. Many members are also trained linguists. They must be smart, obviously. And they must be confident in a way that does not get noticed.

3. We acknowledge that the movie version of this rescue may vary from the real events, but our focus is on the activities of the SEAL team more than on Captain Phillips himself. See, for example, Maureen Callahan, "Crew Members: 'Captain Phillips' Is One Big Lie," *New York Post*, Octo- ber 13, 2013, https://nypost.com/2013/10/13/crew-members-deny-captain -phillips-heroism.

4. Tencent press releases, annual reports, proxies, and shareholder let- ters, accessed March 15, 2019, www.tencent.com/en-us/company.html; Brad Stone and Lulu Yilun Chen, "Tencent Dominates in China; Next Challenge

Is Rest of the World," *BusinessWeek*, June 28, 2017, www.bloomberg.com/news /features/2017-06-28/tencent-rules-china-the-problem-is-the-rest-of-the-world.

5. Zhang Jianfeng (chief technology officer of Alibaba), speech at Alibaba Technology Forum 2016, Hangzhou, "Computing: The Unlimited Imagination," https://yunqi.youku.com/2016/hangzhou/download?spm =5176.8098788.567836.1.

6. For investor confidence, see Dave Ulrich, *The Leadership Capital Index: Realizing the Market Value of Leadership* (Oakland, CA: Berrett-Koehler Publishers, 2015) for capabilities that investors value and that show up as increased market value. For customer commitment and improved revenue per customer, see Dave Ulrich and Norm Smallwood, *Leadership Brand* (Boston: Harvard Business Review Press, 2007). For employee commitment and higher productivity, see Dave Ulrich and Wendy Ulrich, *The Why of Work: How to Create an Abundant Organization* (New York: McGraw Hill, 2011).

7. Arthur Yeung and Sharon Li, annual white papers on National Organizational Capability Survey (2016, 2017, and 2018).

8. For industrial-era capabilities, see Arthur Yeung, *Organizational Capability: Secrets of Sustainable Success* (Beijing: China Machine Press, 2010); Arthur Yeung, *Breakthrough in Organizational Capability* (Beijing: China Machine Press, 2012). For today's required capabilities, see Arthur Yeung and Sharon Li, *DNA of Transformation* (Beijing: CITIC Publishing Group, 2016); Arthur Yeung, Li Bo, and Rebecca Rui, *Transformation in Action* (Beijing: CITIC Publishing Group, 2017).

9. Wayne Brockbank, Dave Ulrich, David G. Kryscynski, and Michael Ulrich, "The Future of HR and Information Capability," *Strategic HR Review* 17, no. 1 (2018): 3–10, https://doi.org/10.1108/SHR-11-2017-0080.

10. Malcolm Gladwell, *What the Dog Saw: And Other Adventures* (New York: Little, Brown and Company, 2009), 167.

11. Interviews with employees and former employees of Google and Facebook by Arthur Yeung and Tencent Research Team, conducted March 14–15, 2017 in person in Mountain View, California and by telephone.

12. See Mobike home page, https://mobike.com/global/.

13. Joseph Kurian A. Manavalan, "Amazon's 'Eat Your Own Dog Food' Approach to Building Platforms," *LinkedIn Pulse*, June 19, 2017, www .linkedin.com/pulse/amazons-eat-your-own-dog-food-approach-building -manavalan.

14. Zhang Yong, CEO of Alibaba Group, open letter to all employees, 2017, http://www.ebrun.com/20170104/209250.shtml.

15. Interviews with employees and former Amazon employees by Arthur Yeung and Tencent Research Team, conducted March 1–22, 2017 in person in China and in the United States and by telephone.

16. Janne Snellmann, chief operating officer of Supercell, interview with Arthur Yeung and Tencent Research Team, conducted January 10, 2017 in person in Shanghai, China.

17. Interview with business leaders of WeChat by Arthur Yeung and Tencent Research Team, conducted June 1, 2017 in person at Wechat Guangzhou office in China.

Chapter 5

1. Dave Ulrich and Justin Allen, "Private Equity's New Phase," hbr .org, August 9, 2016, https://hbr.org/2016/08/private-equitys-new-phase.

2. Cheng Wei, CEO of DiDi, and several DiDi business leaders, interview with Arthur Yeung and Tencent Research Team, conducted March 2, 2017 in person at DiDi's headquarters in Beijing China; Chunbo Lai, senior director of DiDi and head of ride-hailing platform, speech on World of Tech Summit 2017, https://t.cj.sina.com.cn/articles/view/1708729084 /65d922fc034002olg.

3. Interview with various WeChat business leaders by Arthur Yeung and Tencent Research Team, conducted June 1, 2017 in person at WeChat Guangzhou office in China.

4. Jim Yang, Great China general manager at Supercell, interview with Arthur Yeung and Tencent Research Team, conducted April 13, 2017 in person in Shanghai, China; Tencent gaming business leaders, interview with Arthur Yeung and Tencent Research Team, conducted May 5, 2017 in person at Tencent Shenzhen Building in China.

5. Huawei Annual Report, 2017, https://www-file.huawei.com/-/media /corporate/pdf/annual-report/annual_report2017_cn.pdf?la=en.

6. Jeff Bezos, "To Our Shareholders," Amazon annual letter to shareholders, 2011, 2012, in "All of Jeff Bezos' Amazon Letters to Shareholders Together in One PDF," in *Words of Ward, Your Guide to Financial Freedom*, April 20, 2017, http://dameats.com/wordsofward/2017/04/20/all-amazon -letters-to-shareholders-combined.

7. Interview with Alibaba senior managers and industry experts by Arthur Yeung and Tencent Research Team, conducted March 14–20, 2017 in person in Palo Alto, California, and by telephone; Zhonghua, *The Way to IT Architecture Transformation: Alibaba Mid-Platform Strategy and Practices* (Beijing, China Machine Press, 2018).

8. "DiDi of the Past: Tencent Has Support for up to 1000 Servers to Beat KuaiDi + Ali," Guohao, *Shanghai Securities News*, December 1, 2017, http://tech.163.com/16/0809/07/BU0T3R0L00097U7R.html; " How DiDi Beat 30 Competitors in Four Years," August 6, 2016, *Enterpreneur Magazine*, http://www.ebrun.com/20160806/185998.shtml.

9. Cheng Wei and DiDi business leaders interview, March 2, 2017; DiDi recruitment page (in Chinese), accessed March 15, 2019, http://talent .didiglobal.com.

10. Ren Zhengfei (Huawei founder), speech given at Huawei Q4 regional leaders meeting, November 6, 2014, https://tech.sina.com.cn/t/2014-12-25 /doc-icesifvy1782228.shtml.

11. Interview with employees and former employees of Amazon by Arthur Yeung and Tencent Research Team, conducted March 1–22, 2017 in person in China and in the United States and by telephone; Chris Vander Mey, *Practical Lessons on Building and Launching Outstanding Software, Learned on the Job at Google and Amazon* (Beijing: O'Reilly Media, 2012) (also available in Chinese).

12. Janne Snellmann, chief operating officer of Supercell, interview with Arthur Yeung and Tencent Research Team, conducted January 10, 2017 in person in Shanghai, China.

13. Tencent Holdings Limited, "Disclosable Transaction Relating to (1) Subscription for Shares in JD.com, Inc. and (2) Disposal of Assets and Equity Interests in E-Commerce Business," company announcement, March 10, 2014, http://www3.hkexnews.hk/listedco/listconews/sehk/2014 /0310/ltn20140310033.pdf.

14. Jeff Bezos, "To Our Shareholders," Amazon annual shareholder letter, 2008, in *Words of Ward, Your Guide to Financial Freedom*; and Brad Stone, *The Everything Store: Jeff Bezos and the Age of Amazon* (New York: Little, Brown and Company, 2013).

15. Ilkka Paananen, CEO of Supercell, speech given at RovioCon, Helsinki, Finland, 2017; Janne Snellmann interview, January 10, 2017.

16. Employees and former employees of Facebook interview, March 14–15, 2017.

17. Ibid; and Blue Lion Enterprise Research Institute (China), "Case Study: A New Understanding of Facebook Open Platform," January 1, 2016, http://caiwei.yuedu.163.com/source/a5d2f41880d34d42966d24e5dad55 4b7_4.

18. Alibaba senior managers and industry experts interview, March 14–20, 2017; Zhonghua, *The Way to IT Architecture Transformation*.

Chapter 6

1. Curt Coffman and Kathie Sorenson, *Culture Eats Strategy for Lunch* (Liang Addison Press, 2013); Charles B. Handy, *Understanding Organizations* (New York: Oxford University Press, 1976); Edgar Schein, *Organizational Culture and Leadership: A Dynamic View* (San Francisco: Jossey-Bass, 1992).

2. The role of culture as a governance mechanism is the basis of the Nobel Prize–winning work by Oliver Williamson: *The Economic Institutions of Capitalism* (New York: Free Press, 1998); Sidney Winter, *The Nature of the Firm: Origins, Evolution, and Development* (New York: Oxford University Press, 1993); *Markets and Hierarchies: Analysis and Antitrust Implications* (New York: Free Press, 1988). See also William Ouchi, "Markets, Hierarchies, and Clans," *Administrative Science Quarterly* 25 (1980): 129–141.

3. Nicholas Carlson, "Google CEO Eric Schmidt: 'We Don't Really Have a Five-Year Plan'," interview of Eric Schmidt by Seven Perstein, *Tech*

Insider, May 21, 2009, https://www.businessinsider.com.au/google-ceo-eric
-schmidt-we-dont-really-have-a-five-year-plan-clip-2009-5.

4. Chartered Institute of Internal Auditors, "Culture and the Role of Internal Audit: Looking below the Surface," 2014, www.iia.org.uk/policy /culture-and-the-role-of-internal-audit.

5. Satya Nadella, "Starting to Evolve Our Organization and Culture," open letter to employees at Microsoft, July 17, 2014, Microsoft News Center, https://news.microsoft.com/2014/07/17/starting-to-evolve-our -organization-and-culture.

6. Former vice president of Amazon AWS, interview with Arthur Yeung and Tencent Research Team, conducted March 17, 2017, in person in Seattle, Washington.

7. APV, "Alibaba IPO Roadshow Presentation Video," video, YouTube, March 5, 2015, www.youtube.com/watch?v=aK0tqH9ljj8.

8. Jeff Bezos, quoted in Paul Farhi, "Jeffrey Bezos, Washington Post's Next Owner, Aims for a New 'Golden Era' at the Newspaper," *Washington Post,* September 2, 2013. This interview was the first one conducted since his $250 million purchase of the *Washington Post* in August 2013.

9. "Huawei Ren Zhengfei Had Refused to See Morgan Stanley Investment Team: He's Not a Customer," *Dusekeji,* June 11, 2016, http://www.sohu .com/a/82435452_358836.

10. Jim Yang, Great China general manager at Supercell, interview with Arthur Yeung and Tencent Research Team, conducted April 13, 2017 in Shanghai, China.

11. Cheng Wei, CEO of DiDi, and several DiDi business leaders, interview with Arthur Yeung and Tencent Research Team, conducted March 2, 2017 in person at DiDi's headquarters in Beijing, China.

12. Interview with employees and former employees of Google by Arthur Yeung and Tencent Research Team, conducted March 14–15, 2017 in person in Mountain View, California and by telephone.

13. Amazon, "Our Pioneers . . . ," Amazon Jobs website, accessed March 14, 2019, https://amazon.jobs/en/pioneers.

14. Interview with former general manager of Amazon hardware product by Arthur Yeung and Tencent Research Team, conducted March 15, 2017 in person in San Francisco, California; Brad Stone, *The Everything Store: Jeff Bezos and the Age of Amazon* (New York: Little, Brown and Company, 2013); Chris Vander Mey, *Practical Lessons on Building and Launching Outstanding Software, Learned on the Job at Google and Amazon* (Beijing: O'Reilly Media, 2012).

15. Former vice president of Amazon AWS interview, March 17, 2017.

16. Jeff Bezos, "To Our Shareholders," Amazon annual letter to shareholders, 2017, in "All of Jeff Bezos' Amazon Letters to Shareholders Together in One PDF," in *Words of Ward, Your Guide to Financial Freedom,* April 20, 2017, http://dameats.com/wordsofward/2017/04/20/all-amazon -letters-to-shareholders-combined.

17. Jeff Bezos, quoted in Peter Burrows, "Bezos on Innovation," *Bloomberg Business Week*, April 17, 2008, www.bloomberg.com/news/articles /2008-04-16/bezos-on-innovation.

18. Janne Snellmann, chief operating officer of Supercell, interview with Arthur Yeung and Tencent Research Team, conducted January 10, 2017 in person in Shanghai, China.

19. Google's 2014 Founders' Letter, https://abc.xyz/investor/founders -letters/2004-ipo-letter/.

20. Rain Yu Long, chief HR officer and general counsel of JD.com, interview with Arthur Yeung, conducted September 15, 2017 in person at Beijing headquarters of JD.com.

Chapter 7

1. Martin Armstrong, "The Most Common New Year's Resolutions for 2018," *Statista*, January 2, 2018, www.statista.com/chart/12386/the-most -common-new-years-resolutions-for-2018.

2. Zarina Hussain, "How Lee Kuan Yew Engineered Singapore's Economic Miracle," *BBC News*, March 24, 2015, www.bbc.com/news/business -32028693.

3. Lee Kuan Yew, *From Third World to First: The Singapore Story* (New York: Harper, 2012).

4. Jeri Darling, "Reframing Performance Reviews for Greater Impact: An Interview with Accretive Health Chief People Officer, Caroline Stockdale," *People & Strategy*, June 1, 2013, www.thefreelibrary.com/Reframing +performance+reviews+for+greater+impact%3a+an+interview+with . . . -a0343363073.

5. Mercer, "2013 Global Performance Management Survey Report: Global Results."

6. Carol Dweck, *Mindset: The New Psychology of Success* (New York: Ballantine Books, 2007).

7. See Paul R. Niven and Ben Lamorte, *Objectives and Key Results: Driving Focus, Alignment and Engagement with OKRs* (New York: Wiley, 2016); Eric Schmidt and Jonathan Rosenberg, *How Google Works* (New York: Grand Central Publishing, 2014).

8. See Thomas Schulz, *Was Google Wirklich Will* [What Google really wants] (Munich: Verlagsgruppe Random House GmbH, 2015); Danielle Muoio, "Google and Alphabet's 20 Most Ambitious Moonshot Projects," *Business Insider*, February 13, 2016, www.businessinsider.com/20-moonshot -projects-by-google-turned-alphabet-2016-2.

9. Interview with employees and former employees of Google by Arthur Yeung and Tencent Research Team, conducted March 14–15, 2017 in person in Mountain View, California and by telephone.

10. Alibaba Group, "Culture and Values," accessed March 15, 2019, www.alibabagroup.com/en/about/culture.

11. Huang Weiwei, *Dedication: The Foundation of Huawei's HR Management* (London: LID Publishing, 2016).

12. Amazon, "Leadership Principles," Amazon Jobs website, accessed March 15, 2019, www.amazon.jobs/en/principles.

13. Interview with employees and former employees of Facebook by Arthur Yeung and Tencent Research Team, conducted March 14–15, 2017 in person in Mountain View, California and by telephone.

14. Ibid.

15. We are indebted to Charlie Tharp for the valuable insight that reward systems are primarily communication tools that signal what matters most.

16. Dani Dipirro, "Make the 3-to-1 ratio of Positivity Work for You," *Positively Present* (blog), accessed March 15, 2019, www.positivelypresent.com/2010/01/what-is-positivity-.html.

17. Interview with business leaders of Tencent, with Tencent Research Team.

Chapter 8

1. All the examples in this paragraph come from Matthew Syed, "Viewpoint: How Creativity Is Helped by Failure," *BBC News Magazine*, November 14, 2015, www.bbc.co.uk/news/magazine-34775411.

2. Ibid.

3. Interview with former general manager of Amazon hardware product by Arthur Yeung and Tencent Research Team, conducted March 15, 2017 in person in San Francisco, California.

4. Linda A. Hill et al., "The Capabilities Your Organization Needs to Sustain Innovation," *Harvard Business Review*, January 14, 2015.

5. Greg Satell, "Want to Do Corporate Innovation Right? Go Inside Google Brain," *Harvard Business Review*, June 1, 2016.

6. Ibid.

7. Steve Jobs, quoted in Walter Isaacson, *Steve Jobs* (New York: Simon & Schuster, 2011), 552.

8. Michael Schrage, "Just How Valuable Is Google's '20% Time'?," *Harvard Business Review*, August 20, 2013.

Chapter 9

1. Thomas Jefferson Foundation, Inc., "Origins of the Expedition," Monticello, Home of Thomas Jefferson, February 2003, www.monticello.org/site/jefferson/origins-expedition; and Thomas Jefferson Foundation, Inc., "Preparing for the Expedition," Monticello, Home of Thomas Jefferson, February 2003, www.monticello.org/site/jefferson/preparing-expedition.

2. Tencent website, "Culture," accessed March 14, 2019, https://www.tencent.com/en-us/culture.html; Sui Yiyi, "QQ Mail App, Seven-Star Quality Aggregation," Sohu.com, July 12, 2014, http://www.sohu.com/a

/20839670_116068; Hua Mingfei, "QQ Mailbox: How Close to Customer," *Global Entrepreneur Magazine*, June 8, 2012, http://tech.qq.com/a/20120618/000154.htm.

3. Interview with former general manager of Amazon hardware product by Arthur Yeung and Tencent Research Team, conducted March 15, 2017 in person in San Francisco, California.

4. Marin Reeves, Ming Zeng, and Amin Venjara, "The Self-Tuning Enterprise," *Harvard Business Review*, June 2015, https://hbr.org/2015/06/the-self-tuning-enterprise.

5. Interview with employees and former employees of Facebook by Arthur Yeung and Tencent Research Team, conducted March 14–15, 2017 in person in Mountain View, California and by telephone.

6. Janne Snellmann, chief operating officer of Supercell, interview with Arthur Yeung and from Tencent Research Team, conducted January 10, 2017 in person in Shanghai, China.

Chapter 10

1. Interview with employees and former employees of Google by Arthur Yeung and Tencent Research Team, conducted March 14–15, 2017 in person in Mountain View, California and by telephone; Eric Schmidt and Jonathan Rosenberg, *How Google Works* (New York: Grand Central Publishing, 2014).

2. Interview with employees and former employees of Facebook by Arthur Yeung and Tencent Research Team, conducted March 14–15, 2017 in person in Mountain View, California and by telephone; Blue Lion Enterprise Research Institute (China), "Case Study: A New Understanding of Facebook Open Platform," January 1, 2016, http://caiwei.yuedu.163.com/source/a5d2f41880d34d42966d24e5dad554b7_4.

3. Jeff Bezos, "To Our Shareholders," Amazon annual letter to shareholders, 2011, in "All of Jeff Bezos' Amazon Letters to Shareholders Together in One PDF," in *Words of Ward, Your Guide to Financial Freedom*, April 20, 2017, http://dameats.com/wordsofward/2017/04/20/all-amazon-letters-to-shareholders-combined.

4. Alibaba, https://www.alibabagroup.com/en/news/press_pdf/p180809.pdf; "Alibaba 88VIP: Innovation for Super Membership," LieYun.com, January 1, 2019, http://www.sohu.com/a/289628480_118792.

5. Information on Alibaba is from interview with Alibaba senior managers and industry experts by Arthur Yeung and Tencent Research Team, conducted March 14–20, 2017 in person in Palo Alto, California and by telephone; Hou Yi, CEO of Hema, interview by Liang Xiao, *China Entrepreneurs Magazine*, January 11, 2018, http://finance.sina.com.cn/chanjing/gsnews/2018-01-11/doc-ifyqqieu5621980.shtml; Zhonghua, *The Way to IT Architecture Transformation: Alibaba Mid-End Strategy and Practice*;

Nicole Lin, "Why Do Players Quit the Game So Quickly? 10 Suggestions to Reduce Player Churn" (in Chinese), *Beluga Whale*, March 5, 2015, www.baijingapp.com/article/16936.

6. Alibaba interview, March 14–20, 2017; Hou Yi, CEO of Hema, interview by Liang Xiao, January 11, 2018; Lin, "Why Do Players Quit."

7. Janne Snellmann, chief operating officer of Supercell, interview by Arthur Yeung and Tencent Research Team, conducted January 10, 2017 in person in Shanghai, China.

8. Case study and summary from Tencent Research Team (led by Arthur), and information is based on interviews with employees, former employees of those companies, and industry experts conducted from January to June in 2017 in person in China and the United States and by telephone.

Chapter 11

1. Peter James Williamson and Arnoud De Meyer, "Ecosystem Advantage: How to Successfully Harness the Power of Partners," *California Management Review* 55, no. 1 (fall 2012): 34.

2. Beth Kowitt, "The Secret to How Amazon Dominates," *Fortune*, July 18, 2017, http://fortune.com/2017/07/18/amazon-whole-foods-jeff-wilke.

3. Information on Alibaba is from interview with Alibaba senior managers and industry experts by Arthur Yeung and Tencent Research Team, conducted March 14–20, 2017 in person in Palo Alto, California and by telephone.

4. We are grateful for insights from Ron Ashkenas, coauthor of *Boundaryless Organization: Breaking the Chains of Organizational Structure* (San Francisco: Jossey-Bass, 2002); and Mark Nyman, coauthor of *HR Transformation*.

Chapter 12

1. Dave Ulrich, Norm Smallwood, and Kate Sweetman, *The Leadership Code: Five Rules to Lead By* (Boston, MA: Harvard Business Review Press, 2009).

2. "Tencent Announces Strategic Upgrade," Tencent Holdings Limited, October 1, 2018, https://www.prnewswire.com/news-releases/tencent-announces-strategic-upgrade-300721749.htm.

3. Interview with employees and former employees of Facebook by Arthur Yeung and Tencent Research Team, conducted March 14–15, 2017 in person in Mountain View, California and by telephone; Ekaterina Walter, *Think Like Zuck: The Five Business Secrets of Facebook's Improbably Brilliant CEO Mark Zuckerberg* (New York: McGraw Hill, 2016).

4. Jill Shen, "Tencent Creates Technology Committee to Boost In-Company Collaboration," Technode, January 10, 2019, https://technode.com/2019/01/10/tencent-special-technology-committee/.

5. Alibaba Group CEO Zhang Yong internal letter to all employees, "Mid-platform Strategy and Organization Transformation," December 7, 2015, http://www.sohu.com/a/46935967_259281; Zhonghua, *The Way to IT Architecture Transformation: Alibaba Mid-Platform Strategy and Practices* (Beijing: China Machine Press, 2018).

6. Huang Weiwei, *Dedication: The Foundation of Huawei's Human Resources Management* (London: LID Publishing, 2016).

7. Interview with employees and former employees of Amazon by Arthur Yeung and Tencent Research Team, conducted March 1–22, 2017 in person in China and in the United States and by telephone.

8. Ibid; Brad Stone, *The Everything Store: Jeff Bezos and the Age of Amazon* (New York: Little, Brown and Company, 2013).

9. Sonali De Rycker describes Paananen's philosophy in her "Why Supercell's Founder Wants to Be the World's Least Powerful CEO," *Accel News*, May 30, 2017, https://medium.com/accel-insights/why-supercells-founder-wants-to-be-the-world-s-least-powerful-ceo-38bf173d607c.

10. Ilkka Paananen, quoted in ibid.

11. Cheng Wei, quoted in Ma Ping, "Interview with Founder and CEO of DiDi, Cheng Wei: Part I, Understanding DiDi and Data" (trans. Shaolong Lin et al.), *Harbinger*, November 6, 2017, www.theharbingerchina.com/blog/interview-with-founder-and-ceo-of-didi-cheng-wei-part-i-understanding-didi.

12. Leah Fessler, "Didi Chuxing President Jean Liu's Advice for Working Women: 'It's Supposed to Be Hard,'" *Quartz at Work*, February 6, 2018, https://work.qz.com/1196663/DiDi-chuxing-president-jean-liu-beat-uber-at-its-own-game.

13. Tim Cook, "Jean Liu," in "The 100 Most Influential People," *Time* magazine, 2017, http://time.com/collection/2017-time-100/4742753/jean-liu.

14. Cheng Wei, CEO of DiDi, interview by Arthur Yeung and Tencent Research Team, conducted March 2, 2017 at DiDi Headquarter Building in Beijing, China.

15. Kurt Blazek, "An Inspiring Leadership Style: Google CEO Larry Page," *Revolve*, February 3, 2015, www.boothco.com/360-feedback-resources/inspiring-leadership-style-google-ceo-larry-page.

16. Interview with employees and former employees of Google by Arthur Yeung and Tencent Research Team, conducted March 14–15, 2017 in Mountain View, California and by telephone; Eric Schmidt and Jonathan Rosenberg, *How Google Works* (London: John Murray, 2014).

17. We use the term "lean in" to acknowledge Sandberg's key phrase, which she also used as the title of her best-selling book: Sheryl Sandberg, *Lean In: Women, Work, and the Will to Lead* (New York: Knopf, 2013).

18. Brad Stone and Lulu Yilun Chen, "Tencent Dominates in China; Next Challenge Is Rest of the World," *Businessweek*, June 28, 2017, www

.bloomberg.com/news/features/2017-06-28/tencent-rules-china-the-problem
-is-the-rest-of-the-world.

19. David De Cremer and Tian Tao, "Leading Huawei: Seven Leadership Lessons of Ren Zhengfei," *European Business Review*, September 17, 2015, www.europeanbusinessreview.com/leading-huawei-seven-leadership
-lessons-of-ren-zhengfei.

20. Alibaba Group, "Culture and Values," accessed March 15, 2019, www.alibabagroup.com/en/about/culture.

21. Jon Birdsong, "6 Lessons for Leaders from Jack Ma, Founder of Alibaba," accessed March 15, 2019, *WideAngle*, https://wideangle.com/6
-lessons-for-leaders-from-jack-ma.

22. Dennis Green, "Walmart and Amazon's Long-Simmering Feud Exploded in 2017—and It's Redefining Retail," *Business Insider*, December 15, 2017, www.businessinsider.com/walmart-and-amazon-are-business-feud-of
-the-year-2017-12.

23. Jeff Bezos, "To Our Shareholders," Amazon annual letter to shareholders, 1999, in "All of Jeff Bezos' Amazon Letters to Shareholders Together in One PDF," in *Words of Ward, Your Guide to Financial Freedom*, April 20, 2017, http://dameats.com/wordsofward/2017/04/20/all-amazon
-letters-to-shareholders-combined.

24. Cheng Wei, CEO of DiDi, interview by Arthur Yeung, conducted March 7, 2018 at DiDi Headquarter Building in Beijing, China.

Chapter 13

1. Information on WBA business agenda came from public information about the company changes and interviews by Dave Ulrich with business leaders.

2. Information on JD.com's transformation came from Rain Yu Long, chief HR officer and general counsel, JD.com and Shengli Hu, SVP, JD.com, interviews by Tencent Research Team, conducted by phone August 2017.

3. Information on Yonghui's transformation came from discussion, presentation, and interview with Zhang Xuanning, cofounder and CEO of Yonghui Supermarket. Interview conducted by Arthur Yeung, March and May 2018.

INDEX

Note: Figures and tables are indicated by (*f)* and (*t*) following page numbers.

ABOUT THE AUTHORS

Arthur Yeung is a Senior Management Adviser at Tencent Group, where he leads and facilitates organizational innovation and leadership development. Previously, he was the Philips Chair Professor of Human Resource Management at China Europe International Business School (CEIBS) and taught regularly in executive programs in association with Harvard, INSEAD, and the University of Michigan. He also served previously as Chief Human Resources Officer of Acer Group. He is the author of thirteen books and numerous award-winning articles.

Dave Ulrich is the Rensis Likert Collegiate Professor of Business Administration at the University of Michigan's Ross School of Business and a partner at RBL Group (www.rbl.net), a consulting firm focused on helping organizations and leaders deliver value. He has published over thirty books and two hundred articles and book chapters. He has worked with over half of the *Fortune* 200, has numerous lifetime achievement awards for organization, leadership, and HR work, and is listed in the Thinkers50 Hall of Fame.